Swords, Oaths, and Prophetic Visions

Swords, Oaths, and Prophetic Visions

Authoring Warrior Rule
in Medieval Japan

Elizabeth Oyler

University of Hawai'i Press / Honolulu

LIBRARY OF CONGRESS CATALOGING-IN-PUBLICATION DATA

Oyler, Elizabeth.
Swords, oaths, and prophetic visions : authoring warrior rule in medieval Japan /
Elizabeth Oyler.
p. cm.
Includes bibliographical references and index.
ISBN-13: 978-0-8248-2922-3 (hardcover : alk. paper)
ISBN-10: 0-8248-2922-0 (hardcover : alk. paper)
1. Japan—History—Genpei Wars, 1180–1185—Literature and the war.
2. Japanese literature—1185–1600—History and criticism. 3. Historical fiction,
Japanese—History and criticism. I. Title: Authoring warrior rule in medieval
Japan. II. Title.
PL747.33.W3O95 2006
895.6'3209358—dc22

2005022264

University of Hawai'i Press books are printed on acid-free
paper and meet the guidelines for permanence and
durability of the Council on Library Resources

Designed by University of Hawai'i production staff
Printed by The Maple-Vail Book Manufacturing Group

In memory of Jeffrey P. Mass

Contents

Acknowledgments

This book grew out of a fascination with the complexity and richness of medieval Japan instilled in me during my graduate studies and fostered by wonderful teachers. To Jeffrey Mass, I owe my interest in Minamoto Yoritomo, so important a historical figure and yet so elusive in the narratives that I work with as a student of literature. Yamashita Hiroaki of Aichi Shukutoku Daigaku introduced me to the world of *Heike* scholarship and has continued to be helpful ever since. Susan Matisoff, who directed the dissertation from which this book grew and to whom I still look as a mentor and role model, gave me the tools and the confi-dence to approach the vast body of re-told narratives so vital in medieval culture. I deeply appreciate her generous support and guidance.

Two grants were instrumental in providing the time and resources to bring this book to completion. The Japan Foundation funded a six-month affiliation with the Research Centre for Japanese Traditional Music at the Kyoto City University of Arts. There I particularly benefited from working with Steven Nelson, whose lively collegiality and insightful comments on early chapters of this book helped shape my thoughts on the *Heike* and musicality, among other things. I am also grateful to Arai Yasuko, licensed *Heike biwa* transmitter, for the skill and patience with which she introduced me to the practice of her art. This hands-on learning experience provided an important dimension to my understanding of the *Heike*. While in Kyoto, I had the good fortune to come to know and discuss my work with Monica Bethe. Her response to the project and to Chapter Three in particular made this a better work than it would have been otherwise. I am also indebted to Midorikawa Machiko and Michael Watson for sharing their deep knowledge of early and medieval Japanese literature. Michael's work on the *Heike* has long been an inspiration to me, and I am most grateful for our ongoing colloquy in general and his advice regarding early drafts of this book in particular.

A fellowship from the American Council of Learned Societies enabled me to extend my research leave for another nine months, which I had the good fortune to spend in residence at the Kluge Center, Library of Congress. The vast resources of the Library, the generosity of the Asian Reading Room staff, and the camaraderie of other scholars at the Center helped me contextualize my work more broadly. Special thanks also to Pamela Kelley and Ann Ludeman at the University of Hawai'i Press for seeing this project through, and to Terre Fisher for her editorial labors.

I am also grateful for the ongoing support I have received from colleagues at my home institution. Rebecca Copeland has been a constant source of good advice and encouragement, and she and Marvin Marcus gave me constructive responses to early drafts of all five chapters. Nancy Berg helped with Chapter Five. I owe a word of thanks as well to Emi Fujiwara, who helped with tricky *kanji* readings and Haruko Nakamura, who made sure I had access to a wealth of Japanese-language materials. John F. Oyler produced the genealogical charts. Lilla Vekerdy prepared the image used on the book jacket. My husband Mike Finke read through every chapter, and I thank him for both his untiring support and his sharp insights. The strengths of this book have much to do with belonging to a wonderfully positive scholarly community; any failings are solely my own.

Note on Conventions and Sources

This book presents a study of narratives that have enjoyed several incarnations across a number of works and genres. Variant texts of the *Heike monogatari* that include *"Heike monogatari"* in their titles—the Enkyōbon, Kakuichibon, Hyakunijukkubon, Nagatobon, and so forth—are not italicized here. Texts with entirely different names (the *Genpei jōsuiki* and the *Genpei tōjōroku*) are italicized. They are abbreviated as *Jōsuiki* and *Tōjōroku*, respectively, after their first mention. Titles of individual *kōwakamai* are placed in quotation marks, as are named episodes within larger texts. The global narratives discussed in each chapter (the Dream Interpretation, Yoshinaka's Petition, Koshigoe, and Swords) are simply capitalized. References to volumes one and two of the Kakuichibon correspond respectively to the two volumes (44 and 45) of the *Shin Nihon koten bungaku taikei* series containing that text.

Discussion of multiple versions of the same general story requires comparison, which leads to exposition of a number of very similar stories. Where there are differences of significance for this study, variants are explained in detail, since the narratives are unfamiliar to many readers. The intention is to clarify differences between texts and make a somewhat unfamiliar body of medieval work accessible to a wider readership.

A set of appendices is provided to summarize events and relationships discussed in Chapters Two through Five. Appendix A includes a brief narrative description of the Hōgen and Heiji Uprisings. Appendix B contains genealogies for the Seiwa Genji and Itō clans. Appendix C provides a roughly chronological list of editions of the *Heike* variants and other principal works discussed here.

Chapter One

The *Heike monogatari* and Narrating the Genpei War

The Genpei War of 1180 to 1185 stands as one of the most prominent markers on the landscape of Japanese historical memory. Conventionally viewed as the turning point at which cultural, political, and economic power passed from the central aristocracy to provincially based military houses,[1] it has been acclaimed variously as a manifestation of the end of classical culture, the rise of feudalism,[2] and the world's entry into the latter days of the Buddhist law.[3] Although historians point out that social and institutional change was not nearly so radical or sudden as such characterizations suggest,[4] it is nevertheless indisputable that the war began to be memorialized almost as soon as it ended, and the devastation it had wrought became the subject of numerous text and performance narratives that continued to develop over ensuing centuries.

The records emerging from this watershed period in Japanese history introduced a new modality for how Japanese remembered their past. Operating as histories in the broadest sense,[5] they encompassed the traditional roles of both narrating past events and placating the restless spirits of the war's victims. But most importantly, these stories also exhibited a new degree of social and geographical mobility unknown in the canonized texts we associate with the Heian period (794–1185),[6] since they were carried by performers and storytellers between the capital and the provinces. The inclusion of residents of remote locales formerly isolated from the culture of the center contributed to a sense of shared cultural identity. That the tales from the *Heike* described a specific historical event helped to shape a sense of the past that further reinforced that shared identity.

This narrative organization of the actions and actors into "history" reached an apex in the *Heike monogatari* (Tale of the Heike),[7] the monumental tale about the war, its causes, and its immediate aftermath. Its nearly one hundred variants recount diverse aspects of that experience, and all identify the war as the end of an era.[8] Thus the tale's most prominent recensions all focus on the relentless and complete destruction of the Taira clan, who epitomize the excesses of the aristocratic period, and the resultant rise of the warrior class under the Minamoto clan, who set the new direction social organization would take.

The *Heike* had a tremendous impact on the cultural production of the ensuing medieval age.[9] A host of additional new literary works—indeed, entirely new narrative and performance genres—drew both inspiration and narrative content from the *Heike*'s episodes, while simultaneously affecting the perception and interpretation of their *Heike* precursors. Most prominent among these were other long *monogatari*, tales specifically focused on the lives of individual warriors; the ballad-drama *kōwakamai*, which enacted some of the period's most memorable military moments; the placatory *nō* drama; and histories, particularly the *Azuma kagami*. All these new genres articulated and expanded individual *Heike* episodes, bringing them to life in multiple forms.

The retelling of episodes across works and genres is a hallmark of this period, as exemplified by the wholesale movement of storyline, character, and even verbatim text from work to work. So too are synergistic, combinatory relationships among tales: as a group, they created, recreated, and revised the historical stories they told, and this process became a driving force in historical narration. The following study focuses on these concomitant trends in medieval narrative: the centrifugal movement of individual stories into other works and genres (that also traveled geographically and socially) and the centripetal pull of the sheer volume of stories retold (often in the same terms) about the same people and events. The following chapters explore how these elastic yet coherent histories, which accrued cultural weight as they permeated different geographic and social spheres during the Nanbokuchō (1336–1392) and early Muromachi (1333–1573) periods,[10] brought a newly complicated historical perspective into being.

All of the works I consider here tackled the project of representing a difficult past in such a way as to ensure authority and legitimacy. They did so in a cultural milieu in which historiography was inseparable from fiction, religion, superstition, and performance art. This co-mingling of elements we now segregate into distinct disciplines forces us to reconsider our notions of the very concept of historical narration. My approach represents a reassessment of how we know what we know about the past, and what motivations shaped that knowledge. In addition to reconstructing the fullness and texture of medieval historical awareness about the Genpei period, therefore, I also reflect on historicity itself, and how medieval interpretations of the war's meaning reshaped historiographical inquiry and continue to do so even today.

Late Heian History and the *Heike monogatari*

It is impossible to overstate the significance of the Genpei War in Japan's history. Lasting from 1180 to 1185, it was the first prolonged military conflict in generations to affect the region around the capital. Further, as is often the case with civil wars, it pitted family members, friends, and colleagues against each other in deadly combat. Although the war did not bring about immediate change for much of the population,[11] it nevertheless rent the political and social fabric of the country, and, in retrospect, it came to be seen as the turning point in a transition from aristocratic to warrior domination of the social and political orders. As embodied in the monumental *Heike monogatari*, as well as a number of other works and genres partially or wholly engendered by the *Heike*, the Genpei War is one of the most significant premodern events to have shaped the history of the realm, and it continued to serve as a template for nation-building into the modern era.

The ostensible impetus for the war was a call to arms in the name of the disenfranchised prince, Mochihito,[12] who, at the instigation of Minamoto Yorimasa,[13] urged the remnants of the Minamoto to oust former Chancellor Taira Kiyomori and his kin from their positions of power. The Minamoto had been fragmented and almost obliterated following the defeat of their clan head, Yoshitomo, by Kiyomori in the Heiji Uprising (1159–1160). In narrative accounts, Mochihito's call to arms was followed by a pardon from Retired Sovereign Go-Shirakawa that released Yoshitomo's oldest surviving son, Yoritomo, from exile and charged him with punishing Kiyomori.[14] Yoritomo and his younger half-brothers Noriyori and Yoshitsune responded; their rise in the eastern provinces was complemented by that of Kiso Yoshinaka, a cousin, and Yukiie, an uncle, in the north. Following the Taira's hasty retreat from battle at the Fuji River in 1180, things were relatively quiet, with only intermittent skirmishes in the provinces. But in late 1182 the Minamoto under Yoshinaka began to turn back the Taira forces dispatched to Hokuriku (the "north country," here, specifically Echizen, Echigo, and Etchū provinces) to subdue him. Yoshinaka's campaign culminated in a victory at Kurikara, followed by a successful drive to the capital (present-day Kyoto). The Taira were forced to flee to the west, taking with them the child sovereign Antoku and the key symbols of royal authority: the "Three Sacred Regalia" (*sanshu no jingi*)—a mirror, a bead strand, and a sword.

In 1184 what had seemed like a minor rift between Yoritomo and Yoshinaka became a serious rivalry. On the one hand, Yoshinaka's attempts to ingratiate himself with Retired Sovereign Go-Shirakawa in the capital suggested that he had his eyes on becoming the Minamoto hegemon.[15] Simultaneously, however, he allowed his men to wreak havoc on the capital and environs, terrorize the populace, and indiscriminately appropriate goods and personnel, a situation worsened by the fact that the area was suffering from a famine. The embattled but still savvy retired sovereign gave an order for Yoritomo to punish his cousin. Yoritomo sent forces under the leadership of Noriyori and Yoshitsune to the capital to attack Yoshinaka, who was finally killed in battle on 1184/1/21 by Yoshitsune's forces on the shores of Lake Biwa at Awazugahara (in present-day Shiga Prefecture).[16]

Yoshitsune and Noriyori pushed westward, driving the Taira forces further toward the edge of the realm. The final defeat of the Taira came at the hands of Yoshitsune at Dan-no-ura, in the swift-flowing strait between Honshū and Kyūshū. Taking with him the sword Kusanagi, one of the Three Sacred Regalia, the child sovereign drowned, as did many of his Taira kin. His mother was rescued and spent the rest of her life in seclusion as a nun, praying for the repose of her dead. Taira males were executed over the next several years in accordance with the orders of Yoritomo, who had established himself as warrior hegemon in Kamakura (in present-day Kanagawa Prefecture). Rule by warriors through the shōgunal house had finally begun.

Four years after the war's conclusion, Yoritomo succeeded in having Yoshitsune, who had won fame as a victorious general, killed by his own allies in Hiraizumi (in present-day Iwate Prefecture), following a manhunt that had begun shortly after the war. Noriyori was killed in 1193, after a dispute with Yoritomo.[17]

Articulating the *Heike*

Narrative accounts portray the Genpei War as the culmination of a power struggle begun more than twenty years earlier between the scions of the Taira (or Heike) and Minamoto (or Genji) clans.[18] The war, fomented during the Hōgen and Heiji uprisings, is depicted at once as the conclusion of a feud and the beginning of an era in which political authority was attenuated and military affairs came to be overseen by the shōgunal house and its regents based in Kamakura.

The war was a devastating past event that gave rise to complex motivations for telling stories. Among other imperatives, this storytelling sought to "impose a unified meaning upon history"[19] while also serving what we might term a religious function of assuaging the potentially malevolent spirits of the war dead. It is in fact as the placatory recitational art performed by *biwa hōshi* (lute-playing blind male performers) that the *Heike* is most often thought of today.[20]

Problems at the heart of any study of narratives representing this distant period stem from our general inability to grasp their cohesiveness, how they simultaneously served what in modern contexts are differentiated and often oppositional needs or functions. We consequently tend to discuss the *Heike* and particularly its variants in oppositional terms: each variant is marked as history *or* fiction, written *or* performed text, official "Chinese" history *or* popular "Japanese" tale, the product of the religious elite *or* of the masses. While scholars add nuance to this bifurcated model by characterizing both individual variants and the composite text of the *Heike* as existing (and often moving) along a spectrum that stretches between one binary term and the other, the fundamental, two-dimensional model of a line stretched between two poles is rarely challenged. At best, these paired qualifiers define vectors that intersect in the narrative equivalent of three-dimensional space; at worst, they are collapsed into one line, with "Chinese," history, high culture, and writing at one end and "Japanese," fiction, popular culture, and speaking/performance at the other. This study constructs a model in which such linearity is discarded and the network of semantic relations it has been used to represent is reconfigured in more complex and contextually appropriate terms. But first we need to understand the textual history of the various works we call the *Heike,* as well as the critical approaches that have been brought to bear on them in the past. How did the texts of the *Heike monogatari* emerge, how are they connected to one another, and how did later versions derive from earlier ones?

The variant texts of the *Heike monogatari* differ significantly in length, style, and narrative focus. Based on these differences, each has been given a name that refers to some salient identifying characteristic. The Kakuichibon variant, for example, is said to be a transcription of the performance of the *biwa hōshi* Kakuichi;[21] the Enkyōbon is dated to the Enkyō era,[22] etc. Within each variant line, there are often a number of extant physical texts, each of which is further named, generally according to the individual or institution currently in possession of it. Throughout this study, I will be referring to texts by their variant line.[23]

The organization of *Heike* variants differs from text to text and is often inconsistent even within one variant line. The texts generally are divided into *maki* (scrolls, often translated as "chapter," a convention used by McCullough that I follow here). Many are then further divided into *dan* (episodes), also known as *shōdan*, which can also refer to a part of an episode. In texts associated with performance, individual units are traditionally referred to as *ku* (individual performance pieces of significantly varied length),[24] which correspond more or less to a *dan* or *shōdan*. *Ku* are further divided into *kyokusetsu* (patterned melodic sections),[25] units of particular importance in describing the performance style of small sections of text.[26]

This modular organization allows significant structural flexibility,[27] and in fact there was apparently a good deal of rearrangement of *ku* during the medieval period, both in major *Heike* variants as they have come to us today and in peripheral works based on the *Heike*.[28] We often find a lack of rigid ordering, chronological or otherwise, as well as a striking autonomy at the level of the episode or even in parts of episodes. *Ku* usually have descriptive titles; the same is true for *dan* within the written texts for these traditions. The malleability and mobility of episodes are significant for this study, as it is often these pieces—*dan* or *ku*—that are moved to other texts or reworked in other genres.

Many of the texts not so divided are organized in general chronological order, sometimes with dated entries under which the events of that day and other commentary are recorded. Interestingly, this commentary often encompasses narrative material found within a corresponding *dan* from another variant—a citation of precedent or peripheral accounts about a primary character within the *dan*, for example. Still other variants have descriptive titles for pieces resembling *dan*, often added at a later date.[29] These added features have been important markers for the systematic modern categorization of the texts, as we shall see below. But this taxonomic effort has made rigid organizational structures of material whose arrangement was originally fluid and changeable. Narrative pieces originally served as modules that could be used with great flexibility, rather than as prescribed components of a generically defined larger whole.

The *Heike* and the Academy

The *Heike* began to receive scholarly attention as early as the Tokugawa period (1600–1868). The *Sankō Genpei jōsuiki*, an annotation of the *Genpei jōsuiki*, for example, was collated in 1689, and this text became a vital resource for scholars of literature who took up the *Heike* and its variants during the Meiji period (1868–1912). Throughout the Tokugawa period and into the early Meiji, the *Heike* was considered a work of history when, that is, its nature was thought of at all.[30] Once the Meiji was under way and well into until the early Showa period (1926–1989), Japanese intellectuals focused their attention on situating the *Heike* in the context of world literature. The work's potential as, by turns, an epic or lyrical poem, a folk epic, and a national epic captured the imaginations of late nineteenth- and early twentieth-century academics as they labored to create a canon of Japanese literature that would help establish a place for Japan in the cultural landscape of modern nations.

Early literary studies of the *Heike* and other war tales by the pioneering scholars Haga Yaichi and Tachibana Sensaburō[31] identified them as

works of literature in their *Kokubungaku tokuhon* (Reader of national literature, 1891); so too did Mikami Sanji and Takazu Kuwasaburō in *Nihon bungaku shi* (The history of Japanese literature), published the same year.[32] In
their discussions of the *Heike*, these men focused primarily on the recitational texts, and the Kakuichibon in particular. Their work thus largely
reflects the assessment of a single text, thought to be fictional, albeit based
on historical events. That text contained elements that did not coincide
with nineteenth-century ideas about things that could be considered "historical": prophetic visions, heavenly and otherworldly beings, and hyper-
bolic description. Like its premodern equivalents in Europe, the *Heike* was
at this juncture scrutinized, recategorized, and dismissed from the realm
of historiography, and it fell to scholars of literature to define its parameters and its place in Japanese cultural history.

Among the topics of early debate was the *Heike*'s status as an epic,
which engaged prominent thinkers including, for example, Tsubouchi
Shōyō. In his 1893 *Bijironkō* (On rhetoric) he argued that it was not an
epic, but an important precursor of something comparable to the Western
epic. The idea of the *Heike* as a "folk epic" was put forth by Ikuta Chōkō[33]
in his 1906 *Kokuminteki jojishi to shite no* Heike monogatari (The *Tale of the
Heike* as national popular epic). This characterization fed a growing interest in the study of folklore under the leadership of scholars like Yanagita
Kunio and Orikuchi Shinobu,[34] who looked at individual narratives
(either a *dan* or several *dan* about the same character or event) as precursors to a unified, longer tale. Their focus on the hypothesized folk origins
of the *Heike*, which continues to influence our understanding of the work
even today, helped mobilize the attribution of a somewhat misinterpreted
"warrior ideal" to the spirit of the folk in support of Japan's imperial
project in the early twentieth century. This period, however, also saw the
beginnings of a "literary" approach to the *Heike* texts, illustrated most importantly in Yamada Yoshio's foundational *Heike monogatari kō* (Study of
the *Tale of the Heike*, 1911), a careful philological investigation of the *Heike*'s
numerous variants that aimed at creating a genealogy for them.

One primary goal of early scholars was determining textual lineages
for *Heike* variants in an effort to find the origin of the work, an "ur-Heike"
(*gen-Heike*, still a term found in Japanese scholarship). To this end, a handful of contemporary records and references to *Heike* performance and
composition are staples of *Heike* studies. The most famous of these is *dan*
number 226 in Yoshida Kenkō's *Tsurezuregusa*:

> During the reign of the Emperor Go-Toba, a former official from Shinano
> named Yukinaga enjoyed a reputation for learning. But when commanded
> to participate in a discussion of *yuefu* poetry, he forgot two of the virtues
> in the "Dance of the Seven Virtues," and consequently acquired the nick-

name "Young Gentleman of the Five Virtues." Sick at heart, he abandoned scholarship and took the tonsure.

Archbishop Jien [The Enryakuji Abbot] made a point of summoning and looking after anyone, even a servant, who could boast of an accomplishment; thus, he granted this Shinano Novice an allowance. Yukinaga wrote the *Heike monogatari* and taught a blind man named Shōbutsu so that the man might narrate it. His descriptions of things having to do with the Enryakuji were especially good. He wrote with a detailed knowledge of Kurō Hōgan Yoshitsune's activities, but did not say much about Gama no Kanja Noriyori, possibly for lack of information. When it came to warriors and the martial arts, Shōbutsu, who was an easterner, put questions to warriors and had Yukinaga write what he learned. People say that our present-day *biwa hōshi* imitate Shōbutsu's natural voice.[35]

As the earliest statement specifically about the origins of the *Heike*, Kenkō's assertion implies that by his time (ca. 1330), recitation of the *Heike* was an established practice worthy of note by a prominent cultural critic. Although the approximate date claimed by Kenkō is not verifiable, this account does point to the *Heike*'s existence in some form by that time and makes a case for Tendai, and particularly Enryakuji, stewardship of early texts. Moreover, it describes the *Heike* as a work with both written and performance manifestations, an unproblematic claim here but one that would fuel future debates about the *Heike*'s origins and fundamental nature, as we will see below.

Other evidence also supports the *Tsurezuregusa*'s assertion about the textual presence of the *Heike* by the thirteenth century. First, the last date discussed in the *Heike* itself is in 1219, which suggests the *Heike* was codified thereafter. It is also conceivable, however, that there may have been a text sharing that name if not the same content circulating earlier. Also from the thirteenth century, Kujō Kanezane's *Gyokuyō* mentions a *Heike ki* (Heike chronicle) in an entry from 1220, and Fujiwara Teika's copy of the *Hyōhanki* contains a note on the back dating from 1240 referring as well to a *Jishō monogatari* (Tale of the Jishō era[36]), which might indicate the *Heike*.[37] There is some debate about whether other records containing reference to "Heike" written closer in date to the actual events of the Genpei War in fact refer to some early form of the tale or not.[38]

Although a definitive answer about a general date or author(s) for the *Heike* will probably remain unknowable, there is clear evidence that it had entered the cultural sphere by the middle of the fourteenth century as both written and recitational forms. Somewhat less certain is the connection between the texts referred to above and specific variants, as well as the various authors, performers, and/or patrons involved with each, although extensive research has led to some general conclusions about textual genealogies.

The cohort of prolific and influential scholars whose careers spanned World War II and its aftermath built upon Yamada Yoshio's philological project. Most prominent among them were Takahashi Sadaichi, Tomikura Tokujirō, Sasaki Hachirō, Atsumi Kaoru, and Nagazumi Yasuaki. From this generation emerged the most significant paradigm for organizing and analyzing *Heike* variants, which divided them into the read lineage (*yomihonkei*) and the recited lineage (*kataribonkei*), a system that separated all variants into two broad categories based on the oppositional presentation modes of reading (*yomi*) and performing (*katari*).[39] *Yomihonkei* implies a reader (and hence a writer), while *kataribonkei* implies instead a listener (and a performer). This paradigm has been profoundly influential in all subsequent scholarly engagements with the *Heike*, and it has further influenced the way medieval performance "literatures" (with the important exception of *nō*) have been treated. It is also the framework upon which other bifurcations are hung and simplified. The most common of these pairings include: Chinese versus Japanese writing, writing versus speaking, documentary versus lyrical style, and high versus low literature.

Textuality, Lineage, and other Critical Paradigms and Problems

On the surface, the division of variants according to performance mode seems like a useful descriptive model for classifying them. Broadly defined, the *kataribonkei* texts are the constituents of the performance repertoire of the *biwa hōshi* and the *tōdōza* (blind guild),[40] or variants seemingly related to the performative texts;[41] the *yomihonkei* consists of texts that were read rather than recited in performance. *Katari*, however, is a polyvalent term with links to a wide range of narrative traditions: the *monogatari* of the Heian period (including especially the *Genji monogatari* and the *Ise monogatari*, etc.), storytelling in the *setsuwa* (short narrative) vein, and many other forms of non-official narrative. Thus the term, in addition to meaning "performed on a stage," also evokes "stories that are not official history." The *yomihonkei* implies an opposition to the broad idea of *katari*. While on the one hand, the terms *katari* and *yomi* distinguish speaking from reading, juxtaposing the two in this context further exerts a fiction versus history delineation as well. This distinction, while originally descriptive, has tended to become prescriptive, and texts from each line are considered to be basically historical or fictional simply by their classification in one category or the other.

A number of factors contribute to the misleading dichotomy between the read and recited lineage, perhaps the most fundamental being the modern interpretation of premodern textuality. While on the one hand a diversity of writing styles is immediately evident when one looks across the *Heike* variants, the consequent characterizations of each work grow from more general, longstanding ways of treating early texts: they are either "Japanese" (*wabun*) or "Chinese" (*kanbun*) writing. *Kataribonkei* texts are generally thought of as embodying a *wabun* style: they employ the *kana* syllabaries liberally, and they present their tales in a written form that can mostly be read as-is, without significant manipulation of syntactical or lexical units to render them into conventional Japanese. *Yomihonkei* texts, on the contrary, are typified by a much greater reliance on *kanbun*, a writing system imitating Chinese word order that requires particular interpretive skills to facilitate reading it as conventional Japanese. These texts often contain more *kanji* (Chinese characters) and Chinese compounds generally; some are written entirely in *kanbun*. The degree to which *kanbun* is employed, however, differs dramatically from variant to variant and even within variants in both lineages: *kataribonkei* variants use *kanji* as well, and most contain phrases or even long passages (often in the form of embedded documents, such as those discussed in Chapters Three and Four) in *kanbun*. This orthographic difference is, of course, highly marked in the written texts. When read, however, *kanbun* texts would be manipulated to allow them to be read in Japanese, rendering them in a language and form very similar to that of texts written in *wabun*.

The *wabun/kanbun* dialectic is one of the most important framing devices not only for delineating medieval *Heike* variants but also for talking about Japanese writing (and, by extension, literature) generally from its inception through the Tokugawa period. The relationship between the two in early writing in particular has been the subject of much recent scholarly inquiry both in Japan and abroad.[42] Conventionally, *wabun* and *kanbun* have been lined up with other pairings to create a framework for premodern Japanese writing that, on one level, characterizes Japan in relationship to continental culture. China is represented by *kanji*, and Japan by its own written language derived from *kanji* but designed to accommodate the native language. *Kana* (and *wabun*) thus often are treated as a native reaction to and against *kanji* (and continental forms generally). In addition, however, this framework simultaneously—and perhaps more significantly—represents a mapping of those differences onto Japanese (aristocratic, literate) culture and the changes that occur within it, with specific focus on writing, writers, and readers in early Japan.[43] In this sort of configuration, writing is generally divided into public or official (*kanbun*) versus private (*wabun*), and male (*kanbun*) versus female (*wabun*), as are authorial voices and audiences. It is clear that there was some sort of differentiation between styles early on;[44] evidence for named juxtapositions (*onnade* and *otokote* for "female" and "male" writing, for example) exists from the Heian period. What these terms meant in practice, however, is a matter of contention.

Current work on these delineations emphasizes the ways in which their boundaries were permeable and performative, issues that will come into play in later chapters with discussion of (male) lineage and identity within the clan unit. Moreover, some scholars argue that the relationship between writing systems (*mana*, often glossed as Chinese or *kanji*; versus *kana*, rendered as Japanese or syllabic writing per se) is not fundamentally oppositional. Rather, it reflects a correlation between an original (*mana*) and a simplified form (*kana*) patterned on it.[45] *Mana* were full forms, *kana* simplified patterns of them; the example of simplified Chinese characters used in China today in relation to their original forms would perhaps represent a more accurate corollary for the relationship between *mana* and *kana* in the Heian context. This model is complicated by the various syntactical gradations between Chinese and Japanese, what we include today under the rubric of *kanbun* or various forms considered nonstandard *kanbun* (*hentai kanbun*), all of which would have been comprehensible to erudite early readers and writers in Japan.[46] The idea that the Heian period writer saw him- or herself as choosing between Chinese and Japanese, in other words, reflects modern constructs of early language use, not necessarily actual early practice. The multiplicity of conglomerate and hybrid styles from the Heian period and well into the medieval age further points to a greater complexity than conventional interpretations allow; the process of exploring the intricacies of early writing within its contemporary context is an ongoing scholarly project, and one that dovetails productively with the general issue of orality versus writing, which I will be addressing shortly.

The idea of a *kanbun/wabun* dialectic has had a profound effect on *Heike* studies operating within the *yomihonkei/kataribonkei* paradigm. Formality and "Chineseness" tend to be identified as defining stylistic forces behind *yomihonkei* texts, and informality and "Japaneseness" as those behind *kataribonkei* texts. There are correlating assumptions concerning content: We tend to associate public, official, documentary style with the *yomihonkei*, and private, narrative, lyrical style with the *kataribonkei*. This permits a slippage, in which we read "historical" onto the *yomihonkei* and "fictional" onto the *kataribonkei*, a misinterpretation tending to further push the *kataribonkei Heike* texts into the realm of storytelling. Since these texts then meet our expectations of "literature," they become representatives of the (literary) *Heike* as a whole. This characterization operates circularly. The *Heike* is literature because it (or a representative text) looks like literature. As a result, variants less resembling literature, such as the enormously important Enkyōbon, were for many years relatively unstudied.[47] This categorization, therefore, has had the unfortunate side effect of masking the important role the *Heike* in its various forms played as history in its contemporary context.

Beyond these formal elements, narrative style has also been used to distinguish the *yomihonkei* from the *kataribonkei*. Generally speaking, the

kataribonkei is epitomized by numerous digressions—analepses and pro-
lepses at the textual and episode levels—despite the more or less chronological progression within the narrative. The *yomihonkei*, on the other
hand, is considered more specifically chronological, in large part because
many *yomihonkei* variants are organized in something very close to chronological order (the Enkyōbon being a prime example).

The *wabun/kanbun* dialectic further solidifies this characterization:
the mostly *wabun kataribonkei* texts tend to exhibit a paratactic (additive)
sentence structure, while the *kanbun* passages and *yomihonkei* texts generally are more hypotactic (subordinating) and contain parallelisms clearly
indebted to Chinese literary syntax. The argument follows that the *kataribonkei* texts tend to wander syntactically (additive forms being inherently
more open-ended), while the *yomihonkei* texts stick more to logical progression. Given these characteristics, it is tempting to superimpose David
Quint's model for romance and epic onto these two tendencies. The *yomihonkei* texts progress following epic structure while the *kataribonkei* texts
more closely resemble the wandering romance, but again the composite
nature of each text makes this determination difficult on the level of the
work, or even episode.[48] As with the other elements discussed above, these
ideas have some resonance at the level of smaller textual units: lyrical (usually *wabun*) passages that diverge from the main narrative do tend to involve both narrative and physical wandering and speak to the idea of
cyclical time, while straight *kanbun* narrative description tends to move the
plot forward. But these are not specifically functions of the *kataribonkei* or
yomihonkei lineage, and both occur liberally in texts across the spectrum.
We also have to be careful with the idea of cyclical versus teleological progression in a non-Western context. Cosmological ideas privileging cyclical-
ity were more deeply embedded in the early Japanese milieu than in
Western traditions.[49]

The written/oral paradigm is further complicated by the idea of
performance within the *kataribonkei*. The most common image associated
with the *Heike* is that of the *biwa hōshi*, literally "*biwa* priest," a male who
recited episodes from the *Heike* to the accompaniment of the *biwa* lute;
this iconic image far overshadows any conceptualization associated with
the reading of the *Heike* as text. Numerous depictions of blind itinerants
populate the margins of medieval picture scrolls and lists of professions;
twentieth-century scholars have identified these as reciters of the *Heike*,
placing the custodianship of the work in the hands of itinerants, implicitly marginal, poor, blind, and putatively illiterate figures, a characterization that only bolsters the idea that the *Heike* represents the voice of the
folk. But documentary evidence also reveals that something referred to
as the *Heike* was performed in the homes of aristocrats by named performers (including Kakuichi), which suggests control and dissemination

of the work by highly literate religious figures whose institutions served the highest levels of society.

Researchers of the *Heike* today tend to lean toward one of two models for early *Heike* development. Those focusing on the predominance of the *Heike*'s role as historical narration see it as the product of a tradition linked to wandering entertainers and improvisational storytelling, while those emphasizing its religious role believe it emerged within the milieu of placatory ritual in the upper echelons of the Shingon and Tendai establishments and probably developed from a formal written tradition, if not from a specific text.

Both of these paradigms involve an extrapolation backward through Tokugawa period *tōdōza* practice, from which current ideas about performing the *Heike* evolved. Although it is clear that there were blind *biwa hōshi* before the Tokugawa age, the actual origins of performance (and therefore the nature of early *Heike* recitation), and whether or not the earliest performers were exclusively blind, remain obscure. Moreover, the early role of textual fixity and the relationships between textuality and performance are extremely difficult to assess, since texts were associated with performance as early as the late fourteenth century. That is why questions regarding the identity of the *Heike*'s performers and the nature of their performance often bring us back to the larger questions of the *Heike*'s origins: Was it folk or elite? Was it oral or written?

Scholarly research reveals nuances that render these categories ever less sufficient. There is some movement toward the redefinition of terms, but these new alternatives offer refinements of the model rather than significant change.[50] Although throughout this investigation I call the validity of these categories into question, I do not dispense with them entirely. They remain the most prevalent designations used in scholarly discourse, and, more importantly, they represent a backdrop against which to articulate the issue of presentational mode so central to my inquiry.

In sum, then, the description of *yomihonkei* and *kataribonkei* lineages has proved useful to scholars as an initial organizational tool for defining genetic relationships among extant texts. At the same time, however, it obscures other kinds of relationships among texts, particularly those that problematize the ideas about the written and the spoken that form the basis for this opposition. Fundamentally, the scholarly work that invented these concepts involved modernist readings of the past. This work could not help but read back onto the past the twentieth-century implications for the issues of writing and speaking, Chinese and Japanese, official and popular, and fact and fiction. My method will be to set aside the idea of textual lineage, and instead examine *Heike* variants together with other narratives sharing their style and content. We will return again and again to questions of orality and textuality, recasting them as overlapping categories in a newly defined interpretive framework.

Heike variants

Of the numerous variants in the *Heike* corpus, I will be focusing on several prominent texts representing a wide range of narrative structures and thematic foci. They are seen variously as constituents of *kataribonkei* and *yomihonkei* categories. The Enkyōbon is currently considered to be among the earliest *Heike* variants. The colophon of the oldest extant text dates it at 1309, which makes it the oldest *Heike* manuscript of any sort available today. It consists of six books (*hon*) further divided into sections, and it is classified as a *yomihonkei* text.[51] Recently published in annotated and indexed form, it has received significant scholarly attention in Japan over the past several years, in part because of its relative age and also because of its distance, both stylistically and in terms of cosmological and narrative structure, from the Kakuichibon text. In English, the most important work on this text has been that of David T. Bialock, who provides a comprehensive and provocative treatment of, among other things, the Enkyōbon's internal polyvocality and its differences from recited-line texts.[52]

Most familiar to the Western reader of the *Heike* is the Kakuichibon text, since that is the version most often translated into Western languages.[53] It is also the variant most often chosen to represent the *Heike* in Japanese canonizations of classical literature,[54] and it is typical of the *kataribonkei* in structure.[55] The oldest dated manuscript has two colophons, the first dated 1370 and the second 1371. The first colophon, attached to the end of the twelfth chapter, reads: "Twenty-ninth day, eleventh month, third year of Ōan."[56] The second, appended to the "Initiates' Chapter" (*Kanjō no maki*),[57] elaborates:

> On this, the fifteenth day of the third month of the fourth year of Ōan (year of the boar), I hereby convey the twelve books of the *Tale of the Heike* plus the "Initiates' Chapter," the teachings of the masters of our school (*ryū*), and the secret teachings I have received, to Master Shōichi. From mouth to brush it has been passed and written down without missing a character. My age exceeds seventy, and the final years of this fleeting existence have arrived; my life is at its end. Although I pass each *ku* to our disciples, there are those among them who are ill or forgetful, so I set these down to avoid debates. For proof to further generations, I am having this recorded. This book should not be circulated to the outside; the eyes of others may not see it. Further, this text must not be taken by those other than our own apprentices, even if they are close affiliates. If anyone should

turn his back on these precepts, he will be subject to the punishment of the Buddhas. Signed Master Kakuichi.[58]

The 1371 colophon reveals a number of important issues about Kakuichi's personal, social, and even political contexts as a performer. First is the very need for a text: clearly, it was not intended solely as a teaching tool, but also as a record of Kakuichi's art. Contemporary accounts reveal that Kakuichi was much in demand as a performer,[59] so it is not surprising to find his name listed as something resembling an authorial voice of this text. It is likely that he also maintained a high enough socioeconomic place to enable him (or someone acting in his name) to undertake what was certainly the time-consuming and expensive project of recording the text. Beyond this, we can speculate as well about reasons for committing the text to writing: competition, perceived or real, among *Heike* performers or between them and performers of other similar arts; the patron temple Enryakuji's need to establish formal control; the desire on the part of Kakuichi or some listener to record a particularly good version of the tale; and the aspiration to author and/or edit a definitive work. But which of these motivations were most significant is hard to tell. We can assert with certainty only that by 1371, there was a written text of the *Heike*, identified with the performed *Heike* of Kakuichi.

Another important issue raised in the colophon's first line is the assertion of the unproblematic translatability of speaking into writing. Kakuichi's voice is transmitted to paper via brush, not missing a single character. Rather than sounds or even vocalization patterns, what are noted here are words, and specifically words represented textually, as characters. And yet the entire colophon is written in *kanbun*, a patently written style. This general topic will be central in later discussions, but it is significant at this juncture to note the number of presentational modes invoked to give the text authority: it is the faithful transcription of a spoken and sung performance piece of a blind performer, recorded by a sighted non-performer, who wrote in *kanbun*, a formal, documentary style. This kind of provocative interaction between writing and speaking will recur in each of the ensuing chapters. What is more, the colophon's claim of total transmission is possible only through omitting any indication of the musical elements of the performance pieces, thus bifurcating music from word.

Next, the colophon states that the text is to be accessible only to the disciples and close affiliates of the master; the textual object delineates a group of performers and the boundaries of their art and their organization. It is around this time, scholars believe, that the guild which would become so important in the regulation of *Heike biwa* performance was first beginning to take shape.[60] It was patronized first by the Murakami Genji[61] and then by the Ashikaga shōgunal house. The Ashikaga made efforts to

trace their roots to the same Seiwa Genji clan of which Minamoto Yoritomo, the victor of the Genpei War and the first shōgun, had been head.
Hyōdō Hiromi argues that this Minamoto (and specifically Seiwa Genji)
custodianship of the *Heike* as placatory performance points to the important connection between soothing of restless spirits and control of the
country (and its history). This assertion buttresses the centrality of placatory ritual as part of the function of history, and further suggests the important role of shōgunal patronage of at least the Kakuichibon and the
reciters associated with it.[62]

    In addition to these two early texts, another important *Heike* variant
included here is the *Genpei jōsuiki*, a forty-eight scroll work.[63] It is now generally considered to be a *yomihonkei* variant and is one of the most complex
and lengthy recensions. The oldest extant manuscript dates from the
Tokugawa period, but it is thought to have existed in some form during
the early Muromachi years. The *Genpei jōsuiki* is marked stylistically by its
inclusion of several variant versions of individual episodes, a historical discursive practice reminiscent of histories like the *Rikkokushi*.

    I will also make less frequent reference to several further variants.
The Nagatobon *Heike monogatari*, generally classified as a *yomihonkei* text,
exists only in a Tokugawa manuscript, but is thought to be of early Muromachi origin. It comprises twenty chapters, within which there are sub-
divisions by episode. The Yashirobon *Heike monogatari*, a *kataribonkei* text
extant only in a Tokugawa era manuscript, is thought to be representative
of the oldest *kataribonkei* form.[64] It is composed of twelve chapters (with
the fourth and ninth missing in extant texts) and is divided into *ku*. The
Hyakunijukkubon *Heike monogatari* shares many features in common with
the Yashirobon, including the fact that neither contains the "Initiates'
Chapter." It is classified as a *kataribonkei* text. As its title suggests, it consists
of 120 *ku* arranged in twelve chapters. The *Genpei tōjōroku* is a work in eight
chapters only five of which are extant; its colophon dates it to 1337. It contains significant material about eastern warriors, and it is classified as a *yomihonkei* text. These texts are included where they provide counterpoints to
narratives found in the three primary *Heike* variants discussed above.

Other Texts and Genres

Although the *Heike* variants comprise the bulk of the narratives for this
study, they share extensive material with a wider set of texts and performance genres. This sharing is something other than a diachronic intertextual relationship of influence, allusion, imitation, stylization or parody.
The way these other texts also repeat verbatim or near-verbatim content
complicates the boundary definitions of both individual text and genre.
For instance, the *Genpei jōsuiki* has been considered both an independent

work and a variant text of the *Heike*, this is just one example of how hard it is to determine where to draw the line between variants of a textual line and discrete, if similar, texts. Works with their own textual traditions—the *Gikeiki* or the *Soga monogatari*, for example—nevertheless contain long passages very similar to those in one or more of the *Heike* variants. Although the texts as a whole may be unique, these parts create links with other works and emphasize particular moments that bridge both. The question of genre poses another set of concerns. *Kōwakamai*, for example, seems to be a genre, since it is a performance art with a defined repertoire sharing stylistic and thematic characteristics. Yet in their specific content, individual *kōwakamai* pieces represent yet another variation on other texts—while they may be expansions of episodes in longer works, they nevertheless recount the same story in much the same language.

This kind of intertextual relationship is often identified as reflecting oral composition, or, in the case of written texts, residual orality. Thus each variant operates like a performance, with material transformed slightly in each performance or text, but remaining essentially the same; significant scholarship on all the texts considered here emphasizes the importance of short oral tales as source material for longer works. Yet this model is somewhat too simple. As we shall see in Chapters Three and Four, one category of material often repeated nearly verbatim is a document embedded within the narrative, composed in *kanbun* and presented as a written text. Although the presence of a document in a performance piece does not undermine the orality of that piece, it does pointedly introduce the importance of writing and documentation even in the performance milieu. Thus, far from cutting such narratives off from the world of text and writing, works that employ the document device point to the limitations of the oral-versus-written binary.

Indeed, the reiteration of these documents arguably confounds another of the binaries so central to conventional genre definitions: history versus fiction. Embedded documents are recorded in a written style identified with history writing, and they are presented in apparently original form (including dates and signatures). Their inclusion gives the entire work the feel of an eyewitness account, and the fact that they are mostly evidentiary (letters, oaths, records) further evokes the realm of history rather than fiction. That sections containing embedded documents often turn up in nearly identical form across texts and genres points to the significance of the moments they describe within the narrative tradition. The multiple appearances of something looking like an official document in turn works to affirm the document's assertions: if it is included so consistently in so many accounts of an event, it must be true. The chapters of this book look at several places where this truth claim is most important— moments when it is necessary to assert a particular version of a potentially contentious event. Although the dubious historicity of the embedded documents raises questions about the truth claims made, the need to add the flavor of historical accuracy through them points to the significance of the moment in the historical consciousness of the performers, writers, audiences and readers.

The way the *Heike* makes us reconceptualize textual and generic individuality challenges our conventional conceptual tools. In particular I hope to demonstrate the why the modern notion of genre is extremely problematic in considering many medieval arts. This is particularly true for works classified as *rekishi monogatari* (historical tales) and *gunki monogatari* (war tales), where the unifying element is subject matter, and not the kinds of stylistic, formal, or even thematic concerns that we tend to group together under a genre rubric. This study thus focuses on these works primarily as productive elements working in dynamic relationship to create a medieval narrative consciousness about important moments from the Genpei period. From that basis, I proceed to look at the ways in which genre can and cannot be defined for the works I address here.

In addition to the *Heike* variants that provide the focus of this study, I consider four other sustained narratives about the Genpei period, as they contribute to what I will call the works' synchronic intertextuality. The *Hōgen monogatari* and *Heiji monogatari* have textual and performance histories closely tied to the *Heike*, and they seem to have also been part of the *biwa hōshi* repertoire. Dates of composition and authorship are unclear, although both texts have in the past been attributed to various authors, including Fujiwara Tokinaga (dates unknown, but a participant in Yoritomo's 1189 campaign against the Ōshū Fujiwara) and the priest Genyu (dates unknown, Kamakura period Tendai priest). Although prominent figures may have been involved in collating the text, the likelihood of anonymous joint authorship here, as with the *Heike*, is high. Dates for the texts are also hard to establish, and there are enough substantial differences between variants that they range as broadly as those for the *Heike*. The general theories about the date for the earliest *Hōgen monogatari* place it either between 1190 and 1219 (the period in which the Minamoto clan still occupied the position of shōgun), or after 1230, following the composition of the *Gukanshō*, whose author, Jien, is traditionally attributed a part in *Heike* composition. The clearest early evidence for the existence of both texts is found in an introduction to the *Futsūshōdōshū* (1297), which notes that they, along with the *Heike*, were performed by *biwa hōshi*.[65] An entry for 1321 in Sovereign Hanazono's diary, *Hanazono tennō shinki*, comments on a *biwa hōshi* performance of the "Heiji and Heike monogatari, etc." By the end of the thirteenth century, all three pieces were circulating and thought of as a group; most scholars think that this reflects an early to mid-thirteenth-century composition date for both the *Hōgen* and *Heiji monogatari*.[66]

Scholars also divide variants of these war tales into textual lineages in an attempt to define genealogical relationships. They have had less interest than with the *Heike* in separating them into read and recited lineages, although the general parameters set in *Heike* studies tend to be imposed in readings of these works as well. The *Hōgen* has over thirty extant variants.[67] The oldest of these, the Bunpōbon, has a colophon dating it to 1318; this text consists of only the second of the three scrolls. The Nakaraibon, considered part of the same lineage as the Bunpōbon, has three scrolls and shares passages with the Bunpōbon. The Kotohirabon exists in numerous editions and is thought to be a reworking of the earlier variants; it is the basis for annotated versions included in collections of Japanese classics and is considered the most literary.[68] In addition to these main *Hōgen* variants are the Kamakurabon, which is missing its second scroll but seems to be related to the Kotohirabon, and the Kyotobon, apparently also descended from the Kotohirabon. There are later *rufubon* (vulgate or "widely circulated") variants of the *Hōgen monogatari* as well. All of these date to the early modern period.[69]

The *Heiji monogatari* is generally thought to have eleven variant lines consisting of thirty-three texts.[70] The oldest of these, the Yōmei bunkozo manuscript, is incomplete. One notable feature about this text is the relative prominence of Taira Kiyomori and unimportance of Minamoto Yoshihira, the main protagonist of later versions, particularly the Kotohira line.[71] The Kotohira text is the basis for early *biwa hōshi* performances and later popular *rufubon* versions. In addition to these variants, there is an illustrated *Heiji monogatari ekotoba*, which dates from the Kamakura period, and six other variants that reflect significant mixing of the earlier texts.

The *Gikeiki* is an account of the life of Yoshitsune.[72] Its origins are unclear, but it seems to be the compilation of a number of shorter narratives about Yoshitsune's life before and after the Genpei War. The war itself receives only a cursory mention within the text. Most variants are divided into eight scrolls, each of which contains named episodes which, for the most part, are longer than their equivalents in the *Heike*. Although the authorship is unknown, it is possible that some of the narratives in the *Gikeiki* were part of the *biwa hōshi* repertoire.

Scholars generally divide the *Gikeiki* into two parts: Yoshitsune's youth and Yoshitsune's flight from Yoritomo after the war. The first episode in Chapter Four ("The Meeting Between Yoritomo and Yoshitsune") is seen as the dividing point. Unlike most other texts classified as war tales, the *Gikeiki* focuses consistently on a single character and, notably, on aspects of his life that are peripheral to the events in which he achieved historical significance. The episodes in the first half of the work emphasize his bravery and uniqueness as a youth, while the later chapters recount his pathetic flight and death. In this second part he is a much weaker character, and his famous retainer Musashibō Benkei emerges as the most forceful figure. This portion of the text is often cited as the first consistent source of the theme now labeled *hōgan biiki*, or "sympathy for the lieutenant" (Yoshitsune). Manifest more generally as "sympathy for the underdog," this concept would come to be identified as an aesthetic ideal for tragic heroes in Japanese performance arts and literatures throughout the medieval and early modern periods. I use this term cautiously, however, since it plays a role in claims for the uniqueness of Japanese culture and suggests that sympathy for Yoshitsune and other Japanese tragic heroes is qualitatively different from sympathetic portrayals of tragic heroes in other cultures.

The major variants of the *Gikeiki* are conventionally classified into three types.[73] The first, considered to represent the oldest variant line, consists of texts lacking both a table of contents and markers for the individual *shōdan*. The most significant extant texts in this category include the *Akagi bunko Yoshitsune monogatari*, the Tanakabon *Gikeiki*, and the Tenri Library's *Yoshitsune zōshi*. In the second category are the *rufubon*, dating from throughout the Tokugawa period, which differ from these earlier texts by inclusion of a table of contents, individually named *shōdan*, and, as the first episode of Chapter Eight, "The Memorial Services for Tsuginobu and Tadanobu." Finally, there are the printed book (*kanpon*) texts, which include recitational notation and describe the Battle of Koromo River in Tōhoku dialect. There is textual consistency across all variants, although there are numerous small differences in the *rufubon* texts suggesting minor transcriptional discrepancies.

The *Soga monogatari* (Tale of the Soga brothers) recounts a legendary vendetta that occurred shortly after the Genpei War but still during Yoritomo's lifetime. It was a wildly popular tale and most famously is the basis of numerous Tokugawa adaptations for the *kabuki* stage, but even during the medieval period it inspired *nō*, *kōwakamai*, *otogizōshi*, and other tales as well. The *Soga monogatari* relates the revenge taken by the Soga brothers, Jūrō and Gorō, on their father's killer, a close relative who had usurped the position of head of the clan. It is of particular interest for this study because of its similarities to and differences from other accounts of the rise of the Minamoto, as well as the way Minamoto control is articulated within larger narratives about Yoritomo's rise to power, the subject of Chapter Five.

The *Soga monogatari* differs from the other tales and dramatic pieces considered here because it relates a set of events that technically occur during the peaceful early years of the Kamakura government. Yet its themes are close to the hearts and minds of the warrior class: lineage, inheritance rights, family honor, and loyalty that reaches even beyond death.

There are four main variant lines of the *Soga monogatari*. The Manabon, written in a *kanbun*-based form known as *hentai kanbun*, consists of ten *maki*, and is thought to be the oldest text. Scholars think it was composed in the eastern (Kantō) region and was in the stewardship of Agui preachers and monks associated with Hakone shrine.[74] It probably dates from the early to mid-Muromachi period, although there is no definitive author or date of authorship.[75] Scholars believe that its apparently more coherent construction reflects a stronger organizational hand in its editing.[76]

The Taisekijibon seems to be a descendent of the Manabon, but it is written in *kana*.[77] Murakami Manabu suggests that the Manabon and Taisekiji lines evolved more directly from the *shōdō* (Buddhist chant) and *sekkyō* (sermon) traditions, as suggested by textual similarities to works like the *Shintōshū* and by their compact and complex narrative structuring.[78] The Taisekijibon contrasts with the Taisanjibon, which is similarly written in *kana*. The Taisanjibon is also comprised of ten books, but they are much shorter and missing many of the temple histories and episodes devoted to citing historical precedents so common in the other versions. The fourth main variant line is the *rufubon*, the latest and largest lineage; this is also the line included in annotated collections of the Japanese classics and translated into English.[79] It has received considerable attention as well because the antecedents for all later derived texts and performances about the Soga brothers are found in it. The Taisekijibon, Taisanjibon and *rufubon* are referred to by some scholars collectively as *kanabon* (texts written in *kana*) to contrast them with the Manabon. The *rufubon* texts consist of twelve books, and, although like the others they are thought to have originated in the east, their Jōdo sermonizing and episodes about Mt. Hiei link them as well to the Kyoto region; the *rufubon* may have reached its final form in or near the capital.

The *Soga monogatari* was part of recitational repertoires as well, and it is most closely associated with the *goze* of the Hakone region, who were blind female peripatetic narrators.[80] Orikuchi Shinobu posits that the earliest form of the *Soga* was recitational, performed by women, and dedicated to placating the spirits of the brothers; but stylistically, the Manabon suggests to most current scholars that, from early on, this line was part of a tradition of written texts.[81]

We see in *Soga* scholarship a method of categorization reflecting some of the same conceptualizations present in *Heike* classification. Lineages are organized according to two general tendencies apparent in extant texts, one towards the compact *kanbun* style of the Manabon and Taisekijibon variants, and the other towards the more lyrical, "dramatic" (*engekiteki*)[82] *kanamajiri* style of the *rufubon* and other "performance" texts. These categories closely resemble the read and recited lineages, respectively, in *Heike* scholarship, and they seem as well to exemplify some of the common assumptions of the literacy/orality dialectic: the Manabon-derived texts are drier, use more complex terminology (in Chinese), and create a somewhat less coherent individual narrative, while the *rufubon* variants are more lyrical, less clearly ideological, and more dedicated to narration of the brothers' lives. As with the *Heike* divisions, these have relatively permeable borders, and numerous exceptions and outright contradictions can be found within individual texts of both classes; so the distinctions, again, should be viewed with caution.

Kōwakamai, translated as "ballad-drama" by James Araki in the only published monograph in English on the genre,[83] is a performance art from the Muromachi period containing as its mainstay narratives about the military class. We do not have sufficient records to understand how it was performed in its earliest forms in the late fourteenth century, and there is contention about whether or not it started specifically as the warrior art that it became during the Tokugawa period.[84] *Kōwakamai* seems from early on to have involved two performers, both adult males, who recited and danced to minimal rhythmic accompaniment. Although *kōwakamai* contains dialogue, it is narrated rather than performed; individual actors do not fulfill the roles of specific characters. We do not know if this was true of medieval performance as well.[85] In contemporary performance costumes are consistent for all players in all pieces of the repertoire—all wear long *hakama* trousers, and they do not wear masks. The *tayū* role (primary character, similar to the *shite* of *nō* drama) is differentiated from the *waki* (secondary character, similar to the *waki* of *nō*) only by the hat each wears.[86] Scholars believe that early performances were more focused on performative elements, including costuming and movement, than Tokugawa period *kōwakamai*, and that performers included boys and women, whereas adult males would come to dominate the art as it became codified.

Current scholarship tends to link early *kōwakamai* (at least in name) to other medieval popular entertainment. In the late fifteenth century, recognizable references to such pieces come into the written record,[87] where they are identified as *kusemai*. It should be noted, however, that the connection between this nascent *kōwakamai* form and earlier *kusemai* (including that identified as part of the *nō* tradition) is tenuous at best. During this period something resembling the *kōwakamai* repertoire we have today was beginning to emerge as short pieces were consolidated into longer narratives and published as libretti and as texts to be read. By the sixteenth century, some amount of narrative overlap appears between the *kōwakamai* repertoire and that of *jōruri* and *otogizōshi*, an indicator of the continued flexibility among the categories of narrative and performance arts.

Although *kōwakamai* is first and foremost a performance tradition, texts or libretti of individual pieces were also published and illustrated with wood-block prints under the title *Mai no hon* (Book of [kōwaka]mai) as early as the Kan'ei period (1624–1644).[88] Many of the stories within the repertoire derive from episodes from the *Heike*, *Gikeiki*, or *Soga monogatari.* Scholars generally categorize them primarily according to subject (and specifically to narrative subject—Yoshitsune or the Soga brothers, for example). There are two primary textual lineages, the Kōwaka or Echizen line and the Daigashira line. For the most part, differences between texts are minimal and relatively inconsequential for the transmission of overall meaning, but for two of the narratives considered in Chapters Two and Five, they are sufficiently different that I have included both in my analyses.

The *Azuma kagami* differs fundamentally from the other texts in this study because it was compiled specifically to serve as an official history of the Kamakura government.[89] Although its date of composition is unknown, it covers activities of the shōgunate through 1266, making it necessarily posterior to that year. Scholarship generally places it somewhere between 1266 and 1301[90] and credits its sponsorship to the Hōjō family, who served as shōgunal regents following the deaths of Yoritomo's heirs. Several years are missing from extant manuscripts, including 1183 (Juei 2), the year in which the events discussed in Chapter Three occurred.

The *Azuma kagami* is written in the style of an official history, a genre originating with the *Rikkokushi.*[91] Official history as a discursive form was originally developed to celebrate and justify the authority and grandeur of the imperial house; the *Azuma kagami* replicates this effort on behalf of the warrior government. It mimics historical discourse both in its format (organized around dated entries that include replicas of official documents and reports on the activities of the ruling class for that day) and in its style—it is written in *kanbun.*[92] Like earlier histories, it is involved in the project of justification, of providing "the *raison d'être* for the Kamakura government,"[93] an undertaking which necessarily influenced its portrayal of both the current regime and its path to power.

This sort of intentional ideological discourse makes using the text as a historical source problematic, and researchers today do not treat it as a reliable historical record—even as early as the Tokugawa period (1600–1868) scholars were unwilling to take its account of the activities of the Hōjō at face value. Regarding its description of the Genpei War period and its immediate aftermath, the situation is further complicated because there was no meticulous official record of daily events in Kamakura available to the compilers, forcing them to look to sources as diverse as the house records of eastern military families, temple records, the diaries of court nobles, and, perhaps not surprisingly, early variants of the *Heike monogatari*.[94] Yet, since the *Azuma kagami*'s very form suggests historical veracity, its inclusion of materials borrowed from legendary or fictionalized sources likewise lends them an air of veracity. Its incorporation of a wide variety of documentary and narrative sources is what makes the *Azuma kagami* of such interest for this study: it very clearly illustrates the ease with which documents, battle accounts, journal entries, and legends were equally woven into the "history" of the period, a topic that will remain a central concern in the following chapters.

Methodological Considerations: Medievality, Textuality, Performance

In the chapters that follow, I explore how narratives drawn from the above texts and genres collectively create a deep and sustained account of the Minamoto consolidation of power, a tradition that emerged and grew stronger throughout the fourteenth to sixteenth centuries. In doing so, I situate these narratives not only as representatives of individual works or repertoires, but also as constituents of a larger, culturally shared body of ideas about how to interpret the past. The practices that created these narratives blurred many of the borders conventionally associated with Heian period writing and performance: genre, language and writing style, class, and geographic region.

This study focuses on key episodes of internal Minamoto strife from narratives retold across texts and genres during the Kamakura and Muromachi periods. Multiply told tales raise the critical problem of how best to evaluate them as both discrete episodes in larger self-contained works and as a sort of legendary element whose sheer presence exceeds the bounds of those works. Studies of this corpus have tended toward either immanent or genetic interpretive approaches. Both presume a high degree of integrity on the part of any individual text; the boundaries between one text and another are considered fairly clear, and each is treated as a circumscribed, discrete set of written words. This characterization is reflected especially in the naming and categorization of variants within the *Heike* repertoire; their differentiation has been a primary goal of scholarly inquiry. Intertextuality is an important consideration for diachronically situating the work, but ultimately the unit of comparison remains the individual text itself. Questioning these written texts and their autonomy, I believe, will provide a better understanding of the works as a gateway to the broader, more complex cultural space and processes in which the text participates and which endow it with meaning. This loosening of textual boundaries also begins to open up some of the paradigms that circumscribe our understanding of this crucial and complex body of historical narrative. What do we mean by "text," and what is the relationship of one text to others sharing much the same content?

The first issue to consider is the status of the texts available to us for study today. This concern has been productively addressed by scholars of literature, but most fully by those of medieval and less chirographically oriented[95] cultural contexts. These researchers identify several problems with a model based on investigation of the written works per se in cultural situations where the meaning of "text" is extremely fluid and often only loosely connected to written textuality. They provide viable guidelines for defining texts, contexts, and the strategies used for deriving meaning in cultures quite different from our own.

Medieval historian Brian Stock describes the "text" in the medieval European context as: "both physical and mental. The 'text' is what a community takes it to be."[96] For him, it is not only a physical object but also the evaluative and interpretive apparati an audience brings to bear on it; comprehension of its meaning is not necessarily linked to reading or literacy generally. What constitutes a text depends on an agreed-upon understanding of the text's parameters. Its meaning can be derived from written content, but it is also strongly dependent on other layers of meaning conferred by a specific group of interpreters in a specific context. The text can be itself a ritual object, a record of the holy (spoken) word, a finely crafted written narrative, or all of the above.

These multiple dimensions of textuality are of particular interest in connection with the *Heike* and the other works considered in this study, all of which manifest both performative and ritual elements. Even when read rather than heard, voice, music, and ritual context remain inscribed in them and evoke a realm beyond, and to a degree separate from, the written word. The domain of performance is a world where reception of a text is mediated by yet another level or translation as it is interpreted (enacted or vocalized) by a performer (or performers). Through this translation the text is more firmly located in the mind (and on the stage) than it can be by its inscription on a page. Moreover, unlike in the modern context, the meaning of the medieval textual object is merely a starting point for the "text" it preserves, not its full embodiment: it is an artifact that *reflects* the "text," but that "text" itself cannot be fully articulated without performance. That performance in this context involves a ritual dimension adds yet another layer of complexity, to which I will return. Crucially, the content shared among various works telling the same story enables the medieval "text" to create a memorable cultural narrative.

The non-self-sufficiency of the literary text has been underlined by every generation of literary studies since the heyday of the new critics, but the context I am describing points to an additional complication. The texts in question here most certainly overflow the boundaries of the written page, since most of them have several appropriate articulations, often as both performance and written works. And each one stands in close relation to other versions of the same story, which indicates the potential for a composite narrative extending across individual versions. The works in this study are not only not constrained by two covers, but further, not bounded by any sort of textual autonomy: wholesale movement of large narrative segments among versions is extremely common; there is rarely authorial attribution for any work; and there is little sense of an authoritative originary text from which the others have descended. These texts rely on interpretation using both hierarchical as well as lateral paradigms: hierarchically (diachronically), they require the reader or audience to be able to interpret them based on shared cultural and linguistic norms; laterally (synchronically), they also require knowledge of texts that share their story, characters, and often close-to-verbatim narrative. This study explores the interactive dimension of these works in both directions. As we shall see, one vital concern is the idea of interpretive frameworks. In this complex context, logical coherence depends on the ability of the audience or reader to interpret meaning not simply within an individual work, but also across the spectrum of other works with which it interfaces. Thus interpretation itself becomes a vital concern as a new set of hierarchical and lateral relationships is created in emerging and interrelated genres. The interpretive act, in fact, exceeds its role as tool to become a narrative subject as well.

Interpretation is a particularly compelling issue for reasons related to the nature of the texts in question: they are either clearly performance pieces themselves or parts of textual traditions with close ties to performance. An element of aurality is implicit in the experience of a written text with such ties, and thus interpretation tends to rely to some degree on the aural and visual imagination to amplify and color the experience of interpreting. This altering of the reading experience complicates ideas about reading practices. In the conventional (if idealized) case of decoding in written versus performed texts, differing paths to comprehension in each give rise to different parameters for interpretation. Folklorist John M. Foley explains this difference in terms of "referential modes," where in the case of performance, shared traditional knowledge, the performance, and audience fulfill the roles of author, text, and reader in the case of reading.[97]

Foley's comparison is based on a perceived difference between reading and listening experiences. And to an extent, this is valid: the interpretation of a written text depends on our ability to read and re-read, to refer to other texts, to pace ourselves, to derive meaning by visualizing complex sentence structure, and to revel in the beauty of a well-turned phrase. In the reading process, temporality is not entirely linear; it is subject to reversals and looping back to a degree that is much less feasible in a performance arena, where the "text" moves ahead at its own pace regardless of whether the listener chooses to move forward with it or not. By not following the movement of the performance, the listener risks missing part of it.

Foley argues that the mode of referentiality differs for written and oral (or performed) works, with what he refers to as the "immanent tradition"[98] representing the touchstone for the interpretive act in oral traditions. The "immanent tradition" represents interpretive schemes immanent in a culture (rather than an individual text) at the disposal of an informed audience at any given performance of a "text" from a familiar repertoire. His model is based on Wofgang Iser's reader-response theory, with Foley's "immanent tradition" functioning as the equivalent of the author in Iser's paradigm. Although there are problems with this model for the medieval Japanese context, the idea of a shared corpus of stories and characters serving as an interpretive touchstone for multiply told tales is useful.

The most important of Foley's insights for this analysis is his focus on the metonymic relationships among works sharing significant content. The audience knows a body of stories to which particular references in a performance will necessarily point; association is made by virtue of contiguity in the cultural space. Yet Foley invests this metonymic dimension with metaphoric significance. Metonymic association points to "[t]raditional structures . . . [that are] cognitive categories. Reality is configured and expressed, interpreted and reinterpreted, exclusively through the categories set and maintained as the traditional idiom."[99] What appears as metonymic, or accidentally associative, is guided by the metaphoric—cognitive categories that bring meaning to individual tellings. And they are framed, as we shall see, by a constellation of structural tropes embedded in each story: prophetic dreams, symbolic objects, and, perhaps most important in the emergent medieval age, the inherent connection between such established tropes and the idea of documentation. How this set of interpretive parameters is constructed will be the primary focus of this study.

While structure implies hierarchical relationships and static configurations, these are, as Foley indicates, stimulated by lateral relationships between tales—each adds layers of meaning (and weight generally) to the structure, while at the same time altering it to accord with expectations and understandings of the past as time goes by and stories change. One important contention of this study is that these structures and concerns are connected to the idea of an incipient national, or at the very least cultural, identity, as described by Barbara Ruch in her discussion of "audience-oriented repertory literature," works that form the basis for a "national literature." These works constitute a "combination of themes, heroes and heroines, predicaments, ethical dilemmas, resolutions. . . . A national literature is a certain core of literary works the content of which is well known and held dear by the majority of people across all class and professional lines, a literature that is a reflection of a national outlook."[100] Tales from the *Heike* are at the heart of this literature, and as works mobilized in creating narrative frameworks for interpreting history, they were also at the heart of the medieval audience's engagement with its own past.

Ruch's definition points importantly to key features of the audience that increasingly defined the direction of cultural developments: these works were experienced and interpreted by people from a broad range of backgrounds, who, by making connections between their own contemporary reality and the world within the tales, developed shared the critical tools to interpret them both. Brian Stock's description of "textual communities," or groups that "have some way of registering semantic and social relations that are understandable to the speakers, listeners, readers, and writers,"[101] brings one name to this concept. This community is not dependent on literacy, nor are the categories of writing/reading and performing/auditing mutually exclusive or even necessarily useful. What is essential to render a text the property of a given community is a shared set of interpretive skills, deployed within a common interpretive framework.

Below I will examine several ways in which interpretive structures from earlier periods were integrated with others more firmly grounded in the post-Genpei experience and articulated in this group of narratives. I hope to demonstrate the often cooperative relationship between writing and speaking as modes of expression in creating these structures. The interplay between these two is of course vitally important in the Japanese context, where writing had already enjoyed a long history and was the object of sustained critical inquiry, and where the audiences for written texts and performed ones were not mutually exclusive. People with lower levels of literacy were read to, and highly literate people were part of audiences for performances. This diversity in audiences, performers, and texts was made possible by, and also contributed to creating, a narrative that was and is dynamic in form and accessible. We shall see that another significant factor in creating that accessibility was the encoding of interpretive schemes within texts themselves.

Chapter Two

Minamoto Yoritomo

Dreams from Exile

The Barbarian-Subduing General, former Major Captain of the
Right Inner Palace Guards, was a man of great destiny. He quelled
the white waves of the western seas and calmed the green forests
in the far north. Then he dressed himself in brocade *hitatare*, entered the capital, and was appointed *urin taishōgun* (Great General
of the Royal Guards). . . . He renewed Buddhist law and royal law.
He subdued the proud Heike and assuaged the people's grief. He
expelled the disloyal and rewarded the loyal, without favoritism or
regard for proximity or distance. Who would have thought that
the Major Captain, bereft of his mother when he was just twelve,
separated from his father at thirteen, and exiled to Hirugashima
in Izu Province would rise to be such a man of great destiny? Even
he could not have expected it.

—Enkyōbon *Heike monogatari**

*T*he idea of shōgun has long captured the imaginations of both the
Japanese and the rest of the world.[1] The concept is a central tenet of
cultural discourses defining that nation: the shōgun is a great military
leader, a lord over vassals, a man whose stoic masculinity epitomizes certain fundamental cultural beliefs and practices that define "Japaneseness." Minamoto Yoritomo holds the honor of being the first of these
men.[2] Appointed shōgun in 1192 after defeating the Taira in the Genpei
War, he became the prototype for this military office that would reshape
the meaning of "military leader" and, in so doing, redefine the Japanese
political order for centuries to come.

Such an illustrious fate did not seem his destiny thirty years earlier,
however. Following the defeat of his father Minamoto Yoshitomo,[3] he was
sent into exile in Izu, where he languished in obscurity. He only rose again
to prominence after twenty years when he took up arms against the Taira
in a campaign that grew into the Genpei War.[4] With his victory, he was
granted broad jurisdiction over warrior affairs by the central government.

He situated his headquarters in Kamakura, far from the sovereign's capital. From this new base, he granted his retainers positions of power, thus initiating the attenuation of central political power that would propel warriors to the forefront of the political and social spheres. The age of the samurai for which Japan is so famous began, in other words, with the rise of Yoritomo.

Although in this brief account Yoritomo has all the makings of a popular hero, he does not fit traditional definitions of that role. He fought relatively little in the war that brought about the establishment of the Kamakura government, and he is peripheral in most of the tales recounting the conflict. The large number of nō plays depicting the pathos experienced by the men and women caught up in the war for the most part exclude him. His grave is remote and unimpressive, its one dilapidated souvenir stall unoccupied.[5] Compared to the many memorable warriors of his time, ranging from his kinsmen Yoshitsune and Yoshinaka through his Taira rivals—Tadanori, Noritsune, Koremori, to name but a few—he does very little to rank as a cultural hero, either on the battlefield or off. To make matters worse, he is generally loathed for ordering the deaths of his cousin Yoshinaka, and, more importantly, his brother Yoshitsune.[6] Yet it is hard to find narrative or dramatic accounts that hold him culpable for these acts: in contrast to archetypal villains like Taira Kiyomori or Lord Kira of Chūshingura (The revenge of the forty-seven rōnin), he does not figure centrally in the tragic tales of his victims. Blame for his unpardonable acts is formally attributed elsewhere, and he is pushed into the shadows, remaining ever a troubling mystery.

Yoritomo is chiefly remembered for having authored a legal system that significantly altered the political map of Japan.[7] As a political founding father, he redrew the contours of the realm so as to highlight the significance of the provinces. Largely as a consequence of this new emphasis, peripheral people and places were brought to the fore not only as historical and political subjects, but as narrative subjects as well—warriors, peasants, and itinerant performers became the central characters of newly emerging genres and works. As the heir to Minamoto hegemony, the first shōgun, and victor of the Genpei War, Yoritomo more than any other figure represents the impetus for the change that narratives of the period describe. He is the force shaping the people and the events of the war into history.[8]

There is thus a puzzling contradiction in Yoritomo's characterization between, simultaneously, the political and historical founding father and a shadowy, secondary character across the many texts about the Genpei period. This contradiction motivates my book in general and this chapter in particular. How does Yoritomo, the political axis around whom so many plots revolve, fit into cultural narratives of the Genpei period? How do we come to terms with what appear to be his irreconcilable depictions as, on the one hand, ruthless murderer of both enemies and kin, and, on the other, founder of a political order epitomized by a just system of laws, particularly favorable to people outside the aristocratic class? Emerging from these questions is a still larger one concerning the nature of the medieval society that, in its legends, histories, and drama, looked back on the world Yoritomo created as an important starting point. How did medieval people tell this moment of their past, and how does what they told and how they told it reflect their interpretation of Yoritomo's legacy?

The story at the center of this chapter, the Dream Interpretation (*Yume awase*), is one of the relatively few episodes found across a wide spectrum of medieval narratives and drama taking Yoritomo as a subject; this makes it a good starting place for exploring the significance of his character in the cultural milieu of medieval Japan. The episode recounts a sequence of dreams interpreted as foretelling Yoritomo's rise to prominence, set when Yoritomo's fortunes seem darkest: he has been stripped of office and property and is living under guard as an exile in Izu.

Yoritomo in Exile

Yoritomo's exile stemmed from his participation in the Heiji Uprising, where he served in his father's forces as they attempted to unseat Taira Kiyomori from increasingly greater positions of power in the central government. At the outbreak of the insurrection, Yoritomo had barely reached adulthood,[9] and he was the youngest of Yoshitomo's sons of sufficient age to join the fighting. His participation in the conflict was overshadowed by the outstanding martial feats of other warriors, particularly his eldest brother, Yoshihira. As the brief struggle waned and the defeat of the Minamoto became imminent, Yoritomo, his brothers, and several retainers planned to flee east with Yoshitomo in search of sympathetic supporters and sanctuary. Separated from the rest of the party in a snowstorm on Mt. Ibuki, Yoritomo was captured by Taira forces and returned to the capital. Yoshitomo was later betrayed by a retainer in Owari and killed, and Yoshihira was captured and executed. Legend has it that only the entreaties of Kiyomori's stepmother, the Ike Nun, convinced Kiyomori to spare Yoritomo and his younger brothers.[10] Yoritomo was sent into exile in Izu and his brothers were entrusted to temples—all acts aimed at emasculating and disenfranchising the Minamoto line.

It is noteworthy at this juncture that, whether the real reason for banishing (rather than executing) Yoritomo was indeed the Ike Nun's intervention, Kiyomori must have believed that exile was sufficient punishment to neutralize Yoritomo. Although the war tales and later historical memory derived from them tend to portray this act as an example of fatal hubris on Kiyomori's part, there is little evidence to suggest that his assessment of the situation was unreasonable under the circumstances. Given the generally dispersed nature of late Heian families and the vacuum left by the executions of Yoritomo's grandfather (in the Hōgen Uprising) and father on the orders of a generally stable government, banishment was a logical punishment for a man of Yoritomo's rank and age.[11]

The appropriateness of a lenient sentence is even clearer for the younger brothers. Not only were they children at the time of the Heiji Uprising, but they also had been born of several women from families of insufficient rank to represent a political challenge to the Taira. Their weakness both physically and politically was further cast against a backdrop of a lack of family coherence: Yoshitomo had sided against the rest of the family in the Hōgen Uprising three years earlier. With their father and elder brothers executed as enemies of the throne, Yoritomo and his brothers represented a minimal threat to Kiyomori. Their successful cooperation during the Genpei War—a fact that retrospective narrative accounts usually depict as having been pre-ordained by their fraternity—becomes all the more surprising under these circumstances. And although their temporary unity did in fact result in the defeat of the Taira, we should bear in mind that the tendency toward fragmentation that epitomized their overall relations during and after the war (to be considered in detail in Chapters Three and Four) was perhaps the more deeply encoded characteristic of the Minamoto family unit at the time.[12]

Yoritomo's exile to Izu lasted twenty years, and very little documentary evidence remains from that time to suggest what his life was like.[13] This period is elided entirely in most of the *Heike monogatari* variants from the performance repertoire, but it is described in varying degrees of specificity in *yomihonkei* (read lineage) texts, which in fact is one distinguishing features of the line.[14] What can be gleaned from these and other historical sources is that while he was in Izu, Yoritomo apparently maintained correspondence with supporters in the capital, through whom he may have been gauging the political situation there.[15] The most salient episodes from his banishment, however, concern two amorous adventures: affairs first with a daughter of Itō Sukechika, and then with Hōjō Masako. The first ended tragically—when Sukechika learned of the liaison, he forced his daughter to marry someone else and drowned the son she bore Yoritomo.[16] The association with Hōjō Masako, on the contrary, was successful, despite her father's similar ire when first learning of the affair. Unlike her predecessor, she shunned the groom her father had chosen and ran away to join Yoritomo. This relationship formed the basis for the important political partnership between Yoritomo's government and the Hōjō that would last beyond Yoritomo's death.

The prominence of romantic involvements in the narratives of Yoritomo's exile recalls the well-established narrative trope of the amorous
exile-hero.[17] Conventionally, the exiled hero is cast out from the center,
and, in his wanderings in the hinterlands, he discovers lovely women hidden there and staves off despair by enjoying their refined company. An
outcast's romantic tryst with a provincial woman is part of the hero's quest
beyond the bounds of society, but it simultaneously emphasizes his ties to
the capital: the woman is especially attractive because she embodies culture in an uncultured area. Although on the one hand she is a slightly ex-
otic "other," she is accessible because her beauty is conventional, which
necessarily casts her as a reminder of the hero's forced alienation from the
realm of convention. This wandering amorous character, codified in
Heian period literature in such figures as the hero of the *Ise monogatari* or
Genji at Akashi, is a prototype for the young Yoritomo—he is refined, pathetic, powerless, and far from home, which lends his amorous adventures
the texture of other courtly tales of noblemen cast adrift.

In conventional romances, what follows is a heroic return to the
center or a disappointing end in the provinces. Either way, the capital remains the ultimate goal, and success is measured by the hero's ability to
attain it. But Yoritomo's story does not reach a conventional end; the
weight of narrative expectation, in fact, serves primarily to emphasize the
radical difference of his story. Instead of returning to the capital, he remains in the provinces, setting up a household that becomes the basis for
a government. Through this establishment of roots in the east country,
he is able to rise from disenfranchised exile to political hegemon and re-
claim his status as Minamoto heir by producing children. As we shall see,
most narratives describe the moment of Masako's defiance of her father
as providing the impetus for this change: Yoritomo's emergence as the
Kamakura Lord occurs immediately after she flees to his side, and it is
heralded by the Dream Interpretation sequence considered here.

The Dream Interpretation Episodes

The Dream Interpretation narrative explains a dream or set of dreams
prophesying Yoritomo's return from exile and rise to power. It appears in
the *Heiji monogatari*; *Heike monogatari* variants including the Enkyōbon, the
Genpei jōsuiki, and the *Genpei tōjōroku*; the *Soga monogatari*; and the *kōwakamai* piece "Yume awase" (hereafter "The Dream Interpretation"). I will be
looking at two versions of this last piece because of divergences between
the accounts provided by the two *kōwakamai* lineages. For the Daigashira
lineage, I use the Kan'eiseihanbon (hereafter Kan'ei),[18] and for the Echizen lineage, I use the Tenri toshokan/Fujiishibon (hereafter Tenri).[19] In
the remainder of this chapter, I will be fleshing out a complex of themes

found across these variants that articulates the specialness and rectitude of Yoritomo as the founding father of warrior rule.

The variants of the Dream Interpretation narrative are found in texts emphasizing the Minamoto ascent following the Genpei War: *yomihonkei* variants of the *Heike*,[20] the *Heiji monogatari* and the *Soga monogatari*, all of which stress Yoritomo's final rise to power. The *kōwakamai* repertoire, too, shares this focus: most pieces, including "The Dream Interpretation," laud the heroes of the Genpei period and praise the shōgun under whom the warrior class rose to prominence.[21] Thus on one level, the episode should be viewed as part of longer narrative trajectories created by these texts and genres recording the rise of the Minamoto. Yet the multiple appearances of this specific anecdote across such a broad range of works also suggest the importance of this specific moment in the life of Yoritomo. This intersection of larger narratives and the potent layering of versions of this moment within the global narrative is a key fact in the broader arguments to be made below.

The Dream Interpretation narrative marks an important change in Yoritomo's fortunes. Embedded within the narrative of Yoritomo's exile, it appears consistently at the end of Yoritomo's banishment, with one exception—the *Heiji monogatari*, in which it takes place as he goes into exile.[22] In all other variants, it occurs shortly before he has been pardoned, while he is secluded on Izu Mountain with Hōjō Masako, who has fled her father's wrath to join him. The *kōwakamai*, of course, stands as a discrete piece; but as arranged in the *Mai no hon*[23] it is placed at the pivotal point of Yoritomo's story, where he sheds the stigma of exile and takes up arms against the Taira.[24] Most renditions of the narrative involve three characters: a dreamer, Adachi Morinaga;[25] an interpreter, Ōba Kageyoshi;[26] and Yoritomo.

SETTING THE STAGE: YORITOMO'S LOVES

The *Genpei jōsuiki* (hereafter *Jōsuiki*) Dream Interpretation sequence, the most compact of the group, appears in the opening episode of chapter 18 (of 48), "Mongaku Recommends Rebellion to Yoritomo" (*Mongaku Yoritomo ni muhon wo susumuru koto*). The narrative context is as follows: Yoritomo has reached full adulthood in exile in Izu, where he engages in two amorous affairs. He first forms a liaison with the third daughter of Itō Sukechika, and she gives birth to a son, Senzuru. The child is born while Sukechika is away in the capital; when he returns and learns who fathered the child, he is furious and will not accept the "Genji exile" as a son-in-law. He has the child drowned and forces his daughter into a marriage with Ema Kojirō, a local landholder. When Yoritomo learns of this, he is outraged and plans to kill Sukechika, but then reasons, "Where there is a larger goal, smaller resentments should be forgotten."[27] He lays aside his wrath in favor of his main objective: avenging his father's death at the hands of Kiyomori.

At this point Sukechika's son, Sukekane, warns Yoritomo that Suke-chika intends to kill him. Yoritomo calls two retainers, Moritsuna and Morinaga,[28] tells them of Sukechika's plan, and informs them that he will flee. He continues, "It would be foolish to lose my life because of Suke-chika. You two stay here, and no one will know I am gone." He then mounts his steed Ōkage and leaves, taking with him his attendant Onitake. As he travels, he prays:

> All hail, Great Bodhisattva Hachiman! Do not abandon me, the descen-dent of Lord Yoshiie. Make me Barbarian-Subduing General (*sei-i shōgun*), that I might protect the realm (*chōka*) and honor the gods. If you cannot grant that, let me become ruler of the province of Izu, so that I may punish my enemy. If fate does not allow even that, I dedicate myself to your true form, Amida; please take me quickly and help me in the next life.[29]

Moritsuna and Morinaga are able to divert Sukechika, and they later join Yoritomo, who has taken shelter with the Hōjō. Hōjō Tokimasa,[30] the patriarch, is away in the capital, and Yoritomo begins an affair with the el-dest Hōjō daughter, Masako. En route from the capital, Tokimasa prom-ises Masako to a fellow Izu landholder, Kanetaka. When he learns that Masako has given birth to a daughter by Yoritomo, he pretends to know nothing of the relationship and sends Masako off to Kanetaka. Masako es-capes, however, and joins Yoritomo on Izu Mountain, where he has se-cluded himself. Tokimasa and Kanetaka, fearing the militant ascetics of the mountain, decide not to pursue the matter.

Other texts embed the Dream Interpretation narrative within the account of Yoritomo's affairs; these include the Enkyōbon *Heike*, the *Gen-pei tōjōroku* (hereafter *Tōjōroku*), and the *Soga monogatari*. In the Enkyō-bon, the Dream Interpretation appears in the second chapter, in the account of "Yoritomo's Seclusion at Izu Mountain" (*Hyōe no suke Izuyama ni komoru koto*).[31] The account begins with a brief description of Yori-tomo's failed liaison with Itō Sukechika's daughter, in which Sukechika, as someone "indebted to the Heike," severs his daughter's relationship with "the Genji exile." The story continues as in the *Jōsuiki*, though with a slightly more elaborate plea to Hachiman.[32]

The *Tōjōroku* and *Soga monogatari* versions of Yoritomo's affairs are both relatively long and similar to each other. The *Tōjōroku* devotes four episodes (numbers 9 through 12 of chapter 1)[33] to Yoritomo's romances, and the *Soga monogatari*, nine; the similarity between the general narrative indicates an allusive relationship between the texts. The *Soga monogatari* version is the more elaborate, but there are several characteristics unique to the *Tōjōroku* worthy of mention.

The *Tōjōroku* begins with Yoritomo's wish to ally himself with the Itō daughter. He in fact explicitly invokes the example of Ariwara Narihira's affair with the Nijō Consort as precedent for his wooing of the young woman. In asserting that the Itō daughter, like the Nijō Consort, is forbidden as an object of affection for a man of his station, he suggests other associations with the Narihira story: in it, too, the hero's transgressions result in his exile to the east country Yoritomo now inhabits.[34] Yoritomo hopes that the union will gain him Sukechika's support, and while Morinaga at first is skeptical of this plan, the other retainer in attendance, Sasaki Sadatsuna,[35] is supportive. Yoritomo woos the girl, and in time a son is born. The account continues with Sukechika's return from the capital and anger about the match. After a particularly heartrending account of Senzuru's drowning, the Itō daughter laments her fate and an enraged Yoritomo plans to kill Sukechika. But Morinaga and Sadatsuna remind him of his ultimate goal, avenging his father's death: "What a shame it would be to lose one's life over small matters by diverting attention from the real enemy," they remark, and Yoritomo acquiesces and leaves to cast his lot next with the Hōjō.[36] His prayer to Hachiman as he travels is notably longer than in the accounts described above:

> All hail the great Bodhisattva Hachiman! When my ancestor Yoriyoshi went to subdue Sadatō in Ōshū, he dedicated his heir Yoshiie to you, and Yoshiie took the name Hachiman Tarō [First son of Hachiman]. Because of this tie, you have promised to protect the members of our clan (*uji*). I, Yoritomo, am a fourth generation descendent of Lord Hachiman [Yoshiie]. What I ask, Great Bodhisattva Hachiman, is that you give me control of Japan (*Nippongoku*), that you let me smite the enemy of my child, the Lay Monk Itō [Sukechika].[37]

Yoritomo then begins to woo Masako, who, when her father hears of the romance and wants to send her to Kanetaka, runs away to Izu Mountain. Upon learning that she has escaped there, Yoritomo rushes to join her. The text comments that their bond is "unique in this world."[38]

Two of the five *Soga monogatari* episodes describing Yoritomo's affair with the Itō daughter, "The Story of Wang Chao-chün" and "The Story of Sovereign Hsüan Tsung," relate stories from China about the forcible separation of happy lovers as the build up to Yoritomo's parting from Sukechika's daughter.[39] Citing such precedents from literature and legend to comment on the main plot is characteristic of the *Soga monogatari*; to a lesser extent it is an important feature of many of the texts considered here.

In "Yoritomo's Sojourn to Itō" and "The Story of Senzuru," Yoritomo's affair with Sukechika's daughter is described fully. Given the overall concern of the *Soga monogatari*, this attention to the feud between

Yoritomo and Sukechika, seen as the impetus for the situation that causes the Soga brothers' vendetta, is not surprising. Yoritomo's response to the birth of Senzuru raises the issue of his ancestral ties to the east country: "In thinking about the past, he realized that this province was filled with ancient memories, for it was the home of his ancestors; nevertheless, being forced to live there by a [royal] decree, he considered it an unfamiliar, rustic area."[40] The passage goes on to spell out Yoritomo's hope that the child born to him will signify the return of the Minamoto, who will, with the support of the military houses of the east, rise up to confront the Taira. In this text, Sukechika's wrath is fueled by a fear of the Taira, his benefactors, but also by the goading of his wife, the daughter's stepmother. The daughter is sent to Ema in tears, whereupon follow the two Chinese stories.

In "Yoritomo Leaves Itō," Yoritomo is also warned by Sukechika's son (here Sukekiyo)[41] of his father's plan to murder him, and he eventually is convinced to escape. In this version, Sukekiyo rather than Yoritomo lays the plan. In "Yoritomo Flees to Hōjō," Yoritomo prays to Hachiman. His prayer is somewhat more specific than the others in its focus on Genji fortunes:

> In the *Records of the Great Bodhisattva Hachiman* it is written that the Genji will, in these Latter Days of the Law, reside in the Eastern Provinces and subjugate the warriors of the east. However, since many Genji have fallen and the clan has declined, only I, Yoritomo, remain to carry on the legitimate Genji line. If I do not achieve glory, who will reestablish the house of Genji? The world has already entered the Latter Days of the Law, and I have no descendants. Let my opportunity come soon, that I may bring under my command the warriors of the east. If that is not possible, let me live humbly in this province, that I might some day realize my long-cherished desire.[42]

The succeeding episodes of the *Soga monogatari* ("The Story of Tokimasa's Daughters," "The Story of the Mandarin Orange," and "Tokimasa Takes Kanetaka as a Son-in-Law") recount Yoritomo's affair with Masako in more detail than do the other versions. Yoritomo's original intent, according to the *Soga monogatari*, was to woo one of the daughters of Tokimasa's current wife, given his problems with the Itō stepmother.[43] However, Masako, another stepdaughter, became the object of his affections.

Narratives of Masako's life merit an examination in their own right, but for the purposes of this study I limit discussion to the content of her dream. She purchased this dream from her sister, and it bears a striking resemblance to Morinaga's (as we shall see). In the dream, the sister climbed a high peak, placed the moon in one of her sleeves and the sun

in the other, and adorned her hair with a branch bearing three mandarin oranges. Masako understands the dream as alluding to "The Story of
the Mandarin Orange," which relates how oranges were allegedly first
brought to Japan for the mother of the sovereign Keikō during her pregnancy, to assure the safe delivery of the future ruler. Masako interprets
her sister's dream to mean that its possessor will bear sons who, like
Keikō, will rule the land. But she does not reveal this; instead she con-
vinces her sister that the dream is inauspicious, and that the only way to
be free of its predictions is to sell it (which, Masako claims, changes the
substance of the dream). Her gullible younger sister believes her, and
Masako purchases the dream with Hōjō family heirlooms coveted by the
sister—an interesting variation on the connection between lineage and
heirlooms to be explored more fully in Chapter Five.

Masako then begins her relationship with Yoritomo. A girl (Ōhime)
is born, and Masako's father learns of the liaison. Initially upset, he re-
members that an ancestor had married daughters to Yoriyoshi and that
ever since the descendants of Yoriyoshi had flourished in the east country,
so he reconsiders. But because Tokimasa had promised Masako to Kanetaka, he feigns ignorance of the liaison and ships her off to this suitor, a
"Heike warrior." He is secretly relieved that Masako flees (and, as in the
Tōjōroku, it is she who summons Yoritomo to Izu Mountain), and the episode ends with the comment that Tokimasa's "actions, so different from
those of Itō Sukechika, were dictated by his good karma."[44]

The tale of Yoritomo's failed affair with Itō's daughter features a motif
that recurs across the narratives considered in this book: Yoritomo's devotion to Hachiman. In all accounts, he prays to Hachiman as the patron
deity of warriors and the tutelary god of the Minamoto clan. Yoritomo
stresses this family connection when he cites Hachiman as the protector
of his ancestor, Yoshiie; in the *Tōjōroku*, he also mentions Yoriyoshi, and
all texts devote attention to the idea of a Genji line running through
these men and sanctioned by the god. In the *Soga monogatari*, Yoritomo
further claims that the family's rise is foretold in a divine text: the importance of the family for the deity, then, is both invoked in prayer and
confirmed in writing.

The content of Yoritomo's prayer is overtly political—he asks for divine help to rule the land. In the *Jōsuiki* and Enkyōbon, he specifically asks
to be appointed shōgun. His stated goal throughout is twofold: to protect
the realm and please the gods by killing his father's killer, Kiyomori, and
to avenge the death of his son. Yoritomo desires retaliation for the deaths
of his father and son—and who better to ask for divine assistance than the
deity connected to the continuation of the Minamoto line? This doubling
of vendettas highlights the theme of patrimonial lineage so central to the

narrative of Yoritomo's rise. In the *Tōjōroku* and *Soga monogatari* especially, this involves mustering the fighting men of the east under the Genji banner. Thus the god's patronage of Yoshiie and his heirs creates a temporal and cosmological constant that helps solidify the clan's temporarily scattered identity. These concerns all prefigure Morinaga's prophetic dreams.

THE DREAM

The dream occurs on Izu Mountain, while Yoritomo and Masako are hiding there from her father. This is a fitting stage for a prophetic vision: home to religious ascetics, the mountain is a liminal space offering the possibility of communication with the gods. In the *Jōsuiki*, we learn that the couple is now joined by Ōba Kageyoshi,[45] who, upon hearing of their circumstances, has come from Futokorojima to serve Yoritomo. Morinaga is already in attendance. The narrative turns to the Dream Interpretation sequence:

> One night, Kurō Morinaga dreamt that Yoritomo (*Hyōe no suke*)[46] was seated on Yagura Peak at Ashigara, with his left foot on Sotonohama and his right foot on Kikaigashima. From his right and left sides, the sun and moon shone forth. The Ippō Priest (*Ippō bōshi*)[47] came forward offering a gold jar, Moritsuna[48] presented [the Lord] a gold sake cup placed on a silver tray, and Morinaga presented him a sake bottle. Yoritomo drank from it three times. At this point, he awoke from the dream.[49]

Morinaga hurries to Yoritomo's side to recount the dream, and Kageyoshi offers to interpret it. He explains:

> This is a most auspicious dream. You, Lord, will pacify the land as the Barbarian-Subduing General. The sun signifies the sovereign, and the moon the retired sovereign. That they are shining from both sides of you means that the lord of the land (*kokuō*) supports you as general (*shōgun*). Your authority will reach to Sotonohama in the east and Kikaigashima in the west. The sake signifies that you are momentarily deluded, but you will become clear-hearted. In as few as three months but no longer than three years, the stupor will lift and your heart will be clear. Nothing will deviate from what is foretold in this dream.[50]

At this point in the *Jōsuiki* account we learn that Tokimasa, though outwardly angry, is secretly delighted with the match. Yoritomo, for his part, recognizes Tokimasa's value as an ally and also is gladdened. The episode next turns to Mongaku, the ascetic whose procurement of a pardon for Yoritomo from Go-Shirakawa initiates Yoritomo's campaign against the Taira.[51]

In the Enkyōbon version of the dream, Yoritomo straddles the realm from Kikaigashima to Sotonohama from atop Yagura Peak, the sun and moon shine forth from his sides, and he is presented with a banquet by his retainers. Kageyoshi's interpretation includes the assessment, "[the sun and moon shining] forth from your right and left sides means that the sovereign embraces you as general (*shōgun*)."[52] The other predictions are virtually identical to the *Jōsuiki* account. The passage and section conclude again with the comment that publicly Tokimasa was critical of Yoritomo, but secretly he was pleased, as was Yoritomo.

The *Tōjōroku* relates a slightly different dream in the episode entitled "The Story of Morinaga's Dream." Here again, Morinaga dreams that Yoritomo (*Hyōe no suke dono*) is ensconced on Yagura Peak in Ashigara, straddling the realm, facing south, this time with his left foot in the east country (*tōgoku*) and his right foot in the west country (*saikoku*). His retainers set out a feast before him, but the players and details differ somewhat: Ippōbo Toshun brings him a lapis lazuli jug (*heiji*), Sadatsuna presents him with a gold cup, and Morinaga provides a silver decanter. Morinaga takes the silver decanter and faces Yoritomo. After Yoritomo takes three sips of sake, he places the sun and the moon in his right and left sleeves. He then takes three pine saplings and walks south. Two white doves appear from in the sky, nest in his hair, and give birth to three chicks.

Kageyoshi's interpretation is familiar: sitting on Yagura Peak means that Yoritomo will control the land of Japan (*Nippongoku*). Because he is drunk of the wine of delusion (the sips of sake), Kageyoshi says, Yoritomo has been exiled to Izu, lived among the common country folk, and gotten involved in various matters. His left foot in the east means that his control will reach to Ōshū; his right in the west means it will also reach to Kikaigashima. Holding the sun and moon in his sleeves means that he will receive the sovereign's order to serve as Barbarian-Subduing General (*sei-i shōgun*) and also be supported by the retired sovereign. The three saplings symbolize the longevity of his control of Japan (again, *Nippongoku*).[53] The doves nesting in his hair signify that he will have three children. Walking south means that he will wake from his stupor and be successful in his endeavors. Yoritomo responds that, should he in fact succeed in life as prophesied in the dream, he will celebrate by rewarding both dreamer and interpreter with a province.

The *Soga monogatari* version of the episode diverges somewhat from that found in the *Heike* variants. "Morinaga's Dream" opens with the arrival of Kagenobu[54] from Futokorojima at Yoritomo's residence on Izu Mountain, hoping to perform a "meritorious deed" by calling upon the lord.[55] Morinaga is also in attendance. Morinaga awakens in the night and reports to Yoritomo that he has had the following "auspicious revelation" (*ojigen*):

In my dream, you were sitting on Yagura Peak. Ippōbō came forth with a large golden decanter (*kurogane taihenza*), Sanechika[56] laid out matting, Naritsuna placed a gold sake cup on a silver tray, and I, Morinaga, offered you sake from a silver decanter. After you had taken three drinks, you made a visit to pray at Hakone Shrine. You stood with your left foot on Sotonohama and your right foot on Kikaigashima. After placing the sun and the moon in each of your sleeves, you walked southward, crowned with three pine trees.[57]

Yoritomo is overjoyed, and relates that he, too, has had a "strange [prophetic] dream" (*reimu*), in which three doves flew down from the sky, nested in his hair, and bore chicks. He interprets this as a promising sign of Hachiman's divine protection.

A new named episode, "Kagenobu's Interpretation of the Dream" begins at this point. Kagenobu explains to Yoritomo:

[Y]our sitting on Yagura Peak means that you, a descendant of [Lord Hachiman] Minamoto Yoshiie, shall make the eight eastern provinces your home. It stands to reason that you were drinking sake, for in your present situation you are intoxicated by the wine of [delusion]. But you will recover from your intoxication in no sooner than three months, no later than three years, as is indicated by the word "three" in the phrase "three trees."[58]

The narrative at this point relates "The Story of Sake," a rather lengthy detour into the auspicious origins of sake in China, in which Kagenobu elucidates various explanations for the association of the expression "three trees" with sake. His story concludes:

Sake is blessed by the [ruler], the rain and dew that fall from the heavens, and the rays of the moon and sun that shine down from above. Similarly, your blessings, my lord, will extend everywhere. . . . "[T]hree trees" will cause you to forget your worries. You shall bring Japan (*Nippongoku*) under your rule. In the dream you stood with one foot on Sotonohama and the other on Kikaigashima. Surely this means that your rule will extend throughout Akitsushima. That you placed the moon in one sleeve and the sun in the other means that you will undoubtedly receive the support of both the [sovereign] and the retired [sovereign]. That you wore a crown of three pine trees is a sign of the protection given you by the Three Enshrined Deities of the Hachiman Shrine, a sign that you will live a thousand autumns, myriad years. That you walked in a southerly direction means you will, during the present [sovereign's] reign, arrive at the main south entrance of the [. . .] Palace, and proceed to the throne [for an audience with the sovereign]. Your fortune will unfold in this way.[59]

Yoritomo, delighted at this prediction, promises to reward Kagenobu should all he has foretold come to pass.

The *kōwakamai* "Yume awase," classified by modern scholars as a "Yoritomo Congratulatory Piece" (*Yoritomo shūgenmono*),[60] does not include the narrative of Yoritomo's affairs.[61] It is somewhat longer and more complex than the other variants and exhibits a more colloquial style in conversations between its characters.[62] Many of the dream images are by now familiar, but their presentation differs sufficiently to merit a brief sketch of the narrative sequence.

"Yume awase" opens with Morinaga having an auspicious dream while in attendance on Yoritomo in Izu, which he reports to an enraptured audience of Yoritomo and Kageyoshi. He begins with a discourse on the history of auspicious dreams, relating that in India, Queen Maya, taking an afternoon nap, dreamt of a golden-cheeked priest flying into her mouth; this heralded the birth of the historical Buddha.[63] Second, in "our land" (*wagachō*), the sovereign Yōmei's consort dreamt about a golden orb entering her left sleeve, which announced her pregnancy with Shōtoku Taishi. Finally, again in "our land," Saichō dreamt of clutching a lotus flower, and this led to his establishment of the Mt. Hiei temples. Here the dream narrative pauses, and Morinaga and Kageyoshi agree upon the felicitous nature of dreams.

The narrative frame for Morinaga's own dreams in the *kōwakamai* is thus composed of propitious visions from the past foreshadowing the auspiciousness of his own. Moreover, these visions specifically amplify an important theme found in Morinaga's dream: the first two are about births of men who later undergo apotheosis, the third is about another kind of "birth," that of the Tendai establishment on Mt. Hiei. They are favorable visions about positive change and the transformative powers of unique and gifted men.

Morinaga then recounts his own dreams. In the Tenri text there are three, and in the Kan'ei text, four, since it divides the Tenri's second in two. In both versions, the first dream envisions Yoritomo churning the purple, eight-fold clouds of "Higashiyama komatsubara"[64] and holding the gleaming sun. In the second (second and third in the Kan'ei text), dressed in white robe, *tate-eboshi* hat, and *asaikutsu* shoes,[65] he sits on Yagura Peak in Sagami, facing "not east, not south, not west, but north." He places his left foot on Kikaigashima and his right on Sotonohama.[66] Ōba Kageyoshi (or Ōba Kisō hōshi,[67] in the Tenri variant) brings him sake in a jug decorated with a butterfly-shaped closure at its mouth; it is accompanied by a nine-holed abalone.[68] Yoritomo eats a thick bit of the abalone and holds a thin bit as he drinks some sake. He then offers the thin piece to the Kisō Priest (*Kisō hōshi*), who proceeds to perform a felicitous dance (the movements of which are identified by name) before Yoritomo. In the final dream, Yoritomo is holding three pine trees in his right and left sleeves. Morinaga concludes with the request, "Interpret well, Lord Ōba (Kageyoshi)!"[69]

Kageyoshi replies that these are in fact auspicious dreams. The first signifies that Yoritomo will become "the Barbarian-Subduing General" (*sei-i shōgun*) of *Hi no moto*, the origin of the sun, Japan. Seating himself facing north "is read like this: when we write 'north' and 'pile up' (*kita kasanuru*), we read the characters, 'hōjō.' [. . .] This means you will rely on Lord Hōjō in establishing your rule."[70]

In the third dream, the abalone, because it is a creature of the sea, suggests that Yoritomo's influence will extend to all places that can be reached by boat, as well as to places on land that can be reached by horse. His straddling of the realm implies the reach of his power to Sotonohama and Kikaigashima, but also beyond, to Kōrai (on the Korean peninsula), Keitangoku (Mongolia), Shinra (Korean peninsula) and Hakusai (Korean peninsula). These final two appear in the Tenri text but not the Kan'ei text.[71] In the last dream, the three pines represent Yoritomo, Morinaga, and Kageyoshi. "For each inch that they grow, thousands of branches will flourish; their ages will reach a thousand years. You, my young lord, will flourish like that tree for many years."[72] The piece concludes with the remark that "Morinaga's dream account and Kageyoshi's interpretation proclaimed the good fortune of the lord."[73]

The *Heiji monogatari* contains the most significantly divergent version of this narrative, entitled "The Interpretation of Moriyasu's Dream" (*Moriyasu yumeawase no koto*). Appearing toward the end of the third and final chapter of the work, it immediately follows an episode called "Yoritomo's Distant Exile" (*Yoritomo onru no koto*), an account of the commutation of his death sentence to distant exile at the behest of the Ike Nun. The sentence is passed in the capital, and from there Yoritomo departs for Izu. As he leaves, he tearfully thanks the nun for her parental concern after he has been "bereft of his mother since the first day of the third month of last year and his father since the third day of the first month of this year."[74] On his trip to Izu he is accompanied by three or four samurai, among whom is Moriyasu, a faithful retainer of a collateral Minamoto line. The two converse along the route, Moriyasu answering his young lord's queries about local shrines and deities as they make their way east. Moriyasu is loath to part with the prisoner despite worry over the ill health of his own aged mother, whom he has left in the capital. At Seta, they arrive at Takebe Shrine,[75] and Yoritomo requests that they stop there for the night. Late in the evening, Moriyasu secretly reports to Yoritomo a prophetic dream (*reimu*) he has had:

My Lord, [. . .] you made a pilgrimage to the Iwashimizu Shrine.[76] I accompanied you. You were worshipping in the great hall of the sanctuary, and I at the shrine fence. A celestial child of about twelve or thirteen years of age entered the great hall clasping a bow and arrow. He said, "I have brought Yoshitomo's bow and quiver." Then, from inside the treasure hall, a voice resounded, "Place it here. It shall be given to Yoritomo. But first, feed him." The boy went behind a bamboo screen and, upon his return, placed something before you, Yoritomo. It was sixty-six dried abalone. Then the voice said "Yoritomo, eat!" You grasped the abalone and ate the thick parts in three bites. You then threw the remains to me, and I tucked them away. I awoke feeling joyous. The dream . . . means this: the bow and arrow of your house is guarded in the treasure hall of the Great Bodhisattva. Your father temporarily became an enemy of the court (*chōteki*), but this dream reveals your fortunes to be promising. The sixty-six abalone are the sixty-six provinces, which you must take in the palm of your hand. The remainder, which I tucked away, is a promise for the many people in my position [as your followers].[77]

Elated by this news, Yoritomo asks Moriyasu to accompany him just a little further, and Moriyasu decides to follow the young lord permanently. Yoritomo promises that he, Yoritomo, will in return forever bear the karmic burden of Moriyasu's forsaken mother. The party continues its journey into exile.

The placement of the story, the identity of the dreamer, the conflation of the dreamer and interpreter, and most of the specific content of the dream differ markedly from the other renditions. Moreover, this episode does not occur in all variants of the *Heiji monogatari*—it is notably absent from the Kotohirabon line.[78] Its inclusion in the Kujō family manuscript and the *kokatsuji*, or "old print" editions has been a point of debate regarding textual development, since it implies a post-Genpei date of compilation. Most important for this study, the fact that it was a component of some medieval editions accentuates the fundamental role of stories about the Heiji Uprising in the broader Genpei narrative: Yoritomo's rise after the Genpei War is depicted as a development encoded in earlier strife between the Minamoto and the Taira. The inclusion of this proleptic episode pulls the *Heiji monogatari* as a whole into an orbit around the central events of Yoritomo's rise to power. Although in this variant the dream occurs earlier in Yoritomo's life than we have seen in the other versions, it nevertheless appears at the same functional moment: after he has become an exile, and as an indication that he will rise again.

Before moving into an analysis of the sequence as a whole, it will be helpful to flesh out certain striking motifs that occur across variants of the narrative. Perhaps the most noteworthy of these is the focus on geography: we find Yoritomo in most variants straddling the realm from Sotonohama (in present-day Aomori Prefecture) to Kikaigashima (a remote southeastern island where Naritsune, Yasuyori, and Shunkan were exiled by Kiyomori following the Shishinotani affair in 1177), locations representing the eastern- and westernmost extremities of the realm.[79] The *Tōjōroku* contains the more general *tōgoku* and *saikoku*, but all variants depict Yoritomo's broad reach, emanating from his seat on Yagura Peak.

Located in Sagami Province (present-day Kanagawa Prefecture), Yagura evokes the land to which Yoritomo had been exiled in 1160 as well as ancient ideas about the edges of the realm: it was through nearby Ashigara Pass that Yamato-takeru entered the eastern lands in order to subdue them in the *Kojiki* and *Nihon shoki*. The area is thus geographically significant both for the specific moment of Yoritomo's emergence from exile and historical cartographies of the realm's eastern regions. Yoritomo's wide stance in the dream translates quite literally as reach in the military sense: he places each foot at an edge of the realm, marking the boundaries of his control.

Next, we encounter a catalogue of important retainers, three of whom present Yoritomo gifts. The jar (*heiji*) is a homophone of the Taira family name,[80] a pun also used elsewhere in *Heike* narrative.[81] There is no commentary about the jar, perhaps because the allegorical significance of its presentation to Yoritomo is transparent; subduing the Taira is, after all, one of the acts for which Yoritomo is best known.

The gold sake cup and the silver tray on which it sits provide an earthly echo of the sun and moon shining at Yoritomo's sides. The motif of the three sips from the cup foretells the three months to three years it will take for recovery from Yoritomo's stupor to occur. A commonly used magical or otherwise special motif in traditional narrative, the number three is often linked to pledging certainty, particularly in marriages. Yoritomo's sojourn in the mountains that occasions this dream, of course, is spurred by his yet unrecognized marriage to Masako; here the idea of pledges bleeds as well into his devotion to his cause.

Yoritomo promises rewards to his supporters should his future unfold as the dream predicts—a vow foreshadowing his actual administrative methods as Kamakura Lord after the Genpei War. The idea of Yoritomo's political role is of vital importance; in all cases, it is noted that he will subdue the realm. In the *Jōsuiki* and Enkyōbon, the "realm" is identified by the terms *chōka* and *tenka*, respectively; in the *Tōjōroku*, and *Soga monogatari* we find *Nippongoku*; and in the *kōwakamai*, the very similar *Hi no moto*. In all cases, it is as shōgun that Yoritomo will take on the responsibility of controlling the country.

In the *Soga monogatari* and the *kōwakamai*, the two most elaborate versions (and the two that explicitly note the auspicious nature of dreams), we find interesting additions that support the themes already developing within the aggregate narrative. In the *Soga monogatari*, the doves are linked specifically to Hachiman's protection of the Minamoto, and Lord Hachiman Yoshiie is evoked as Yoritomo's ancestor; this echoes as well, of course, Yoritomo's recounting of the Minamoto lineage in his prayer to Hachiman and Tokimasa's recollection of Yoriyoshi and Yoshiie. The visit to Hakone Shrine probably reflects the importance of that shrine generally in the *Soga monogatari* narrative, but in so doing, it also stresses Yoritomo's location: he is firmly grounded in the east.

The southward journey, a sign that Yoritomo will be received by the ruler, is unique to the *Soga monogatari*, but it recalls the interpretations elsewhere of the sun and moon images as connoting the support of the reigning and retired sovereigns. "The Story of Sake" represents a significant divergence, but it is tied into the narrative shared by the variants through the explanation of the "three trees" that crown Yoritomo. These recall the three saplings of the *Tōjōroku* account, as well as the various other trinities in this cycle: three sips, three doves, three chicks, Masako's three mandarin oranges, and the Lord-Dreamer-Interpreter triumvirate.

In the *kōwakamai*, the interpretation of the remainder of the dream overtly evokes the written word in its explication of Yoritomo's north-facing posture as indicating his reliance on the Hōjō; the sequence uses the term "to read" (*yomu*) to explain the interpretation of this image. Such an interpretive strategy requires a comprehension of the written character set and an awareness of intricate wordplay within that set.

Finally, in the *kōwakamai* the dream interpretation sequence seems less precisely correlated to the dreams themselves than in the other variants. Yoritomo's straddling of the realm, the most salient example, is skipped entirely, and the abalone's status as a sea creature is substituted as proof of the reach of Yoritomo's future power; the abalone's conventional association with longevity is not mentioned at all. Likewise, Yoritomo's sharing of the abalone with the Kisō Priest has the pragmatic function of eliciting a performance rather than being a symbolic representation of his future benevolence toward his supporters.

The Dream Interpretation: Narrating the Rise of the Warriors

The Dream Interpretation narrative, as we have seen, marks a critical moment in Yoritomo's change of fortunes and provides a legitimizing context for his rise to power following the Genpei War. As one episode in longer independent narratives, it represents a diachronic marker of Yoritomo's change in fortunes, a turning point in each story. Thus in the *Heiji monogatari*, it is a final hopeful foreshadowing of events twenty and more years in the future, while in the other texts it is the first step in the creation of a world under Yoritomo's control. Yet as an episode flexible enough to occupy slightly different moments within individual narratives or stand alone as a *kōwakamai* piece, it tends to draw attention to itself as a discrete narrative unit as well. In both its combinative aspects and as a self-standing narrative whole, the Dream Interpretation sequence proves a rich thematic nexus, a matrix of associations out of which the Yoritomo of history will be born. The remainder of this chapter traces these associations and how they operate in both the episode itself and the longer narratives in which the dream is embedded.

Among the variants of the Dream Interpretation sequence, a coherent image of Yoritomo's future rise to power is realized through a number of closely related tropes that can be seen generally to elucidate two interwoven themes: the idea of Minamoto family identity and continuity, and the concept of the realm of Japan, over which Yoritomo will be granted control as "shōgun." Both of these issues are closely affiliated with conceptualizations of authority: the divine and earthly authorities that sanction Yoritomo's rise, and Yoritomo's prophesied authority over the land. Underlying these is a metahistorical concern with authenticating certain views of the past. What tools do tellers use (and what responses are elicited in readers and audiences) as a means of creating an acceptable history of a new political order?

The dream topos is used to animate a complex of symbols that gives meaning to central historical themes—the transfer of power to Yoritomo, the establishment of the shōgunate, and the rise of the military class to rule a newly imagined realm—in the context of narrations of the Genpei War.

MINAMOTO IDENTITY: THE GREAT WARRIOR CLAN OF THE EAST

One of the primary themes running through this study is the conceptualization of the Minamoto clan as a continuous lineage spanning Japanese history and supporting the political and social structures defining that history. Yoritomo's rise to power is in a way the culmination of Minamoto identity, since he is the first to gain a meaningful political position that is also heritable. His rise is inevitably framed by the military greatness of his ancestors, particularly Yoshiie; references to this great warrior fill the war tales.[82] The ongoing importance of being Minamoto is further demonstrated in the medieval and early modern periods by the Ashikaga and Tokugawa shōgunates' preoccupation with connecting their own lineages to that of the first shōgun. The idea of the shōgunal house belonging to the Minamoto remains an important marker of warrior identity until the modern age, despite the fact that Yoritomo's own line ended with the death of his son Sanetomo in 1219.[83]

The name derives further significance from its association with the royal family: as one of the monikers granted sloughed-off princes of the blood, "Minamoto" immediately indicates this illustrious link.[84] According to historical records, the Minamoto comprising the "Seiwa Genji" lineage took shape as a military house beginning in the mid-Heian period, rising to relative prominence under the patronage of the Fujiwara regents.[85] As governors and subordinate provincial officials, men with the Minamoto family name gained distinction as enforcers of central authority, and as members of the military guards they also served the throne in the capital city. Yoriyoshi and his son Yoshiie were particularly celebrated as great warriors, in large part for their successes in the Former Nine Years' War (1056–1062) and Latter Three Years' War (1083–1087) in northern Honshū. Constituents of this same kin group mobilized to become leaders during the Hōgen and Heiji uprisings.[86]

Yet these figures alone did not add up to the idea of a great, sustained military dynasty. Following the Latter Three Years' War, Minamoto fortunes waned. As victor in that conflict, Yoshiie had been forced to remunerate his supporters from private coffers when the central government refused compensation for what it considered a private dispute. Although this act of altruism is cited as a source of future support for Minamoto by the descendents of Yoshiie's beneficiaries during the Genpei campaign, its immediate effect was to financially weaken Yoshiie and the mainline Seiwa Genji. The Hōgen Uprising proved even more devastating: Yoshitomo sided against his father and brothers, and, as part of the horrific settlement of that conflict, was ordered to execute his entire kin group, which had supported the losing side. In the waning years of the Heian period, in other words, the mainline Seiwa Genji was not particularly important to the court politically or supported by it financially, nor was it acting as a unified family in the sporadic military actions of the time.[87]

In the Dream Interpretation narrative, however, Minamoto lineage is a feature of all renditions, albeit to varying degrees. At the most basic level, famous members of the Minamoto line are invoked liberally. Yoritomo's prayer to Hachiman mentions Yoshiie in all versions, and, in the *Tōjōroku*, it invokes Yoriyoshi as well. In the *Heiji monogatari* dream sequence, Yoritomo receives Yoshitomo's sword from the gods. In the *Soga monogatari*, he ruminates that the east country had been a hereditary stronghold of the Minamoto, but because he arrived there as an exile, he never felt at home until the birth of his son, Senzuru. This male heir of course represented the potential continuation of the line that would give meaning to both Yoritomo's position in the lineage and the space of the east country in which the child was born. Later in this version, Hōjō Tokimasa's willingness to accept his daughter's choice of spouse is based on the good relations his own ancestors enjoyed from marriage into Yoriyoshi's clan. Thus, in these narratives Yoritomo is consistently and conspicuously identified as a Minamoto.

Although his Minamoto heritage is most strongly evoked in the *Soga monogatari* (one of the later texts), it is present in all versions, demonstrating that the attraction of the idea of the Minamoto lineage increases over time. And these later accretions affect readings of the other works as well—even though the theme is not as fully developed in early texts like the *Tōjōroku* and the *Heiji monogatari*, its presence even in a nascent form reinforces the importance of the Minamoto family identity across the broader body of texts. The result is a successful projection of the lineage back to Yoshiie, a "history" reified by its repetition in so many sources. Intertextuality, in other words, works in both directions: in addition to later texts alluding to or even borrowing from earlier ones, the very coherent view of the Minamoto lineage in the later *Soga monogatari* is *read back onto* earlier versions of essentially the same story, giving form and substance to the older, less lengthy descriptions.

On a slightly abstracted level, substantiating the Minamoto lineage is precisely the narrative problem the auspicious dream addresses. Yoritomo is the heir apparent to Yoshitomo, and his banishment to Izu is a very public marker of his impotence in every sense—he has been stripped of his rank and title and placed under guard. In the *Soga monogatari* he specifically identifies his position as impeding him from doing what he, as Minamoto inheritor, should do: continue the line. His failed affair with Sukechika's daughter provides an eloquent illustration of just how thoroughly his clan has been emasculated. When his son, the male progeny of the "Genji exile," is drowned Yoritomo is powerless to protect the child or, at this point, wreak vengeance. His first attempt at restarting the line has been a tragic failure.

Against this backdrop, his second liaison seems destined for failure as well. Masako's father, at first ill-disposed to harboring Yoritomo in so intimate a capacity, sends his daughter off to another suitor. But there are also important differences: the child born this time is a girl (which perhaps lessens her grandfather's ire), the woman is willful, and the patriarch is not murderous. This new situation is the context for the felicitous dream foretelling a change of fortune. Significantly, the dream comes in the wake of Yoritomo's invocation of the clan deity, Hachiman. This connection sets up metaphoric associations that both position the lineage within broader, more significant socio-political realms and shore up its claim to antiquity and unity in the east.

DIVINE AUTHORITY: HACHIMAN AND THE MINAMOTO

The most often cited origin of the relationship between Hachiman and the Seiwa Genji is the dedication of Yoriyoshi and Yoshiie to the god, cemented during the Latter Nine Years' War when Yoshiie takes the name "Hachiman Tarō" ("first son of Hachiman") in honor of the deity. Yoshiie's relationship to Hachiman is invoked throughout the war tales; it is recalled by each Minamoto hero in turn when he goes into battle or confronts other difficult circumstances, as Yoritomo does here. Not surprisingly, the initial devotion to the god demonstrated by Yoriyoshi and Yoshiie as forefathers of the Seiwa Genji is closely identified with Hachiman's status as the patron god of war and warriors: these early devotees defined their identities as warriors by claiming Hachiman as their tutelary deity. Several generations later, Yoritomo tapped into the potential of this affiliation, starting with his patronage of the Tsurugaoka Hachimangū in Kamakura. Originally built by Yoriyoshi as a branch of the Iwashimizu Hachimangū in 1063, it became an important symbol of Yoritomo's new headquarters in Kamakura when he relocated and expanded the shrine in 1180. His government offices and the dwelling places of his most prominent retainers were built on the avenue leading to the shrine complex. Where the royal palace was the locus of power both politically and geographically in the capital at Heian-kyō, Hachiman's shrine served that role in Kamakura. Thus the history given sustained meaning in stories like the Dream Interpretation was also consciously being crafted by Yoritomo himself as he drew formal attention to Hachiman, his ancestors' connection to the god, and the site of Kamakura as a home for Hachiman to rival Iwashimizu.

In all the Dream Interpretation variants, Hachiman's sanction is a necessary element in Yoritomo's rise. Yoritomo's invocation of the god throughout the works figures Hachiman as his patron deity, and the prayer itself immediately precedes his change in fortune. Further, Hachiman's doves are integral to the dream symbolism in the *Tōjōroku* and *Soga monogatari* accounts (in both cases they appear in conjunction with pines, conventional symbols of longevity and prosperity). The connection between divine sanction and military might in the *Heiji monogatari* is more direct than in these other renditions; indeed, it is manifest in the appearance and speech of the god himself: Hachiman informs the dreamer that he is vouchsafing the bow and arrows of Yoshitomo for the time when Yoritomo will rise and use them to protect the throne.

Although the good fortune foretold Yoritomo resonates throughout the Dream Interpretation variants, the *Heiji monogatari* dream of Hachiman as custodian of Yoshitomo's bow and arrows is somewhat anomalous. It has deep connections, however, to another cycle of stories about the rise of the Minamoto under Yoritomo that impinges on both this narrative and that considered in Chapter Five: "The Young Samurai's Dream" (*Seishi ga yume*), appearing, among other places, in the Kakuichibon and the *Jōsuiki*, concerns the circulation of military accouterments within the realm of the gods as symbols of divinely sanctioned authority. It is articulated through many of the same images as the *Heiji monogatari* Dream Interpretation and bears brief consideration here.

"The Young Samurai's Dream" appears shortly after Kiyomori's transfer of the capital to Fukuhara in both accounts (Kakuichibon, chapter 5; *Jōsuiki,* chapter 17). The narrative relates the portentous dream of a samurai in the service of the Taira retainer Minamoto Masayori (and ultimately in service to Kiyomori). In the dream, an assembly of deities discusses the sword of commission (*settō*), a blade given by the sovereign to his general (*shōgun*) to represent the general's authority to subdue all enemies of the court. The patron deities of the Minamoto (Hachiman) and Taira (the Itsukushima deity) debate the fate of the sword. It had originally been in the possession of Yoshitomo, but because he turned his back on the government, it was passed for a time to Kiyomori, who in turn abused the authority it represented. Now Hachiman requests that it be returned to Yoritomo, Yoshitomo's heir; the assembly of deities (in the Kakuichibon led by Hachiman and in the *Jōsuiki* by Amaterasu) decides to honor this request. When this dream is revealed by the dreamer, it is interpreted as an inauspicious sign for Kiyomori.[88]

Insofar as this ominous dream appears to a Taira retainer, its circumstances are quite different from the *Heiji monogatari* narrative; nevertheless, in content the two dreams are strikingly similar and certainly grounded in the same root story. In both, weaponry (the sword; the bow and arrow) is used metonymically to evoke politically sanctioned military authority. Hachiman's role as keeper of the weapons, the foregrounding of the importance of protecting the realm from its enemies, and the idea that a deity can stand in for a family are all elements shared between the narratives.

While I do not want to dwell too long on this somewhat peripheral story, its overlap with the Dream Interpretation cycle is significant on a number of levels. First, it highlights one of the many ways the metaphoric connection between Hachiman and Minamoto lineage is articulated consistently in the broader sphere of Genpei narrative. Second, it points to another central set of symbols that work within this sign system: the bow and arrow, and the sword. This combination of the Minamoto name, the patronage of Hachiman, and the significance of military prowess define the Minamoto as the military clan the gods have delegated to protect the throne and the realm in the role of shōgun.[89]

MINAMOTO YORITOMO, GREAT BARBARIAN-SUBDUING GENERAL

Yoritomo's rise to the position of shōgun is the center of the Dream Interpretation story. The key points of Kageyoshi's interpretation are that Yoritomo will be named to that position, that he will subdue the realm, and that he will be endorsed by the royal authorities. The *Jōsuiki*, Enkyō-bon, and *Soga monogatari* variants of Yoritomo's prayer to Hachiman also feature his desire to attain that position.

The development of the idea of shōgun articulated in Yoritomo's rise is of particular import. Although attaining this post is foretold as Yoritomo's destiny, "shōgun" is in fact not the most common epithet for him in the war tales: he is more often the Former Assistant Commander of the Military Guards (*Hyōe no suke*) or the Kamakura Lord (*Kamakura dono*). That said, Yoritomo's status as "shōgun" clearly is a matter of narrative concern here. What is the specific meaning of the term in the medieval narratives about the Genpei period, and why is so much attention dedicated to delineating that meaning in the Dream Interpretation variants?

The term "*sei-i [tai]shōgun*" and its abbreviated version were originally imported from China centuries before Yoritomo's lifetime. Shōgun designated a commander of forces, appointed by the sovereign, sent out to quell disturbances in the realm's hinterland, the dwelling place of barbarians.[90] Prior to its appropriation in the medieval war tales, this title was not the political, permanent position it would become, but rather an appointment tied to a specific military campaign against outsiders (*i, ebisu*). This shifts in the war tales; now the shōgun is still defender of the throne, but he defends it instead against "enemies of the court" (*chōteki*)—a rhetorical move that domesticates what formerly were foreign enemies and the territories they inhabited,[91] a topic I will return to in the next section.

Although in the war tales "shōgun" is sometimes used to mean, simply, "general," we increasingly find *[sei-i tai]shōgun* used to denote the particular permanent and alienable position held by Yoritomo as head of the Kamakura government, just as it is in the Dream Interpretation narrative. While the title did eventually become durable, this definition is doubly anachronistic here: Yoritomo was not officially appointed shōgun until 1192, nearly a decade after the defeat of the Taira, and he himself never considered the title permanent.[92] In fact, he resigned it immediately after the appointment, preferring to refer to himself as *Utaishō* (Major Captain of the Royal Guards), an established, aristocratic position to which he had been appointed earlier, and the highest office in the traditional hierarchy to which he was ever promoted.[93] In other words, he chose to define and aggrandize his political clout in terms of the conventional order, and "shōgun" in all likelihood represented too low a position to be considered viable for this purpose. We are thus left with the question of why an inaccurate appellation is so central to the narrative of Yoritomo's rise and what its use has meant to audiences both in the medieval period and today.

The term shōgun became associated specifically with the position of Kamakura Lord after Yoritomo's death, replacing "Kamakura Lord" (*Kamakura dono*), by which Yoritomo is frequently identified in contemporary sources. Shōgun as a political institution was in fact established as a product of the jockeying for control after Yoritomo's death by the Hōjō and the Hiki, both relatives of Yoriie, Yoritomo's successor. Each family wished to enhance its own power, but neither was in a position to directly challenge the Minamoto heir for leadership. This situation was resolved according to the time-honored practice of aristocrats close to the sovereign: the strongest contenders—in this case the Hōjō—established themselves as shōgunal regents and controlled the official actions of the appointed shōgun from that position.[94] For the regents, then, the stability and legitimacy of the position of shōgun were of paramount importance, for only through that position were they empowered. The death of Sanetomo, the last Minamoto shōgun in 1219, did nothing to disrupt this system—in one great irony of the Kamakura period, "[t]he shogunal title, which was never very important for the Minamoto, became indispensable for the Hōjō. A succession of child (or figurehead) shoguns would henceforth justify their own permanent regency. It thus became expedient to reinforce the Minamoto memory even as the Minamoto line was dying out."[95] While the Minamoto line ended just twenty years after Yoritomo's own death, the idea of shōgun—justified through the righteous military history of the Minamoto clan—therefore remained.

The problem for this study lies not so much in the system itself, but in the specific designation "shōgun" for this position. Identifying the Kamakura-based warrior hegemon as shōgun redefines the term by politicizing and institutionalizing it. In the Dream Interpretation narrative, designating Yoritomo "shōgun" becomes a vital element in the story of the rise of the warrior class, and specifically, the warriors of the peripheral eastern regions where Yoritomo staked his claim to power.

MAPPING THE REALM

The importance in the Dream Interpretation sequence of the east country in particular and the peripheries more generally is given form in the striking dream of Yoritomo perched on Yagura Peak and straddling the realm from Sotonohama to Kikaigashima. The dream's focus on physical geography suggests an important new narrative space being opened within the cultural imagination for the post-Genpei world, one that eschews the capital city as its point of reference in favor of Yoritomo's base of operations in the east. It is this narrative milieu that grants the term "shōgun" its cultural weight.

In the Dream Interpretation stories, the dream and its readings occur in the context of exile. As mentioned above, by the medieval period exile was a long-standing narrative trope with specific associations. Here it plays an important role in structuring the story and further is underscored by historical reality: Yoritomo had been banished and was living in Izu, one of six established sites for "distant exile," the harshest punishment save execution that the government could impose.[96] In theory, he was culturally and politically in the outback of the realm, living in a place that the center controlled bureaucratically, but which was very much beyond the

cultural pale of Heian aristocratic society. The dream vision occurring in
this context predicts not his return from exile, but rather his mastery of
the realm from a remote eastern locale. This is a very different narrative
development from classical models, where exilic experiences might create
plot but the larger story always required a return to the capital for a successful conclusion. In the Dream Interpretation, however, the east is
opened up as a narrative space where action not only occurs, but where it
might also begin and end. Moreover, in reassigning meaning to the established trope of exile, the Dream Interpretation narrative also addresses
the problem of overcoming the literal emasculation of the Minamoto line
that was the impetus for Yoritomo's exile, since exile actually gives Yoritomo the opportunity to restart the lineage.

The idea of the east as a new origin or center is figured most clearly
by the image of Yoritomo sitting on Yagura Peak. This image, interestingly,
is not new: it is in fact similar to a prophetic dream reported in the *Gōdan-
shō* and the *Ōkagami,* which both record an otherwise unconnected prophetic dream wherein sitting on a peak near the capital is interpreted to
suggest a great destiny.[97] An important difference here is that the peak
upon which Yoritomo sits is far from the capital. His perch on Yagura
marks it, quite literally, as the eastern seat of authority he will attain.

This assertion suggests a momentous shift in meaning for the clus-
ter of tropes and symbols in play in the Dream Interpretation narrative.
By naming a peripheral site like Yagura as a new sort of center, the tale
highlights its potency as a liminal site.[98] Yagura is not simply an outlying,
unknown place, but rather a space where changes and reversals can occur. This is achieved narratively by assigning new meanings to tropes like
the exile experience, prophetic dreams, and the terms "Nippon" and
"shōgun." The liminality of Yagura Peak (and, metonymically, the east
country and Kamakura) thus activates the transformative, metamorphic
nature of the metaphors underlying these conventional topoi, making
possible a profound reinterpretation of the idea of the realm at this critical moment of social reorganization.

From Yagura Peak, Yoritomo's realm is vast, and it is recorded in strikingly
similar terms in almost all variants—from Kikaigashima to Sotonohama—
with the additional extension to continental regions in the *kōwakamai.*
Significantly, the image is described as one of expansive reach, not defensive barrier.[99] Moreover, both the *Tōjōroku* and the *Soga monogatari* explicitly give the land between these points a name: Yoritomo will be shōgun of
Nippongoku.

The term Nippongoku is old. It was originally one of several appella-
tions referring generally to the realm of the early Japanese, and it can be
found in such formative texts as the *Nihon shoki* and *Kojiki.* Although it did

not by any means supplant all the other names for the realm during the medieval period, the war tales represent one medium where it predominated and in which it is defined in geographic terms reflecting a *medieval* realm—the westernmost border marks the barrier against Mongol invasions, while the easternmost points to its assimilation of the generally fractious Ōshū region.[100] In the *kōwakamai*, the latest of the texts considered here, the significance of Nippongoku receives protracted attention; Kageyoshi's careful interpretation reveals that Yoritomo's holding the morning sun represents his rule over the "origin of the sun." By drawing attention to the places that will be meaningful in the future—the east country from which the shōgunate will rule military affairs and the borders which will be clarified in part by threat from the Mongols—this interpretation transforms the world of the Genpei period to reflect a later reality.

The medieval realm is also evoked in these works by the symbol of the abalone that Yoritomo receives in the *Heiji monogatari* account, an image echoed in the *kōwakamai*.[101] Recall that Yoritomo's possession of the sixty-six abalone is interpreted as symbolizing his control over the sixty-six provinces. The "sixty-six provinces" is a common stand-in for "the realm" in texts of this vintage;[102] it is further linked specifically with Yoritomo in the pilgrimage practice known as *rokujūrokubu*, or the "sixty-six part circuit," which began during the Muromachi period and gained widespread popularity among members of all classes during the Edo age. The practice consisted of copying the sixty-six sections of the Lotus Sutra and then offering them at each stage of a country-wide sixty-six circuit route. The "Record of the origin of the sixty-six part circuit" (*Rokujūrokubu engi*), a Muromachi period document, cites as the origin for this practice a pilgrimage undertaken by a group of holy men under the leadership of the priest Raichō, an alternative pronunciation for "Yoritomo." Not surprisingly, this Raichō is none other than an earlier incarnation of Yoritomo, and his followers are all former incarnations of the men who would be reborn as his most intimate retainers.[103] As a reward for their good works, the group was reborn as leaders of the land. Although their tale has stronger ties to the Koshigoe narrative considered in Chapter Four,[104] the concept of the sixty-six-point circumscription of a sixty-six-province realm through the peregrinations of Yoritomo's former incarnation resonates strongly within this narrative about his emergence as shōgun, as does the image of the lord surrounded by retainers who both celebrate him and are rewarded by him.

In the frame narrative, it is the retainers Morinaga and Kageyoshi who recount and interpret the dream(s) before Yoritomo. In the *Tōjōroku* and *Soga monogatari*, Yoritomo recognizes their importance by offering them rewards should the dream come true, and in the sake-pouring episode of the dream, the retainers attending Yoritomo further reinforce the importance of the lord's relationship with his men. The link between lord and retainers is made even more explicit in the *kōwakamai*, the latest text and the one most closely associated with celebrating the warrior class. The retainers help Yoritomo nurture the growth of the realm, symbolized by the three pine trees, and they share in governance as symbolized in the distribution of the abalone.

Yoritomo's role as a general over men, however, relies on his own submission to the sovereign, without whose sanction any military action would be considered seditious. In most variants, the sovereign's approval is symbolized by the sun and the moon, with the sun representing the sovereign and the moon the retired sovereign. This association is conventional, and this image is consistent throughout all accounts save the *Heiji monogatari*, in which the sovereign is suggested more obliquely by the reference to the Minamoto role in protecting the realm from its enemies. In the *kōwakamai*, there is a somewhat different configuration of images implying the sovereign's support: Yoritomo stirs the clouds and holds the sun.[105] He stands at "Higashiyama komatsubara," a location commentators cannot identify, but speculate might refer to the eastern hills of the capital.[106]

The *kōwakamai*, probably the latest of these works, reflects a subtle but significant change in its definition of Yoritomo as the possessor of a named realm. This account appropriates and alters the trope of the sun (standing for royal authority) to represent the land ruled by the sovereign yet held by Yoritomo (*Hi no moto*). He has at once assumed the position of the sovereign (possessing the realm) and asserted the sovereign's sanction for that position (the sun shines forth). There are several points of metonymic slippage here—the sovereign, like the sun, evokes the realm, Yoritomo possesses and, by straddling the realm, represents its dimensions. This suggests a tantalizing claim to legitimacy hinging on a seemingly paradoxical idea: on the one hand, Yoritomo operates under royal sanction, while on the other, he appropriates it for himself. He is at once like the sovereign and subordinate to him.

As we have seen, the global narrative comprised by these recensions creates a coherent representation of Yoritomo's future greatness by incorporating conventional tropes into new narratives and by expressing new ideas through established modes of presentation. The idea of shōgun, in particular, is reshaped by its association with the Kamakura Lord. On the one hand, it still very much connotes protector of the realm and defender of the throne; but it is transformed as well into a much more exalted position, one that mirrors the greatness of the sovereign. The lord's presence makes possible the action played out by his supporters. The idea of the realm "Nippongoku" likewise is modified to substantiate the greatness, not of the center but of the eastern provinces. Further, it is the shōgun governing from the east who clearly defines its borders. Yoritomo becomes the symbol through which new narrative space and new narrative subjects are brought into play.

Reading Dreams

The Dream Interpretation narrative thus articulates a vitally important segment of one of Japan's most central cultural narratives—the rise of the warriors from the east country to supplant aristocratic society, directed by the first shōgun, Yoritomo, heir to the Seiwa Genji line. But this is a story that functions by assigning new meanings to and amplifying the valence of terms, which, newly prominent, will define cultural consciousness. To be sure, such a transvaluation is not unique to historical narratives; but history, arguably, represents the discursive arena in which such new definitions have the greatest implications. For new tropes to work in the creation of cultural narratives, they must be presented in terms that audiences are equipped to interpret and internalize as essential parts of their past. There has to be a negotiation, in other words, between the familiar and the new such that the new becomes normative. We have seen above how the layering of novel meanings on established images and the stringing together of those images work to create a story; let us now turn to the method of narration itself, since it is through telling the tale of the auspicious dream that Yoritomo's story was inextricably woven into the long history of the realm.

The centerpiece of the Dream Interpretation episode is the recounting of the dream and its interpretation. In the *kōwakamai*, this fragment constitutes the episode in its entirety; when stripped down to its basics, the framing stories fall away, and the dream vision becomes pivotal in the performance repertoire. This points not to the relative unimportance of the framing stories but rather to how deeply they are embedded in cultural memory; the moment of change for Yoritomo evokes the larger story, which, even though unspoken, is nevertheless known. Yet this choice suggests that what is most fundamental to this narrative of historical change is the prophetic dream and its explanation.

Prophetic dreams are a common feature in the narrative and historical tradition of early Japan. Women's dreams of being passed an object by a lover reveal impregnation;[107] dreams about occurrences at shrines or temples direct the dreamer to support those institutions; and occasionally a deity will appear and speak directly to the dreamer, as in the *Heiji monogatari* version of the Dream Interpretation. Dreams, like other sorts of prophetic visions and spirit possessions, were seen as points of communication between the phenomenal world and the various other realms with which it came into contact: those of the gods, of the restless dead, and of the aggrieved living whose enmity causes their spirits to wander. As Morinaga points out in the *kōwakamai*, prophetic dreams had a long and illustrious history both in "our realm" and in older continental cultures, and they often accompanied significant cultural events. They provide reliable predictions and warnings to the dreamer, serving as barometers of the degree to which the everyday, terrestrial world is in harmony with the cosmic order.

Not surprisingly, the cultural importance of prophetic dreams in everyday experience renders them equally vital in the narrative traditions of early and medieval Japan. Prophetic dreams propel or paralyze characters in the *Heike* and other war tales, but also in the *Genji* and the memoirs of Heian period scribes and diarists; whether the world is a conscious fiction or a narrativized reality, the vitality of prophetic dreams—as well as their role in motivating narrative—is consistent.[108] Because they are connected with suprahuman knowledge, these dream express a perspective "higher" than that of the story's characters and relate the point of view of the "author" in both textual and cosmic senses. Dreams thus represent an element that works at once at a basic textual level and at a metatextual one, as they simultaneously move the plot and comment upon and justify its development. They presume knowledge of the ending, and this knowledge is specific to the narrator rather than his heroes, who are left to make sense of visions or predictions that are hard to decipher within the context of those heroes' present reality.

Within a text, therefore, the interpretation of a dream is invaluable in navigating the complications of the narrative world. Only by correctly understanding this essential sort of otherworldly, authoritative commentary can a character move forward successfully.[109] This is particularly true when the dream is as portentous as Morinaga's: although Yoritomo's success is predicted in the dream, he is not empowered by it until Kageyoshi interprets it. The foregrounding of the act of interpretation is a significant characteristic of all the variants; where the episode stands as a titled section, it is referred to not simply as the "dream (*yume*)" but rather the "dream interpretation (*yume awase*)." In the *Tōjōroku* and the *Soga monogatari*, it is specifically the interpreter whom Yoritomo promises to reward should the prediction prove true. Thus while on one level the Dream Interpretation is about Yoritomo's future fortunes, his reconfiguration of the realm, and the importance of the warrior class, then it is also very centrally about the vital importance of interpretation.

Interpretation here is enacted in, and seems specifically to comment upon, the functioning of both the oral/aural and the written realms. On the one hand, Kageyoshi hears the dreamer's account and then is asked to explain it. Rather than reading a text and making sense of the words, he is hearing a story and making sense of a set of vignettes played out on the screen of the dreamer's mind. Immediacy is important: the authority of the dream is predicated on the unmediated nature of the message, and the profundity of a prophetic dream depends largely on the directness of the communication from the world beyond. The role of the interpreter as decoder thus becomes problematic. As a mediating element, interpretation challenges the immediacy of the vision, and by extension, it comprises the directness traditionally associated with oral transmission, which, because of its ephemerality, requires a greater degree of transparency in communicating its meaning than writing. The need for interpretation raises the question, what about this sort of communication situation necessitates (and lauds) interpretation?

The interpreter of dreams, the reader of cosmic signs, turns out to be a reader in a much more mundane sense. Indeed, the activities of reading and writing are deeply implicated in this episode. Interpreting the "morning sun in the east" as "the origin of the sun" and therefore "Japan" involves transforming dream symbols into *kanji* and then reading them; the explanation of "piling up attention in a northerly direction" as a reference to the Hōjō operates similarly. In some sense, then, dream interpretation stands as a metaphor for reading and so suggests the infiltration of modes of expression steeped in the practices of "written culture" into the oral/aural realm.

Yet I think something at once simpler and more meaningful is occurring here. The dream interpretation is an after-the-fact positing of a long-before-the-fact prediction of Yoritomo's ascension and an assertion of a teleological principle to the messy, contradictory story of the Minamoto. It is a mirror in the text for what the text as a whole accomplishes: mastery of the narrative and cultural anxieties aroused by the challenge of grasping a changing world, endowing the present order with the sanction of the gods and tradition, and using those to create a sense of cultural identity. The detour through writing (the ability to "read" *kanji* encoded in the dream) helps legitimize a particular interpretation of the dream, but what really matters is how all modes of communication and cultural codes are mobilized to achieve the overriding goal of reframing the present historical moment. In the endless circulations and repetitions of stories from the Genpei period, we can not only see the result of that process, we can, moreover, witness it taking place and sense the anxieties driving it.

Interpretation as a metatextual issue will be mapped across all the narratives treated in this study, but perhaps nowhere more explicitly than in the Dream Interpretation narrative. Although this story grants Yoritomo a far more central role as a narrative subject than will the others, he nevertheless is *not* the primary actor here—that role is shared by the dreamer, Morinaga, and the interpreter, Kageyoshi. It is they who do all the telling in a story in which nothing but telling actually occurs. They both present and then explain the truth that is at the story's center. They are, in effect, internal alter-egos for reciters, actors, and writers (as tellers) and readers and audiences (as interpreters).

Chapter Three

Kiso Yoshinaka

Petitioning Hachiman

A lthough Yoritomo became the *de facto* hegemon of warrior affairs as a result of the Genpei War, the position was very much in contention during the conflict itself. His most serious rivals were members of his kin group, and two of them posed critical challenges to his claim to both clan and warrior headship. The first of these was his cousin, Kiso Yoshinaka (1154–1184), an ambitious provincial warrior who had been raised in Shinano by a hereditary retainer after his father's death in 1155. Although Yoshinaka's mobilization of troops began, like Yoritomo's, in response to Prince Mochihito's call to arms, Yoshinaka represented a much more immediate threat to the Taira, since he was closer to the capital. The Taira dispatched a punitive force to control him, which he defeated at Kurikara and Shinohara. In 1183, he entered the capital, where he routed the Taira and, according to the *Heike*, was welcomed as a savior by Retired Sovereign Go-Shirakawa and the central aristocrats. Shortly after his arrival, however, his ruthless appropriation of supplies in the famine-weary capital region, compounded by his inability to navigate the vicissitudes of high-level political life, resulted in his alienation from both capital dwellers and Yoritomo, who feared his cousin's ambitions. With the sanction of the retired sovereign, Yoritomo sent forces from Kamakura to punish Yoshinaka, who died in battle on the shores of Lake Biwa in 1184, little more than six months after his triumphant arrival in the capital. The forces defeating him were under the command of two of Yoritomo's brothers—Yoshitsune and Noriyori.

Yoshinaka's appearance in Genpei narrative raises vital concerns about the Minamoto lineage. As the first Minamoto to push his way to the capital, Yoshinaka brought the clan to the fore militarily and politically after twenty years of obscurity precipitated by the Heiji Uprising. In narratives of his life, Yoshinaka's heritage as a Seiwa Genji is always emphasized, yet his almost immediate alienation from Yoritomo during the Genpei War reveals deep divisions within the celebrated Minamoto family unit. He occupies a difficult position historically: by heredity, he was an ally in the clash between the Minamoto and Taira clans, yet in his individuality and ambition, he challenged the very idea of a coherent "Minamoto" identity.[1] Moreover, as a member of a collateral line directly vying for power with the main heir, he represented a potential alternative version of the Minamoto destiny that defied the story of Minamoto unity. Yoshinaka's career thus points to one of the most troubling issues in the story of the Minamoto ascendancy: how to address the tension between the historical fact of parricide on the one hand and the romanticized reanimation of the Minamoto clan through its victory in the Genpei War on the other.

This chapter and the next explore cases where the dissonance between narrative exigency and historical event is addressed in accounts of the fractious struggles within the Minamoto clan. Specifically, they discuss instances when heroes compose written oaths as proof of their sincerity and rectitude, to assert a place for themselves within an idealized Minamoto family. Two vital moments in Minamoto relations motivate the writing exercises. First is Kiso Yoshinaka's articulation of his position within the clan as he begins his campaign (considered here), and the second is Minamoto Yoshitsune's defense of his actions as he tries to situate himself relative to Yoritomo following the war (Chapter Four). When faced with the need to explain what might be considered self-serving actions, each hero resorts to similar means of establishing his legitimacy—swearing loyalty by writing documents.

Although not entirely absent from earlier narrative, the use of formal written documents in the war tales as evidence of inner honesty represents a new concern with document writing and its significance in warrior society.[2] These chapters demonstrate how a new set of interpretive tropes for medieval culture use documents to guide the audience in determining rightness or wrongness of a character's actions within individual narratives, and, by extension, in history.[3] The ways documents are situated in texts and the kind of documents used are key to understanding some of the tensions in historical accounts of this period. First, however, let us consider Yoshinaka more broadly within the contexts of the Genpei War and the post-Heiji Minamoto clan.

Setting the Scene: Kiso no Yoshinaka's Call to Arms

Kiso Yoshinaka emerges as a player in the Genpei War as the tapestry of Taira power begins to unravel.[4] In the Kakuichibon variant, his name first appears on a list of Minamoto clansmen who might be marshaled to aid Prince Mochihito[5] in the "An Array of Genji" episode of chapter 4.

Positioned immediately after Retired Sovereign Takakura's pilgrimage to Itsukushima ("The Imperial Journey to Itsukushima" and "The Imperial Return"), this moment represents a turning point in the narrative, when the center is crumbling and what will follow is a completely different sort of order.

The arrival of Yoshinaka as a narrative subject in an unsteady world is preceded by a series of episodes that present growing indications of the realm's incipient disintegration. The general scene of the early chapters of the Kakuichibon is the sphere of the aristocrats living in the capital and the Taira's initially successful integration into this milieu. The narrative leaves the center only to accompany important characters either on pilgrimages to temples and shrines, from which a return trip is almost immediate; or into exile, from which return at all is uncertain. Both of these movements emphasize the importance of the center. Pilgrimage is productive; something is gained by leaving the center, visiting a sacred site, and returning, as is shown in Kiyomori's initial pilgrimage to Kumano ("The Sea Bass"). Exile, on the other hand, represents a generally counterproductive narrative topos, signifying removal from the center to a liminal site without the promise of return and reintegration (a convention challenged in the narrative of Yoritomo's rise, as we saw in Chapter Two).[6]

Although the tale opens with Kiyomori's successful pilgrimage to Kumano, what follows is a succession of infelicitous and unproductive journeys. Most notable, perhaps, is the string of banishments whose inappropriateness signals that the government is out of equilibrium. It begins with the expulsion of Abbot Meiun and the Shishinotani conspirators in chapter 2 and progresses through the exile of the ministers of state and the retired sovereign in chapter 3 and Mongaku in chapter 4. These removals of primarily central political figures (the itinerant Mongaku is a notable exception) from the capital one after another mark the downward spiral of Kiyomori's fortunes as order is disrupted and legitimate authority is dispersed.

These clearly counterproductive removals are accompanied, moreover, by a series of pilgrimages bearing negative results, a striking reversal of the expected cycle of departure and return.[7] Shigemori's pilgrimage to Kumano, during which he pleads with the deity to either take his life or cause his father (Kiyomori) to rectify his behavior, is particularly significant. His return from that trip signals the onset of his swift and fatal illness that leaves the Taira bereft of its one reliable voice of reason. Retired Sovereign Takakura's pilgrimage to Itsukushima also can be seen in this light. Although his father, Go-Shirakawa, is released from house arrest upon Takakura's arrival back in the capital, this moment also immediately precedes his brother Mochihito's rebellion, which results in the prince's death. Further, it comes just a year before the retired sovereign's premature death, ostensibly caused by sorrow over the Taira clan's ill-management of political power. This moment also marks the transfer of the capital, one of the narrative's most clearly unproductive movements. Kiyomori decides to take his infant grandson, the sovereign Antoku, along with the trappings of royal authority to Fukuhara, thus abandoning Heian-kyō, the city that had housed the capital for four hundred years. This event coincides with the emergence of Minamoto from the provinces to challenge the Taira.

These physical departures from a center that has become disordered deliver critical narratorial commentary on the degeneration of the aristocracy under Taira control. Serving as a primary interpretive guide for the audience or reader of the larger tale, they point, through geographic metaphor, to a void that Yoshinaka will try to fill. This is just the first step in the narrative of a de-centered world reorganizing itself, a theme that will remain important throughout the tale. There is a clear (original and originary) center, but imbalance at the axis causes dispersal and shifts narrative attention to alternative power configurations and new power-holders like Yoshinaka dotting the landscape beyond the capital's perimeter.

Other complementary narrative devices further articulate the disarray into which the world has fallen. Two of these are familiar from Chapter Two above, namely, the comparison of events to Chinese, Japanese, or sometimes Indian precedent to assess their significance within larger schemes of political and cosmological meaning; and the appearance of omens or visions within the narrative that position textual events in relation to the divine order. Although these frames are most vitally important in recitational texts like the Kakuichibon variant, they appear often enough in the other versions considered here to represent an important topos within *Heike* narrative generally. They often work in tandem, as in the case of the felicitous appearance of the sea bass in "The Sea Bass" (1.3)[8] an omen in itself and in keeping with the precedent of King Wu of Zhou. Both omen and precedent also structure Meiun's banishment ("The Exile of the Tendai Abbot," 2.1). Chinese precedent is cited in recounting Shigemori's firm admonishment of his father, and a dream frames the Kasuga deity's displeasure in "The Unadorned Sword" (3.12), foretelling the death of Shigemori. The general mayhem resulting from friction among groups of monks, the royal house, and the Taira are signs in and of themselves (representing an imbalance between Buddhist and earthly authority), and they are followed by more of the same: the appearance of the weasels in "Strange Occurrences" (5.3) and Mochihito's inaccurate physiognomy reading in "An Array of Genji" (4.2).[9]

Although this rich layering of traditional tropes gives texture to the general deterioration created by Kiyomori's ruthless handling of governmental power, other signs of the times are harder to interpret conventionally, including the arrival of Kiso Yoshinaka.[10] Appearing at the end of this stream of indications that the center is losing its socio-political potency, the account of Yoshinaka's rise involves reorganizing historical meaning, since he represents a complete contradiction of the aristocratic world in (and on) whose terms history had been narrated.

The initial weakening of Taira power in the "An Array of Genji" episode is immediately compounded by ill omens in "The Matter of the Weasels" (4.4), in which Retired Sovereign Go-Shirakawa orders a written interpretation of a divination that follows the unusual appearance of weasels in the Toba Mansion. He is told, "joy and sorrow will visit His Majesty within three days."[11] The interpretation proves correct: On the following day, he is released from house arrest (cause for joy), but then immediately learns of Mochihito's rebellion (cause for sorrow). The larger narrative moves to the hounding of Mochihito and the battles in Nara that result in the deaths of the prince and numerous others. Indications of upheaval continue, including the transfer of the capital to Fukuhara; events surrounding Yoritomo's uprising in the east; the burning of the Nara temples by Taira warriors under the command of Kiyomori's son, Shigehira; and the death of Retired Sovereign Takakura,[12] son of Go-Shirakawa and father of the sovereign Antoku.

The introduction of Yoshinaka as a new narrative subject into this already volatile context requires readers to rethink their habitual modes of interpretation. On the one hand, any narrative must function within established patterns to allow historical continuity, an issue particularly important for a realm grounded in the idea of a divinely-sanctioned, unbroken royal lineage. However, the newness of the subject matter concomitantly requires adaptation of these themes to changed, contemporary realities—not only the political and social changes wrought by the Genpei War itself, but also developments in the warrior world in the years between the end of the war and the time when it became codified as narrative. The refraction of the past through the eyes of a society a century or more posterior to it creates a need for explanation, which in turn necessarily complicates the framing of the historical narrative. Thus we find a complex interaction between earlier modes of contextualizing history, historical exigencies central to the events being narrated, and newly important modes of expression stemming from the (later) performance milieu. In the case of Yoshinaka, document writing becomes one important trope through which this change is articulated.

Writing and the Rise of Yoshinaka:
The Circular Letter, Kanetō's Oath

As a provincial and an outsider even within his kin group, Yoshinaka is problematic to a far greater degree than his cousin Yoritomo.[13] His actual ties to the capital are more tenuous and his ambitions potentially greater, and he fails in a way spectacular and unparalleled elsewhere in Genpei War narratives. His military strength derives from connections to provincial families of relatively low rank, and he is the son of a woman with no strong familial backing of her own. This said, he nevertheless shares with Yoritomo the Minamoto lineage inherited from their grandfather, Tameyoshi, and he is clearly a man able to mobilize support under the general banner of the Seiwa Genji line. Although his actions after entering the capital are overtly condemned, his death is romanticized as fully as any other Genpei War death save Yoshitsune's. Tracing how the narrative negotiates the two sides of his character provides some of the clearest indications of how historical interpretive schemes are restructured in Genpei narrative.[14] Most important among these is the depiction of his ability—and later, his failure—to articulate his position through official documents, despite being characterized as an unrefined and unlettered provincial.[15] In the Kakuichibon text, this issue is first addressed in "The Circular Letter" (6.5), in which he raises troops.

THE CIRCULAR LETTER

In the brief pause between the episodes eulogizing Retired Sovereign Takakura and those about the death of Kiyomori, the Kakuichibon introduces Yoshinaka with relative fullness in "The Circular Letter." This episode describes Yoshinaka's youth and his reason for raising troops. It begins as follows:

> Meanwhile, there began to be talk of a Minamoto in Shinano Province called Kiso no Kanja Yoshinaka. This Yoshinaka was the son of the Crown Prince's Guards Captain Yoshikata, who was the second son of the late Rokujō Police Lieutenant Tameyoshi. After the slaying of his father, Yoshikata, at the hands of Kamakura no Akugenda Yoshihira on the sixteenth of the eighth month in the second year of Kyūju (1155), the two-year-old child's weeping mother had carried him in her arms to Shinano Province, where she had gone to Kiso no Chūzō Kanetō and said, "Please raise the boy as you think best; make a man of him." Kanetō had labored hard at his ward's upbringing for more than twenty years, and the child had grown into a man of surpassing strength and matchless valor. . . .
>   Escorted by his guardian, Yoshinaka had often visited the capital to observe the activities and behavior of the Taira. He had gone to the Hachiman Shrine for his coming-of-age ceremony at the age of thirteen, and there, in the presence of the bodhisattva, had prayed, "My great-grandfather Yoshiie became the son of this august divinity and assumed the name Hachiman Tarō [Hachiman's eldest son]. I shall follow in his footsteps." Then he had put up his hair in front of the shrine and taken the name Kiso no Jirō [Second Son] Yoshinaka.[16]

This initial description immediately marks Yoshinaka as peripheral. Not only is he characterized as a member of the provincial Minamoto clan,[17] he is further marginalized by his father's death at the hands of a kinsman from the main line[18] and his subsequent removal to the remote locale of Kiso beyond the reach of his father's killer.[19] The appellative "Kiso" further marks him geographically and subtly also in status: he is in hiding from the relatives who would kill him, thus suppressing his patrimony. He is brought up as a member of a household of lower rank than his own, one steeped in military arts but lacking the refinement of the central aristocracy; for want of a father of rank to match his ambitions, Yoshinaka lacks the sophistication that should be his. This failing in his upbringing will prove fatal. His extreme reliance on military might rather than political tact proves to be his undoing in the end, since he becomes unable to gauge the appropriateness of his behavior when he finds himself in a position of power. In this respect (and in many others), he stands in stark contrast to Yoritomo, another orphan, but one better able to broker his status as primary heir *(sōryō)*[20] of the previous generation's patriarch into a return from the political edge to reconfigure the very idea of the "center." That these two immediately are at odds over Yoshinaka's role[21] is not surprising in light of the contentiousness between their lines one generation back. As the Taira begin to fall, the two find themselves in parallel positions—both precarious, both potentially powerful.

Yoshinaka's awareness of his own marginality and his attempts to navigate a course to change this status are ongoing concerns in tales about the entire course of his life, but they are particularly relevant in accounts of the early stages of his military career, when he raises troops and launches his campaign. This is marked within the Kakuichibon from his introduction into the text. His seemingly self-conscious choice of the Iwashimizu Hachiman Shrine as the site of his coming-of-age ritual, and his adoption of the name "Jirō," in particular, demonstrate his concern about identity, lineage, and legitimacy. He draws attention to his ancestry as he first steps forward as an adult. In careful imitation of his ancestor Yoshiie,[22] he identifies himself as a member of the clan under the protection of Hachiman. By taking the name Jirō, he further invokes the directness of his genealogical ties to the former Minamoto patriarch, to whom he also shows deference by acknowledging the priority of the man known as Hachiman's first son [Tarō].

The issue of Minamoto identity is accentuated in all narratives about the origins of Yoshinaka's campaign, but it is treated somewhat differently in other versions. In the earlier Yashirobon and Hyakunijukkubon *Heike* variants, the account of Yoshinaka's connection to Kanetō is included, but the descriptions of his military prowess found in the Kakuichibon are sketchier in these variants. The early texts also do not assert his coming-of-age at Iwashimizu Hachiman Shrine or the connection with Hachiman

Tarō. The Enkyōbon and the *Genpei jōsuiki* do not contain this episode, either; they do, however, actively identify Yoshinaka as Yoshikata's second son, a potential alternative source for the choice of "Jirō" as his adult name.[23] Yoshinaka's elder brother, Nakaie, had been in the capital when their father was killed, at which point he was adopted by their kinsman Yorimasa. When Yorimasa raised arms against the Taira in his bid to instate Prince Mochihito as sovereign, Nakaie and his sons were killed. The Enkyōbon does not mention Yoshinaka's knowledge of or opinions about this brother at this juncture, although later it depicts Nakaie's death as one of the causes for Yoshinaka's actions.[24]

Some texts also include a more extensive discussion of the death of Yoshinaka's father, Yoshikata. According to the *Genpei jōsuiki* and the *Azuma kagami*, once he had murdered Yoshikata, Yoshihira tried to have Yoshinaka killed as well, but the toddler was protected by other warrior families, and eventually was delivered into the hands of Saitō no Bettō Sanemori, who entrusted him to Kanetō in Kiso. The *Azuma kagami* account has Kanetō taking the child because his wife was Yoshinaka's wet nurse; this account is not included in the *Heike* variants.[25] In the Enkyōbon, Kanetō clearly hides the identity of the child; the *Jōsuiki* does not include the disguising of the child's identity, but does relate his early wish to avenge his family name by attacking the Taira (significantly, not the Minamoto kin connected to his father's killer). Each of these variations will be taken up again in more detail as part of the discussion of Yoshinaka's Petition, but some general observations are worth noting here. First, as mentioned above, the issues of identity, lineage, and friction within the Minamoto clan are important themes to greater or lesser degrees in the narrativizations of Yoshinaka's call-to-arms. Second, around the time of the Kakuichibon there appears to be a general movement, starting in variants from the late fourteenth century, toward explaining the name "Jirō" as a reflection of a self-conscious linkage to Hachiman; this suggests a marked concern with asserting his status as a member of the Minamoto clan. However, variants without the coming-of-age narrative continued to emerge as well. All that can be noted diachronically at this point, therefore, is that the foregrounding of Hachiman and Yoshiie in this narrative seems to be a later development but not an inevitable one, and throughout the medieval period, the issue of Kiso's relationship to the Minamoto main line continued to be charged with either overt or subtle tensions.

Following the relatively brief account of his upbringing in Kiso, the narrative turns to Yoshinaka's preparations for raising arms. The Kakuichibon account states:

> One day, Yoshinaka summoned his guardian, Kanetō, to hint at something he had on his mind. "I hear that Yoritomo has rebelled and taken over the

eight eastern provinces, and that he is getting ready to march on the capital from the Eastern Sea Road and drive out the Taira. I want to subjugate
the Eastern Mountain and Northern Land circuits and dash ahead to con-
quer the Heike. To tell the truth, I have a fancy to be called one of the Two
Commanders of Japan."

    Kanetō was overjoyed. "That is just why I have looked after you all
this time," he said, with a respectful bow. "Those words prove you are
Yoshiie's descendant." . . .

    "The first step is to send around a circular letter," Kanetō said.[26]

    The act of writing, then, represents an important moment in Yoshi-
naka's self-definition. His intentions from the outset clearly represent a
challenge to Yoritomo as he claims a position within the Minamoto clan.
Yet his ambition is framed by this interaction with Kanetō. Significantly,
Yoshinaka reveals his desires to his guardian before moving forward, and
his plan for mustering forces proceeds only in accordance with Kanetō's
guidance. When Yoshinaka asks for advice, Kanetō urges him to compose
a *megurashibumi*, or circular letter, an inquiry to powerful warrior leaders
in the region to determine their level of interest in and potential com-
mitment to Yoshinaka's cause.[27]

KANETŌ'S OATH

The pattern of (invited) advice followed immediately by the composition
of a document is noteworthy here, since we find it recurring as well at
other critical moments throughout Yoshinaka's life. This is true in the
case of the petition discussed below, as well as his letter to the monks at
Enryakuji ("Kiso's Letter to the Enryakuji," 7.10). And there are other
permutations of this pattern in the narrative of Yoshinaka's rise. In one,
Kanetō rather than Yoshinaka composes a document, but its contents
and narrative significance are similar. The Enkyōbon recounts that
shortly after Yoshinaka reveals his ambitions to Kanetō, Kanetō is summoned to the capital and interrogated by the Taira, who fear Yoshinaka
may be harboring seditious intentions. They question Kanetō, but finally
let him go with threats against Yoshinaka if the rumors of rebellion prove
true. Importantly, in parting, they make him write a *kishōmon*, an oath
swearing his fidelity.[28] The oath is included, allegedly in its original form,
in the Enkyōbon variant; this is one of many documents quoted in the
war tales ostensibly verbatim and in its entirety. It is not, however, contained in historical document collections, nor do contemporary journals
or other records refer to it, a general trend I will discuss below.

    Kishōmon are written oaths sworn to the gods and buddhas (rather
than to any earthly authority), and they therefore lie within the greater
cosmological jurisdiction to which all sentient beings are beholden. Here,

Kanetō's signing of the oath satisfies the Taira and allows him to return to Kiso (apparently unaccompanied); but it causes Kanetō significant internal turmoil. Ill at ease, he decides to entrust Yoshinaka to Nenoi Yukichika, a sympathetic local lord, in part as a strategic move to protect his ward, but also to remove Yoshinaka from the sphere of potential karmic retribution should he, Kanetō, act in violation of his oath. His dilemma is one we will continue to encounter—a protagonist placed in a position in which his sincerity is doubted, often in a context that can be construed as a formal arena, such as an audience with a power holder, a visit to a shrine or temple, or an interrogation. He is then either given the opportunity to plead his case or prevented from doing so, and the outcome of the episode (whether his petition is received or not) suggests the trajectory his life will follow.

The *Jōsuiki* provides an expanded version of Kanetō's *kishōmon* that further emphasizes the importance of signing this written oath. When Kanetō is called to the capital, he has the opportunity to orally refute charges that he and Yoshinaka are planning a rebellion. Kanetō's explanation to his Taira interrogators is as follows:

> "Yoshinaka was only two years old when his father Yoshikata was killed at Ōkura in Sagami by his nephew, Akugenda Yoshihira. Yoshinaka's mother, adrift in worry for the child and fearing Yoshihira, brought me the boy and asked me to raise him as best I could. Bearing in mind her sorrow, I have brought him up until now, and I know these rumors of rebellion are empty. Or is this someone's slander? But if you command it, let me go back home, and I will have my sons arrest him and bring him to you."
>
> The inquisitor responded, "If we are to let you go, you must write an oath [*kishōmon*] to the effect that you will bring back Yoshinaka. If you do not [write it], we will only release you after your sons have brought him here."[29]

Perplexed, Kanetō reasons, "This is not an oath that I write from my heart. The gods will not hold this against me. The gods will forgive what I say under this sort of duress."[30] The narrative continues that Kanetō wrote the oath on the back of an ox-head talisman (*goō hōin*) from Kumano, and a direct quotation of the oath itself follows.

References to ox-head talismen first appeared in the Heian period, when they were employed to ward off fire, cure disease, and insure safety and prosperity.[31] During the Kamakura period, they came to be used for writing oaths, a practice that peaked during the Sengoku period. The oldest extant ox-head talisman is dated 1266, and it is inscribed with an oath.[32] Kanetō's talisman, like the several others mentioned in the *Heike*, is associated specifically with a member of the warrior class swearing a written oath. Whether or not anachronistic here, it points to a concern with written oath-taking that certainly resonated with a medieval audience.

That Kanetō would swear such an oath, combined with the careful narrative attention dedicated to his rationalization about breaking it, both point to the significance of the act of writing in the realm of bearing witness. Significantly, it is breaking this oath, rather than his earlier lies, that causes him the most concern. Speaking and writing are both notable parts of the interrogation scene. Kanetō is permitted to explain his position *verbally*, but he is also forced to *write* an oath before the gods. The oath is an act of inscription, and by writing on the back of a talisman, he fixes his words visually and materially—an interesting (but by no means unusual) necessity for a promise made to the invisible gods.

Of course, the oath also clearly indicates the more practical parameters for this confrontation; it stands as proof of his honesty to his interrogators. And they, first and foremost, will decide Kanetō's and Yoshinaka's earthly fates. This issue is the greatest cause for worry and the reason that propels Kanetō to swear a false oath at all. Kanetō's ability to rationalize his actions here, however, also points to the fragility of this apparatus. The oath, written under duress, does not reflect sincerity. Composing the oath allows Kanetō to serve the higher goals of his heart, though these goals directly contradict the language of the oath. Worldly authorities attach special significance to the written word, but Kanetō trusts that the gods will see beyond it. Coming to this conclusion requires him to navigate self-doubt—he writes the oath because such an order "would be hard to run away from," but it gives him pause in a way that his earlier spoken untruths do not. Moreover, once he returns to Kiso, he entrusts Yoshinaka to Nenoi Yukichika "in order to accomplish his true goal but not turn his back on his oath."[33] Ultimately, he expects the gods to recognize the sincerity of his intentions in supporting Yoshinaka against the Taira.

Although this particular *kishōmon* is peripheral to the narratives at the heart of this study, it is remarkable for its narrative consonance with the other oaths and petitions that continue to appear at crucial points in the accounts of Yoshinaka and, as the next chapter reveals, Yoshitsune. Presented as an embedded document, a verbatim quotation of what Kanetō ostensibly wrote, there is a sense that the oath and oath-swearing is a *mis en abyme* for the text's drive to establish its own veracity and sincerity. In a narrative about bearing witness, documentation becomes both text and metatext.

Sincerity is a factor as well in a second type of documentation, the petition. While neither interrogation nor petitioning were new to the judicial system at the time of the Genpei War, their prominence in narratives about the war meant to be read and heard broadly was. What this tells us about the culture creating these narratives, and what it suggests about how audiences and performers interpreted the importance of written documents, are questions to bear in mind as we turn to the narrative of Yoshinaka's Petition.

Yoshinaka's Petition: Mediation and Knowledge

Yoshinaka's petition is one of many documents of questionable veracity found in the *Heike*. It appears in neither the *Gyokuyō* nor the *Gukanshō*,[34] two sources often cited as alternative versions of Genpei history. As mentioned earlier, however, this episode does appear as a *kōwakamai* piece, which provides a different generic point of reference.

In the Kakuichibon,[35] once Yoshinaka raises an army, he moves to fortify his boundaries by placing troops at strategic points along the route that the Taira will follow in their pursuit of him. In "The Expedition to the Northern Provinces" (7.2), we learn that a large Taira force has begun moving up the Hokuriku Road under the command of Koremori, Michimori, Tsunemasa, Tadanori, Tomonori, and Kiyofusa, all high-ranking members of the clan. They face a much smaller enemy—Yoshinaka's troop strength is consistently listed at 50,000. At this juncture, the Taira seem destined for victory; the felicitous appearance of Benzaiten in the form of a white dragon in response to Tsunemasa's *biwa* performance at Chikubushima ("The Visit to Chikubushima," 7.3) is quickly followed by their victory at Hiuchi ("The Battle at Hiuchi," 7.4). In response to the Taira offensive, Yoshinaka hastens to bolster his defenses, dividing his troops into seven units under the command of his lead generals. He positions them to form frontal and rear forces for a confrontation at Tonamiyama in Echigo. He himself leads 10,000 of these warriors and sets camp at Hanyū, north of Tonamiyama.

The next episode in the Kakuichibon, "The Petition" recounts Yoshinaka's dedication of a petition (*ganjo*)[36] to Hachiman. This is the first embedded document credited to Yoshinaka in the Kakuichibon,[37] and it clearly marks his ascendancy as a Minamoto general. It appears in all major versions of the *Heike* and also the *kōwakamai* "Kiso's Petition" (*Kiso no ganjo*). These multiple, similar appearances mark the event as an essential element in narratives about Yoshinaka's career; they also highlight this specific moment as part of Genpei history.

The Kakuichibon version of Yoshinaka's Petition finds Yoshinaka planning his strategy from his Hanyū encampment after dividing his men into seven groups. He remarks:

> The Heike must be planning to cross Tonamiyama Mountain to the plain
> for a frontal attack with their huge army. . . . Victory in that kind of battle
> depends on numbers; we will not win if we let them exploit their size. If we

send standard bearers ahead with white flags, they will see them and stay in
the mountains. "Here comes the Genji vanguard!" they will say. "Their
army must be huge. They know the terrain and we don't; we will be surrounded if we burst out onto the plain. Our rear is safe while we stay on this
rugged mountain; we had better get down and let the horses rest awhile."
In the meantime, I will pretend to try to engage them; and as soon as night
falls I will drive their whole army down into Kurikara Valley.[38]

The general strategy, then, is to ambush the larger Taira forces in the
mountains, where they think they are safe. Note at this point Yoshinaka's
prediction that the Taira will choose to stay in the mountains because
Yoshinaka's forces "know the terrain and we [the Taira] don't."[39] This
passage introduces a set of terms repeated throughout this version as well
as the others considered here: *annai(sha)*, "to be (one who is) knowledgeable," versus *buannai*, "to lack knowledge." This pairing is underlined here first by Yoshinaka himself, who immediately suggests that his
side possesses the requisite knowledge and that he recognizes its importance. The possession of knowledge at critical moments, as we shall see,
remains a vital concern in all the variants.

The opening of the episode differs slightly from variant to variant.
The Enkyōbon, which is not divided into episodes, lists the occurrences
described in the Kakuichibon's episode under an entry dated Juei 2
(1183/6/1). Yoshinaka learns that the Taira main force is heading
through Tonamiyama, and he realizes that he must keep the enemy in the
mountains to avoid a battle on open terrain, where his smaller army would
be at a disadvantage.[40] He then predicts that the Taira will stop in the
mountains to rest their horses if they see Minamoto standards and mistak-
enly think that they are about to engage a large force.[41] In the Hyakunijukkubon, in contrast, this part of the narrative is included in *ku* (episode) 62,
which precedes the primary *ku* considered here, number 63, "Kiso no
ganjo."[42] In *ku* 62, Yoshinaka divides his troops and sets out his standards;
his prediction of the Taira reaction is not included, but this tactic is again
intended to keep the enemy in the mountains.[43]

The Nagatobon, like the Enkyōbon, is not divided into episodes, so
I have chosen to define the beginning of this episode as coinciding more
or less with the narrative of the other variants. It is important to bear in
mind that this artificial division is meaningful for considering a particular piece of the narrative shared with other variants, but that it does not
reflect the flow of the text of the Nagatobon itself.

In the Nagatobon, Yoshinaka has arrived at the Hannya [*sic*] Plain
and learned of the superior size of the Taira forces. Here again, he asks
his men for suggestions about tactics, and requests that someone knowledgeable advise him. A retainer named Miyazaki describes the terrain.

He counsels Yoshinaka to divide his forces and trick the Taira into thinking the Minamoto army is larger than it really is, which will make them decide to stay in the mountains. Yoshinaka is pleased with this plan.[44]

In the *Jōsuiki*, the episode "The Petition to Ima Hachiman," like the Hyakunijukkubon, opens after Yoshinaka has determined a strategy for the upcoming battle and is encamped at Hanyū. In the preceding episode, "Division of the Minamoto Forces," he splits up his forces and sets out standards to fool the Taira. The *kōwakamai* opens with his arrival in Echigo and then moves to his planning of strategy; as in the other variants he sets out his standards to fool the Taira. The text notes that this is part of his plan, which suggests the kind of intention spelled out more clearly in some of the other texts.

The important issue of possession versus lack of knowledge is also more clearly articulated as the narratives continue. In the Kakuichibon, the Taira respond exactly as Yoshinaka had predicted; again Yoshinaka's knowledge is expressed as "*annai.*" Upon seeing the Minamoto standards, they declare:

> Here comes the Genji vanguard! . . . Their army must be huge. They know the terrain and we don't; we will be surrounded if we burst out onto the plain. Our rear is safe as long as we stay on this rugged mountain. There seems to be good forage and water here; we had better get down and let the horses rest awhile.[45]

In this version, their response is centered squarely on the importance of possessing knowledge. Of particular interest is the wording, which mimics so closely Yoshinaka's prediction; they behave exactly as he said they would. Yoshinaka's forecast is played out not only in their actions but also in their words. The exact repetition here is important to bear in mind, since it resonates with the theme that runs throughout this episode of Yoshinaka's ability to interpret his surroundings accurately (and here, to anticipate the Taira response).[46]

In the remaining variants, this section is presented in very similar terms. In the Enkyōbon, Yoshinaka's prediction of the Taira reaction is more succinct than that in the Kakuichibon, but the description closely follows the Kakuichibon wording.[47] The Enkyōbon narrative continues with the comment that the Taira did nothing to prepare for the upcoming battle. In the Hyakunijukkubon and Nagatobon descriptions the Taira also act as predicted, stopping at Sarunobaba to rest their horses.[48] In the *Jōsuiki*, in accordance with Yoshinaka's plan, the Taira dismount in the mountains; here the response does not match Yoshinaka's prediction word-for-word, but it is very close to that found in other variants. The *kōwakamai* records this section using somewhat different wording: "The

mountain is rugged and the valley deep; they can't surround us. This is a
good place to feed and water the horses, so let's make camp here."[49] In the
Hyakunijukkubon and the *Jōsuiki,* this action marks the end of the preceding episode and the text's entrance into the narrative of Yoshinaka's Petition proper.

At this juncture, all versions except the Enkyōbon return to Yoshinaka and
his troops. The Enkyōbon, however, lingers on the Taira movements. The
Taira call a diviner from their midst, who tells them, "An attack before the
ninth month[50] will be unsuccessful. Pull back and fortify the rear guard."[51]
However, one of their leaders, Kageie, in a hurry to complete the campaign and return to the capital for rewards ahead of a rival,[52] decides to ignore the divination. Following quickly on the comment that the Taira did
nothing to prepare for battle, this characterization of their camp and
Taira leadership presents a stark contrast to Yoshinaka's more thoughtful
approach to the upcoming engagement. As if to intensify this juxtaposition, the Enkyōbon immediately returns to Yoshinaka's camp, where he
performs his own sort of divination. He arrays thirty horses with saddles
and *shide* (paper streamers), dedicates them to Tenman, the deity of the
place, and asks that if the god favors him in the upcoming battle, the
horses be caused to enter the enemy camp in formation, and if the god
does not favor him, that the horses be made to scatter. The horses enter
the Taira camp in formation, much to the surprise of the Taira. One of
Yoshinaka's men retrieves them, and Yoshinaka confidently prepares for
battle.[53]

This interlude represents a different sort of knowledge acquisition,
but one that resonates later in the episode. Divinations are closely linked
to omens; and, as with the questioning of the local person about the terrain, this part of the narrative concerns interpretation. In both cases,
knowledge is acquired actively. Yoshinaka asks the god for a sign, and the
diviner is called to interpret between his lord and the divine authorities.
The leader proves his character by choosing to accept or ignore the sign.
Yoshinaka's humility before a local person of lower rank differs markedly
from the Taira's overconfident flaunting of signs from the gods. This is the
sort of situation in which each demonstrates his relationship to the cosmological order, a topic Yoshinaka will raise in his petition. The Taira here act
against divine will, and Yoshinaka acts in accordance with it.

With the Taira resting in the mountains, Yoshinaka next begins to plan for
battle. In the Enkyōbon and Nagatobon, he sets out with twelve retainers
to survey the land; in the other four variants, this movement from the encampment is not explicitly mentioned, but his surveying of the land is.[54] As
he looks out over the surrounding area to assess his position, he spies the

vermilion *torii* gate of a shrine on Natsuyama, a nearby peak. He then calls upon a person knowledgeable about the area (*annaisha*) and asks him to identify the deity enshrined there. According to the Kakuichibon, the local man responds, "Hachiman. This is Hachiman's land."[55]

All versions identify the shrine as Hachiman's; and an additional remark that Hanyū is Hachiman's land appears in the Hyakunijukkubon, the *Jōsuiki*, and the *kōwakamai*.[56] The man to whom Yoshinaka speaks is distinguished in slightly different terms from variant to variant, but all refer to him as connected to the place and therefore knowledgeable about it. In the Enkyōbon and Nagatobon, he is a person from that place (*sato no osa*), as he is in the *kōwakamai* (*sato no hito*). In the Hyakunijukkubon and Kakuichibon, he is a person with knowledge (*annaisha*), and in the *Jōsuiki*, he is a retainer who is also a resident of that province (*tōgoku no jūnin*).[57]

Yoshinaka's query regarding the shrine demonstrates his ability to understand his position vis-à-vis an unfamiliar environment. Here again, he defers to a local because that person has knowledge where he himself does not. By relying on the *annaisha*, Yoshinaka is able to locate himself in terms appropriate to the environment; this scene echoes his earlier calling upon his men for advice on strategy in the Enkyōbon and Nagatobon. Moroever, his inquiry bears important fruit. He learns that the shrine is dedicated to Hachiman, the tutelary deity of his clan and the god of warriors and war. This knowledge enables him to position himself within the unfamiliar geographical terrain of Echigo and the equally unknown historical territory of battling his way from the provinces to the capital.

Yoshinaka immediately interprets the proximity of a shrine to Hachiman as auspicious, but he pauses again to call upon an interpreter to confirm his evaluation and to help him plan his next steps. The interpreter this time is his scribe, Kakumei, whom he asks if it would be appropriate to present a petition to the god "as a prayer for the moment as well as for posterity."[58] Kakumei assures Yoshinaka that a petition would in fact be fitting, and he dismounts to compose it.

Kakumei is a steady presence in the narrative of Yoshinaka's early campaign, an invaluable companion serving as Yoshinaka's key diplomatic interpreter as he moves towards the unfamiliar political and cultural center embodied by the capital. Kakumei's interpretive importance is conventionally indicated within the worldly contexts of aristocratic and monastic society, two groups outside Yoshinaka's range of experience but with which he must interact.[59] Where Yoshinaka needs to establish connections with these central power holders, he relies on Kakumei, who both advises him on the appropriateness of actions and then composes missives in Yoshinaka's name. Although Kakumei's actual historical presence is hard to pin down,[60] all versions present a history for him in this episode that articulates his role both as Yoshinaka's interpreter and as a character in his own right:

Kakumei was attired in a dark blue *hitatare* and a suit of armor with black leather lacing. At his waist, he wore a sword with a black lacquered hilt and scabbard; on his back, there rode a quiver containing twenty-four arrows fledged with black hawk's-wing feathers. His lacquered rattan-wrapped bow was at his side; his helmet hung from his shoulder-cord. He took a small inkstone and some paper from his quiver, knelt in front of Lord Kiso, and began to write the petition. What a splendid combination of the civil and martial (*bunbu ryōdō no tassha*) he seemed!

This Kakumei, the son of a Confucian scholar-family, had formerly served at the Kangakuin, where he had been known as Chamberlain Michihiro. Then he had become a monk, with the name Saijōbō Shingyū. He had been a frequent visitor at the southern capital, and it was he whom the Nara monks had commissioned to reply for them when letters were sent to Mount Hiei and Nara after Prince Mochihito's arrival at the Onjōji. Kiyomori had taken violent exception to the sentence, "The Novice Kiyomori is the dregs of the Taira clan, the scum of the warrior class." "How dare that rascally Shingyū call me the dregs of the Taira clan and the scum of the warrior class? Seize him and put him to death," he had said. So Shingyū had fled from the southern capital to the northern provinces, become Lord Kiso's scribe, and taken Taifubō Kakumei as his name.[61]

Kakumei is more or less equally prominent in all versions, although the order in which his dress and history are described varies from text to text. The description of his attire is generally consistent, as is his past, where included. In all cases, he dismounts and pulls paper and inkstone from his quiver, and he is praised as an exemplar of both civil and martial arts. There are certain small differences: in the Enkyōbon and Nagatobon, his history is not included, but his attire is.

The *Jōsuiki* and the *kōwakamai* embellish a bit—the *Jōsuiki* narrator notes that this was the same Kakumei who wrote Yoshinaka's petition to the Shirayama god, a missive included in chapter 29, episode 3. When he begins to write, Kakumei unfolds the paper, and, "just as if he were copying something of old,"[62] writes Yoshinaka's words. In the *Jōsuiki*, Kakumei's dress is depicted after the petition. This description concludes with the comment that, "in his left hand he held the petition, in his right his brush; what a paragon of the civil and martial he was!"[63] The *kōwakamai* further highlights him as writer: When Yoshinaka decides to write the petition (here he does not ask for Kakumei's advice), Kakumei dismounts, pulls ink stone, brush, and folded paper from his quiver. His dress is described, he is praised as a paragon of the two skills, his history is recounted, and the petition appears. The text concludes with praise for his calligraphy.[64]

In all versions of the narrative except the *Jōsuiki*, Kakumei appears first as a warrior, described in the formulaic the "dressing the warrior" pattern so commonly found in battle narratives.[65] The "dressing the warrior" motif, of course, usually draws attention to characters about to participate in a significant battle; winners and losers are both frequently "dressed." Scenes of dressing are highly marked narrative moments; the length of the description and the particular items described often indicate rank and the more sustained importance of the character. Here, Kakumei's *hitatare*, armor, and bow and arrows are described, but his mount and its saddle are not. His distinguished armor and rattan-wrapped bow are consistent with a character of some wealth and refinement. Mizuhara Hajime suggests as well that the solemnity of his dark blue and/or black attire emphasizes his status as a monk.[66]

In the performance tradition, the account of his attire is performed in the *kō no koe* (strong voice) and *kudoki* (plain chant) *kyokusetsu*.[67] This patterning is somewhat uncommon for dressing sequences, which are usually performed in the *hiroi* (picking up) *kyokusetsu*. The difference, however, is not inconsistent, since *kō no koe*, although higher in register, like *hiroi* represents a raised pitch relative to the surrounding narrative.[68] Both *kyokusetsu* are generally associated with the *hiroimono* (martial) mode.[69] Kakumei's dressing stands out in performance, musically marked as conventionally military.

Importantly, however, despite being "dressed" as if for battle, Kakumei is preparing not to fight, but to write. The "dressing the warrior" trope here clearly finds a different sort of use than is customarily the case. In addition to his armor and arrows, he carries paper, ink stone, and in two cases a brush, all of which are the accoutrements of a scholar rather than a warrior; yet he pulls these items from his quiver. The fact that he is described as a master of both (clearly differentiated) civil and martial arts further emphasizes the bifurcation of the two occupations. Moreover, his status is described in terms of his scholarship and his intellectual, rather than military, lineage;[70] in the Hyakunijukkubon and Kakuichibon, this comes immediately after his battle dress. Notable especially is mention of his affiliation with the *Kangakuin*, the prestigious academic institution established by and for the Fujiwara clan to provide housing, tutoring, and early education for its sons to supplement their studies at the government-sponsored *Daigaku*.[71]

In all texts except the *Jōsuiki*, the first real image of Kakumei is of someone who is at once a scholar and a warrior. Scholarship, equated here specifically with writing, is juxtaposed with archery. This pairing, though seemingly natural from a modern point of view, contrasts with the more common conjunction of military arts and music (and to a lesser extent poetry) we see typifying the best of the Taira warriors in the *Heike*.[72] Kakumei and his lord Yoshinaka are clearly not seen as embodying the same courtly talents as the Taira, who stand as the last remnants of a fading aristocratic culture specifically marked by music and poetry. That world, this passage suggests, is being reconfigured according to an entirely new set of terms. As a monk and later as Yoshinaka's scribe, Kakumei's ability to compose documents marks him as a scholar, a learned, public mediator. The description of his past in this delineation of his character stresses the significance of mediation that transcends his former life as a monk and his current role as Yoshinaka's scribe; writing here is about official communication, and Kakumei's writing is of great importance. That the later *Jōsuiki* and *kōwakamai* variants embellish the description of Kakumei's role as scribe further suggests that this issue became even more significant over time.

The most salient indication of the importance of writing in this episode, however, is the inclusion in all variants of the petition itself.[73] It is set off from the text by the formal entreaty at its beginning (*kimyō chōrai*) and its date and signature at the end (1183/5/11; *Minamoto Yoshinaka uyamatte mōsu*). The style in which it is composed contrasts sharply with the surrounding text: it is most commonly written in *kanbun* or a modified version of it (what is generally termed *wakan konkōbun*).[74] The language is formulaic and sprinkled with expressions taken directly from Chinese and Buddhist texts. Although the high concentration of what we tend to see as formal Chinese expressions does not inherently mark the text as "written" rather than "spoken,"[75] the inclusion of the petition in this form emphasizes its status as writing. This is clearly a document *as document*, intended to be interpreted as a transcription, or in performance, a reading of the petition.

Within the medieval context, the invocation of gods before battle was relatively common.[76] A general hoping for victory would perform rituals designed to win a deity's (or deities') support for his campaign. Composing a *ganjo* was but one important method for garnering this sort of divine assistance used by members of the warrior class during the medieval period. *Ganjo*, more commonly referred to as *ganmon*, are written missives couched in the conventional terminology we see here. They present both a promise of faith and a prayer for divine assistance. The idea of presenting written petitions to the gods of war stretches back to the Nara period, as does the closely related idea of rituals directed at those gods to bring victory in battle.[77] Generally, after a *ganjo* was written, it would be read before the god and burned ceremonially as a dedication.[78]

Although the request in Yoshinaka's petition ("I beseech the unseen and seen buddhas to lend their strength and the holy gods to exert their powers. Secure my victory at once! Drive the enemy back in every direction!")[79] refers specifically to the upcoming battle, it is embedded in a catalogue of other, perhaps even more important requests and assertions that reveal much about how Yoshinaka is positioning himself. The petition opens:

> All hail! I touch my head to the ground in obeisance.
>
> The Great Bodhisattva Hachiman is the lord of the Japanese court, the ancestor of our generations of illustrious sovereigns. To guard the throne and benefit mankind, he manifests himself as the three august divinities and assumes the temporary guise of the three deities.[80]

This description of Hachiman as the ancestor of sovereigns refers to his identification with Sovereign Ōjin, a conflation common to Hachiman origin tales.[81] The "three august divinities" refer to the three bodies the Buddha manifests (*hōshin, ōjin, keshin*), and the three deities are the avatars of Hachiman, ancestor of sovereigns and tutelary deity of the Minamoto.

The petition continues with an invective against Kiyomori (the "Taira Chancellor"), who is portrayed as "a foe to Buddhist law and an enemy to royal law."[82] Other scholars have discussed the centrality of the theme of righting relationships according to Buddhist and royal law in the *Heike* narrative, and the invocation of "Buddhist law and royal law" here is consistent with that general thematic thrust.[83] It also resonates with the divinations performed earlier in the Enkyōbon variant: The Taira are clearly out of balance with karmic and worldly power structures, while at this point Yoshinaka's behavior suggests that he is acting within acceptable parameters. Here, he identifies Kiyomori as a threat to the natural order, and then he situates himself in opposition to Kiyomori: "Though humble, I spring from warrior stock; though inadequate, I pursue my father's calling. The thought of the Taira Chancellor's foul deeds prohibits selfish calculation: I entrust my fate to Heaven and dedicate my life to the state."[84] The line, "though inadequate, I pursue my father's calling" is taken from the *Book of Rites*; it appears as well in the document discussed in Chapter Four. This use of a quotation from a Chinese text situates Yoshinaka in proper relationship to the throne, which he has already aligned with Hachiman, his tutelary deity. Further, he frames his personal connections to the sovereign and Hachiman by invoking the will of "Heaven," the metonym for the Buddhist cosmological order. The petition then claims that the fortuitous appearance of the shrine had given him hope for his campaign: "My tears of joy overflow; my gratitude is profound."[85]

The *ganjo* then turns to a recitation of Yoshinaka's lineage and the family's close connection to Hachiman:

> Ever since my great-grandfather, the Former Mutsu Governor Yoshiie, dedicated himself to Hachiman's service and took the name Hachiman Tarō, all of his descendants have worshipped at Hachiman's shrines. Many years have passed since I first bowed my head before the god as one of their number. In undertaking this great task now, I am like a child measuring

the vast ocean with a seashell, like a praying mantis opposing a mighty chariot with its forelimbs.[86]

By invoking Yoshiie, the petition reaffirms Yoshinaka's assertion of himself as heir to Yoshiie's military prowess. He emphasizes the shared clan identity (and ostensibly goals) of Yoshiie's descendants, who devote themselves to Hachiman worship. This rhetorical move, of course, recasts the family in terms of unity and continuity where we already know there has been murder and mistrust.

This passage is followed by phrases borrowed from the Chinese canon: The syntax and vocabulary generally evoke the Chinese; the metaphorical comparisons are presented in parallel structure, and the choice of source texts reflects a late-Heian engagement with Chinese texts common among the erudite.[87] While the inclusion of such wording may not indicate significant broad-based internalization of the texts themselves, it does indicate a general privileging of the Chinese texts in this type of public document. The *ganjo* ends with an entreaty to the god to support Yoshinaka's campaign and show him a sign if the "prayer has been accepted, if the visible and invisible powers will protect [him]." In all versions except the Enkyōbon, the petition is dated 1183/5/11 (in the Enkyōbon, it is 1183/6/1) and signed "Minamoto no Yoshinaka."

Yoshinaka's signature clearly and formally identifies him as a member of the Minamoto clan, inheritor of Yoshiie's military prowess and special connection with Hachiman. In the name of the clan and its favored relationship with Hachiman, he enjoins the deity to recognize his prayer and to show him a sign that it has been received. He presents this claim as one who is no longer the fugitive orphan, the child victim of severe internecine strife taken in and hidden by Kanetō, but rather a full-fledged member of this family with an illustrious history of service to the throne.

The *kōwakamai* ends at this point, after noting that everyone praised Kakumei's calligraphy. The other variants, however, go on to describe the dedication of the *ganjo*. It is presented at the shrine,[88] together with "top arrows" from the quivers of Yoshinaka and twelve of his lead warriors.[89] In the Enkyōbon, Nagatobon, and *Jōsuiki*, the petition and arrows are delivered to the shrine by a man wearing a rain hat, a degree of detail that gives those accounts the ambiance of an eyewitness account.[90]

The Kakuichibon narrative continues: "Might it be that the Great Bodhisattva recognized the supplicant's peerless sincerity from afar? Most reassuringly, three wild doves (*yamabato*)[91] flew out of the clouds to flutter above the white Genji banners."[92] Doves appear in the rest of the *Heike* variants as well, and are referred to variously as wild doves, sacred doves (*reikyu*), and once, in the *Jōsuiki*, as white doves (*shirohato*). Their appearance manifests Hachiman's recognition of Yoshinaka's "undivided devotion." The terms used to describe this state are consistent throughout: Yoshinaka has an undivided (*futatsunaki*) heart (*kokoro*), intention (*kokorozashi*), or both.[93]

While the other five texts conclude this episode with the dedication, the Kakuichibon and Hyakunijukkubon follow it with almost identical accounts of two precedents for this marvelous demonstration of Hachiman's favor. First is Sovereign Jingū's invasion of Silla, when, in response to her prayers, "Three [sacred] doves appeared in front of her shields and the foreigners suffered defeat."[94] Next is a description of the campaign by Minamoto Yoriyoshi, "the ancestor of these Genji,"[95] against Sadatō and Munetō, in which he invoked the god to empower a fire in front of the enemy position. In response, "a wind instantly engulfed the enemy in flames and burned down Sadatō's residence. . . . The rebels were later defeated, and Sadatō and Munetō were ruined."[96] In the Hyakunijukkubon, Yoriyoshi's son, Yoshiie, is instead cited as an ancestor who made this invocation.[97] The misattribution is an interesting narrative slip, since it points to the greater significance of Yoshiie for Yoshinaka and the idea of Minamoto clan identity generally.

Both of these earlier campaigns resemble Yoshinaka's: a small force faced by a larger enemy of outsiders. In the case of Jingū, the others are foreigners (*ikoku no ikusa*)—not surprising, given the location of the battle. In the case of Yoriyoshi, peripheral brigands are the "other" (*izoku*). For Yoshinaka, the "otherness" of the enemy is far less clear: the Taira are central aristocrats who have established blood ties to the throne. Although, as discussed in Chapter Two, the war tales are one site where provincial "others" become domesticated enemies of the throne (*chōteki*),[98] the opposite is happening here. Yoshinaka proclaims his role as defender of the throne against a large, outside force—the Taira who are alienated by this very assertion. That the Taira are compared to foreign or undomesticated enemies makes them "other" to Yoshinaka's rightful order. The narrative concludes, "Mindful of these precedents, Lord Kiso dismounted, doffed his helmet, washed his hands, rinsed his mouth, and made obeisance to the [sacred] doves with a confident heart."[99]

Yoshinaka dismounts and makes obeisance in all variants, but only these two cite precedents. All three remaining texts note that the Taira, looking on from afar, are terrified by this sight, which literally makes "the hair on their bodies stand on end."[100] This marks the end of the Kakuichibon and *Jōsuiki* episodes; the Haykunijūkubon continues to describe the battle and Yoshinaka's overwhelming victory. The other two texts, the Enkyōbon and Nagatobon, are not divided into episodes, so this break is not clearly delineated in them. However, there is a nominal shift indicated in both texts—the next sentence begins with the deictic expression "Some time later, . . ." (*saruhodo ni*).

Variation and Consonance:
Interpretative Strategies and Making Meaning

On the thematic level, several elements stand out across the variants to assert the correctness of Yoshinaka's actions and Hachiman's sanction of them. At a very fundamental level, the narrative builds structures that link Yoshinaka to the Minamoto line, establish the political and cosmological rectitude of his military project, and demonstrate his ability to interpret signs correctly.

Yoshinaka's connection to the Minamoto main line is, in reality, tenuous. As mentioned above, his father was rather dramatically alienated from it through his murder by the *sōryō*-apparent of the main line. Yoshinaka himself grew up in obscurity and, most likely, even in hiding. Additionally, when he began to raise troops, he also raised the suspicions of his cousin Yoritomo such that Yoritomo demanded a meeting, at which Yoshinaka gave his son to Yoritomo as a son-in-law, and, in effect, a hostage. Within narrative traditions and the historical record, therefore, Yoshinaka's relationship to the mainline Seiwa Genji is strained at best. Probably as a consequence of his alienation and marginality, it is vital to Yoshinaka's military project that he establish his credentials as a general, which means asserting his position within the Minamoto line.

The idea of continuous lineage is highlighted in Yoshinaka's reasoning for writing his petition. In addition to being a prayer responding to the moment, it is also intended to serve "the coming generations." In other words, Yoshinaka is positioning himself within a lineage that projects both back into the past and forward into the future, in which the rifts are overwritten by a narrative of continuity made manifest in the clan's ongoing relationship to Hachiman. The temporal gaps are diminished against this atemporal constancy, which in turn is reified through the concept of lineage. Yoshinaka thus asserts a view of the past and the present that mitigates the clearly less coherent reality he inhabits. Although this resembles teleological epic narrative in that it "overgoes" the difficulties of a messy reality by creating a seamless narrative,[101] it is important to remember here that Genpei narrative asserts hegemony in not entirely teleological ways. Not only does the forward-moving trajectory of Yoshinaka's campaign efface contesting narratives, but his assertion of the atemporal relationship to Hachiman also removes serious moments of contention in his own and his clan's past. The recontextualization of the movement of time within a transcendent cosmological reality, then, is another way in which difficulties are recast and diminished in this and other Japanese narratives.

The issue of Hachiman's sanction is closely connected to the idea of Minamoto family unity and Yoshinaka's place within the clan. It is not surprising, therefore, to find Hachiman figuring so prominently in all versions of the narrative. The consistency of his presence across the variants is demonstrated most concretely in the shrine Yoshinaka spots on Natsu-yama and in the form and content of the petition itself. Yoshinaka formal-izes his relationship in writing and within this document asserts his privileged connection to the god. His identification of Hachiman as the ancestor of the Minamoto and the royal family reminds the audience or reader of the (albeit distant) blood relations between the two, a blurring we encountered in Chapter Two as well. More importantly, however, the document configures the appropriate relationship between them. The Minamoto are defenders of the throne, and Hachiman, as a divine repre-sentative of the royal family, marks the rectitude of that relationship in his sanction of the Minamoto line.[102] Clan coherence is the locus of narrative coherence in the broadest sense; this is where all the divergent variants re-veal themselves to be tellings of one and the same story. In all but the *kōwakamai*, the god's response through the appearance of sacred doves represents acknowledgement of the petition and the petitioner.

As we saw above, another vital issue raised in the variants is the acquisition of knowledge. Knowledge per se is articulated throughout the text in the juxtaposition of *annai* versus *buannai*. But it also encompasses the idea of the "local" (*sato no osa; sato no hito; jūnin*), someone familiar with the area. In all variants, the centrality of knowledge acquisition is evident in Yoshi-naka's inquiries about the identity of the shrine, but it is also an important element in his strategic planning, when he predicts that the Taira will stop in the mountains because they do not possess knowledge of the local ter-rain. This is especially clear in the Enkyōbon and Nagatobon. What follows in all texts supports his assessment: he is able to lay a trap for the Taira, because they lack knowledge (*buannai*). There is a clear correlation, there-fore, between battlefield success and knowledge in all versions of this nar-rative.

But the most central act of knowledge acquisition in all variants is Yoshinaka's summoning of Kakumei to compose the petition. It is, after all, the petition that brings the god's favor and Yoshinaka's victory. This critical moment is not marked by use of the terms *annai* and *buannai*, however, even though the role Kakumei plays here is very much that of the *annaisha*, the possessor of knowledge. How he differs from the other *annaisha* underlines his interpretive methodology, and marks his actions as commentary about interpretation, not just of divine signs but also of the narrative itself.

I have already noted how Kakumei is foregrounded as a scribe and how his role as a writer of documents differentiates him from the Taira noblemen. Unlike those artistic writers, Kakumei functions as a multi-tiered interpreter, one who communicates between people, between people and gods, and, importantly, between the audience and the story. This role is articulated most fully in the *kōwakamai* (the latest variant), which devotes extra attention to Kakumei's act of unfolding the paper to write. Even more importantly, it ends not with the appearance of sacred doves, but rather with praise for Kakumei's calligraphy, which suggests a growing emphasis on writing, and a de-emphasis of other interpretive modes. Nevertheless, the missing conclusion, with its overtones of the god's beneficence, is understood by the ending of this variant. The piece is felicitous not only because Kakumei writes well, but because the audience knows the petition will garner the god's favor and the following battle will be won. The Hyakunijukkubon tells the same story through yet another juxtaposition: in its rendition, the *ganjo* writing and the ensuing victory are contained in the same *ku*. And in all variants, the story turns on Kakumei's act of writing.

Importantly, however, it is not simply the narrative *about* his writing but the presence of the actual document that forms the center of the episode. The document is emphasized formally in both its written and performative manifestations. As text, it is set apart from the surrounding narrative as a verbatim quotation; it employs a much greater number of *kanbun* expressions than the general narrative, and it is signed and dated, which lends it an air of concreteness. In performance the document is recited in a melodic vocal pattern that is designated for *yomimono*, or works containing important documents.[103] In both performance and written narrative, the petition marks a pause in the action, and in this pause a document is presented that enables the audience to interpret a significant event. Like Kanetō's *kishōmon*, the *ganjo* is offered in a rarified arena, a place where Yoshinaka's mettle and, more importantly, his intention, are being tested. Although Yoshinaka's undivided sincerity is what the god recognizes here (a reunion, perhaps, of Kanetō's divided heart and words), that sincerity is given form and meaning in the petition.

Kakumei as petition-writer thus serves as simultaneous interpreter between Yoshinaka and the god, shifting hermeneutic practice to a praxis of translation. This shift is mirrored in another layer of the piece as well. A vital part of the presentation of a *ganjo* is always its oral recitation before the shrine, a moment not specifically recounted in any variant. On the one hand, this omission probably reflects the obvious assumption that such a document would be read, but it also accentuates the element of documentation per se in this episode. That said, we cannot escape the element of performativity associated with many of these texts. On this level of presentation, the inscription is recited. The performer acts both as narrator (before the audience, outside the narrative) and as presenter (before the god, within the narrative). This doubling resonates with the art of Genpei narrative generally, wherein the performer becomes mediator between the character (and audience) and the god(s) as he performs the placatory tale. The way the document reaches outside the text to give the medieval audience a familiar, temporal, and fixed interpretive structure is paralleled by the way the performer, as interlocutor, reaches into the text and brings to life the recited document, which, when presented to the god, causes him to respond.

What can these variant texts, when considered as representatives of a more general narrative of Kiso Yoshinaka's rise, tell us about the medieval interpretation of his story? Diachronically, we see a general movement toward emphasizing the role of Kakumei as scribe and the increasing importance of writing. Yet in all variants, the idea of written documents as a vital medium of communication with the god remains consistent, and the petition's insertion in document form also signals this importance to the audience. By continually underlining the power of the document (and the act of writing) when used sincerely to gain divine sanction, Genpei narratives help shape a new, comprehensible interpretive scheme for an audience that took documentation, especially as proof in legal disputes, to be the norm.[104] It was a powerful tool, giving materiality to a version of the past that, because of its fixity, had the potential to overwrite unspoken problems with that past. By this means Yoshinaka here creates a Minamoto history that effaces the facts of tremendous internecine strife. The very stability of the document's description and the consistent foregrounding of the writer across variants both suggest the growing importance of written documents as proof of sincerity in medieval Japanese society. This in turn points to the ways these associations can be used within narrative and performative traditions to direct interpretation at important but problematic narrative moments.

Chapter Four

Yoshitsune at Koshigoe

Fealty Oaths, Fall from Grace

*M*inamoto Yoshitsune is indisputably Japan's favorite cultural hero. The lead general in the Genpei War, he played a decisive role in the destruction of Yoritomo's enemies and enjoyed renown among warriors and capital-dwellers alike. He was a fearless leader, guiding his men into battle against what seemed like impossible odds, first at Ichi-no-tani and then at Yashima and Dan-no-ura. In each campaign, he emerged victorious. His devotion to his men rivaled that of his ancestor Yoshiie, and he inspired equal reverence from them. His legendary valor and popularity worked to his disadvantage in the end, however. Almost immediately after his victory at Dan-no-ura, he found himself the target of Yoritomo's suspicions, and four years later, under siege by Yoritomo's supporters and down to only a handful of his own retainers, he was forced to commit suicide in Hiraizumi, having already been placed under censure by the government and denied all support beyond that of his closest followers.

Yoshitsune's precipitous change in fortunes, one of the defining moments in narratives of his life, is the focus of this chapter. It occurs at the end of the war, when he arrives in Kamakura to deliver prisoners of war (the highest-ranking Taira general, Munemori, and his son, Kiyomune) and receive rewards from Yoritomo. Yoritomo has the prisoners taken into custody and detains Yoshitsune on the outskirts of Kamakura at a place called Koshigoe. The various accounts of this moment differ much more markedly than those in earlier chapters (the Enkyōbon and *Jōsuiki*, in fact, include a contradictory narrative of it), but in the most famous incarnation of the "Koshigoe" story, Yoritomo refuses a formal audience and sends Yoshitsune back to the capital as his deputy. Yoritomo's rebuff of Yoshitsune here is extreme: there is neither welcome for the victorious general, nor a reunion between the brothers. It is a surprising turn of events—up until this point in the war, Yoshitsune has received nothing but praise.

What caused the apparently sudden falling out between the brothers, and how is such a damningly fractious rift handled in historical narratives?

Yoshitsune looms large in medieval historical and artistic traditions. His legendary life stands out as the most complete of any Genpei figure. His infancy, his youthful experiences at Kuramadera, his involvement in the Genpei War, and his flight to Hiraizumi make up a longer linear story from which the cross-section of the Koshigoe narrative is taken. Especially important is the rift between Yoshitsune and Yoritomo that becomes evident in the final years of the war. A brief review of his story helps to contextualize the Koshigoe incident and place it in relation to the narratives of the other lives considered in earlier chapters, across which similar or identical patterns of meaning reinforce each other in the larger cultural milieu. In addition to the *Heike* variants considered so far, this discussion also includes the long narrative text *Gikeiki*, chronicling the life of Yoshitsune. The *Gikeiki* operates in interesting dialogue with the *Heike*,[1] and both provide foils for the other new text considered here, the pseudo-history *Azuma kagami*, a documentary work that nevertheless draws significant content from the legendary narrative traditions. The intertextual borrowings between histories, war tales, performance traditions, and legendary biography articulated in the Koshigoe story reveal a permeability of textual and generic borders that helped propel the widespread transmission of this story and contributed to the particular way the historicity of this difficult and important moment took shape.

Yoshitsune in the Medieval Imagination

Yoshitsune's life is the subject of more stories during the medieval period and beyond than any other single historical figure in Japan. Shorter narratives of all stages of his life appear in various medieval *monogatari, kōwakamai,* and *nō,* as well as in the dramatic arts of *kojōruri, kabuki,* and *bunraku* during the Edo period.[2] His life story is also the subject of the *Gikeiki,* literally the "Record of Yoshitsune," and he is considered the third of three great heroes whose rise and fall form one of the important structural frameworks of the *Heike monogatari.*[3] Extant texts about him in other traditions, both medieval and early modern, seem to derive from material collected in the *Heike* and the *Gikeiki.*

Where the *Heike* provides ample description of Yoshitsune's battlefield heroics, the *Gikeiki* almost completely elides Yoshitsune's involvement in the Genpei War,[4] recounting instead broad-ranging legendary material concerning the rest of his life.[5] Although there are no records concerning its composition, scholarly opinion agrees that it probably represents a collation of episodes about the hero circulating during the Kamakura and early Muromachi periods strung together to create a coherent whole.[6] In addition to the many fanciful accounts of Yoshitsune's exploits, he is also mentioned in his capacity as Yoritomo's representative during and immediately after the Genpei War in the contemporary records *Gyokuyō* and *Gukanshō*, as well as in the *Azuma kagami*.

Yoshitsune was the youngest son of Minamoto Yoshitomo. Born in 1159 to Tokiwa, a relatively low-ranking consort, he was still an infant at the time of the Heiji Uprising. After Yoshitomo was branded a traitor and enemy of the court, Tokiwa was forced to seek protection for herself and their three sons. Legend has it that Taira Kiyomori, having been granted responsibility for the disposition of punishments following the uprising, was captivated by Tokiwa's beauty and decided to spare her sons if she would in return become a member of his household,[7] at which point her sons were sent to temples to become monks. The older two, Zenjō and Gien, both took vows, but later joined Yoritomo's rebellion; Yoshitsune ran away from the temple to which he had been entrusted before taking the tonsure.[8]

Tokiwa's initial flight from Kiyomori, her subsequent capture, and the sparing of the boys comprise the subject of numerous narratives and dramatic pieces, as does Yoshitsune's life at Kuramadera, where his mother had sent him for religious training. The *Gikeiki* claims that it was at Kuramadera that Yoshitsune, known by his childhood name Ushiwaka,[9] first demonstrated signs of superiority as a scholar and a future hero. Under the tutelage of the monks there, he showed signs of semi-miraculous strength and wisdom. According to the *Gikeiki*, "he spent every day with his teacher, reciting sutras and pouring over Chinese classics. When the sun sank in the west, he read on with the teacher until the image lamps flickered out."[10] This text further records a visit by a Minamoto retainer who informed Yoshitsune of his familial heritage and reminded him of his responsibility to the spirit of his deceased father, at which point the object of Yoshitsune's devoted study immediately changed from the scripture to the art of war. He made nightly visits to Kibune Shrine, where he entreated the deity Hachiman to "preserve the Genji,"[11] and he promised to erect "a magnificent shrine endowed with twenty-five hundred acres of fields"[12] if his aspiration to punish his father's enemies were realized. Each night he engaged in mock swordplay, cutting down trees and bushes he dubbed with the names of prominent members of the Taira clan.

In addition to the *Gikeiki* account of Yoshitsune's training at Kuramadera, there are also other legends about military training of a more otherworldly variety. Among these are "Chapter on the Flute" (*Fue no maki*)[13] from the *kōwakamai* repertoire, which narrates his nightly training by *tengu* (goblins) who transmit secret military strategy to him.[14] Another *kōwakamai* piece, the "Record of the Future" (*Miraiki*),[15] presents Yoshitsune's relationship to the supernatural in similar terms, but in this case, the *tengu* show his own future in a prophetic night visit. Assuming the roles of the various people he will encounter in his attack on the Taira, they act out Yoshitsune's life in an uncanny play within a play that represents a rehearsal of history as it will develop; the "Record of the Future" is thus another manifestation of the prophetic dream motif we saw in Chapter Two, with the audience's past being inscribed as the narrative subject's future. Importantly, this dream concludes with the warning to Yoshitsune: "After [the destruction of the Heike], Lord Ushiwaka, do not incur the wrath of your elder brother. Do not place trust in Kajiwara [Kagetoki]. If there is discord between you brothers, your luck will run out. If there is discord within the six familial relations, the protection of the Three Sacred Regalia will not be assured. This is the end of what we can tell you. The rest is unknown."[16] The "Record of the Future" introduces several problematic issues that also will be addressed by the Koshigoe narrative: the brothers' discord, the involvement of Kajiwara Kagetoki, and a preoccupation with the fate of the Three Sacred Regalia.

The veracity of most accounts of Yoshitsune's life at Kuramadera is of course highly questionable, but these works nevertheless constitute an important segment in his life story. Like Yoritomo and Yoshinaka, he spends his youth cut off from the center, in a locale and a situation in which his Minamoto identity is suppressed. In most accounts, he only actually learns of his family history as he grows up, and inevitably the source of this information is an outsider. The narrative of his coming into knowledge has some interesting parallels and contrasts with Yoritomo's and Yoshinaka's. All are urged by nonrelatives to embrace their family destiny and overthrow the Taira. For Yoritomo and Yoshinaka, this is a call to action after a long period of waiting, but for Yoshitsune it represents a new awareness of who he is and what his destiny might be. Yoshitsune starts from a position of general ignorance, and it is his inability to navigate a path to knowledge (despite his extensive study at Kuramadera and his demonstrated intellectual competence), that eventually causes his downfall.

At age fifteen or sixteen, Yoshitsune fled Kuramadera to the northern territory of Ōshū, which was then under the control of Fujiwara Hidehira, a long-time ally of the Genji. In 1174 the Fujiwara stronghold at Hiraizumi enjoyed great affluence under Hidehira, and Yoshitsune was apparently welcomed and offered support. When Yoritomo raised troops in 1180, Yoshitsune proceeded from Hiraizumi to Kisegawa, where he met his brother on the twenty-first of the tenth month, according to the *Azuma kagami*.[17] Yoshitsune spent the next three years with Yoritomo in Kamakura, while Yoshinaka and his troops moved toward the capital. By the middle of 1183, Yoshinaka had successfully routed the Taira, but his excesses convinced Yoritomo to dispatch Yoshitsune and another brother, Noriyori, to chastise their cousin. Their eastern forces quickly routed

Yoshinaka from the capital; his death then opened the path for Yoshitsune and Noriyori to gain Retired Sovereign Go-Shirakawa's sanction for their pursuit of the Taira, granted on the twenty-ninth day of the first month of 1184, according to the *Azuma kagami* and the *Heike* variants.[18]

Yoshitsune's reputation for excellence as a military commander emerges from his two-year offensive against the Taira. The battles for which he is famous were fought in two relatively quick campaigns, the first against the Taira encampment at Ichi-no-tani and Ikuta-no-mori, lasting four days from departure from the capital to the Taira's retreat; and the second, nearly a year later, against the Taira position at Yashima, which led to the sea battle of Dan-no-ura. This operation took less than two months. Between these engagements, Yoshitsune was stationed in the capital, and during this period animosity seems to already be brewing between him and Yoritomo. In the sixth month of 1184, Yoritomo requested that the court grant Noriyori governorship of Mikawa Province (present-day Aichi Prefecture), completely passing over Yoshitsune.[19] Moreover, Yoritomo entrusted the pursuit of the Taira to Noriyori, leaving Yoshitsune in the less visible position of Kamakura representative to the central government in the capital.

Perhaps because of this set of circumstances, Retired Sovereign Go-Shirakawa awarded Yoshitsune both rank and title later that year. While the retired sovereign's intentions in doing so are unclear at this point, scholars of literature and history alike have speculated that his motive was to spark discord between Yoritomo and Yoshitsune.[20] Whether this causal relationship was actual or simply an anachronistic attribution is difficult to ascertain (all records describing it were composed at a much later date), but accounts of the brothers' discord are consistent. The *Azuma kagami* notes Yoshitsune's dissatisfaction with the disposition of awards in the sixth month.[21] Following Yoshitsune's appointment to Junior Fifth Lower Rank,[22] Yoritomo relieves him of military duties.[23] Yoshitsune is not called back into military service until Noriyori's failure to defeat Taira Tomomori and his forces at Shimo-no-seki sufficiently frustrates Yoritomo into reinstating Yoshitsune as military commander.

Yoshitsune's remarkable crossing from Honshū to Shikoku to effect a land-based attack on the Taira at the beginning of 1185 rivals his daring descent down the Hiyodorigoe cliffs backing the Taira stronghold a year earlier; both were rash actions that the more staid among Yoritomo's commanders generally did not support. Yet both were overwhelmingly successful—and ultimately decisive—in leading to the final Minamoto victory. Although in narratives focused on Yoshitsune (as most are), his bravery is lauded, we are also given indications that his boldness was seen as impudent and perhaps even insubordinate. At several moments in most renditions of the Genpei War, he is at odds with Kajiwara Kagetoki,[24] an eastern warrior whom Yoritomo has entrusted as both a commander and liaison between Kamakura and the troops on the field.

Despite Kagetoki's disapproval, Yoshitsune's daring and decisiveness led to Minamoto victory; at Dan-no-ura the Taira were completely destroyed. Their casualties included the child sovereign Antoku, as well as many of his Taira relatives. Clutched in the arms of his grandmother (or in the *Azuma kagami*, the arms of the gentlewoman Asechi no tsubone),[25] Antoku sank to his death, taking with him the sword Kusanagi, one of the Three Sacred Regalia. It was never recovered. Yoshitsune returned victorious to the capital, where he took up his duties as Kamakura's representative and married the daughter of Taira Tokitada, one of the Taira prisoners. This act alienated Yoritomo, who had already endorsed Yoshitsune's marriage to a daughter of one of his own retainers, Kawagoe Shigeyori.[26] Yoritomo's anger is manifest in his order of the twenty-ninth day of the fourth month for his warriors not to obey Yoshitsune, according to the *Azuma kagami*. At this point, Yoshitsune begins protesting his innocence, first through a fealty oath (*kishōmon*) sent from the capital, and then by journeying to Kamakura to plead his case in person.

This juncture is critical in the narration of warrior history, because it is the first moment in the brothers' relationship where there is clearly strife without reconciliation, and it stands as the turning point after which hostility and destruction prevail. Although this portrayal is consistent throughout the variants considered here, it is most striking in the *Gikeiki*, where it is manifest not only thematically, but also structurally—it occurs halfway through the narrative. As a narrative subject Yoshitsune is transformed here from a brash and impetuous warrior into a contemplative, hesitant, and melancholic tragic hero in the aristocratic mold.

Although the Enkyōbon and *Jōsuiki* describe a meeting between the brothers at this juncture, in other accounts Yoshitsune journeys to Kamakura, but he is not permitted to enter his brother's encampment. He spends several weeks at its outskirts sending his brother fealty oaths, which Yoritomo ignores. Yoshitsune eventually composes a long petition, the *Koshigoe jō* (hereafter, the Koshigoe petition) swearing his loyalty, which Yoritomo also rejects, and Yoshitsune is forced to return to the capital without having seen his brother. Since this falling-out is the topic of the Koshigoe narrative, I will pursue its implications no further here; its profound historical meaning, however, should be evident even so. At this point, brothers from a family claiming worthiness as defenders of the throne on the basis of familial lineage and filial devotion have reached an impasse in their own relationship so great that the next step is planned assassination.

Once he returns to the capital, Yoshitsune is quickly stripped of many of his land holdings. Although he is granted the governorship of Iyo, he sees this as a merely nominal award. Moreover, relations between Yoritomo and the brothers' uncle Yukiie deteriorate at this time, and Yoshitsune sides with Yukiie. The two are forced to flee an attack from Kamakura, and they head towards Shikoku and Kyūshū, where most of their ships are destroyed in a storm that also kills many of their few remaining supporters. The two go their separate ways, and Yoshitsune successfully disappears for a time; in 1187, he makes his way to Ōshū, where he is greeted warmly by Fujiwara Hidehira. Hidehira's health fails, however, and he dies before the end of that year. His son, Yasuhira, is eventually convinced by repeated entreaties from the central government that Yoshitsune's death would be to his own benefit. He attacks Yoshitsune, who, cornered and down to only a few men, kills himself, his wife, and their daughter on the thirtieth day of the intercalary fourth month of 1189.[27]

The "Reverse Oars" Debate

Throughout the Genpei narratives, Yoshitsune is characterized as a fearless, devotion-inspiring leader. His brashness puts him on the edge between bravery and foolishness, and the precariousness of this position opens him to criticism. Though proving key to the success of each action, his descent from Hiyodorigoe to Ichi-no-tani and his crossing the straits between Watanabe and Yashima were seen as suicidal by his compatriots. Although the narrative voice in the war tales does not censure his actions per se, by the final battles, Kajiwara Kagetoki does, and their disagreements form the basis for what the tales record as a devastating blow to the relationship between Yoshitsune and Yoritomo.[28] In all the extended narratives considered here, there is clear friction between Kagetoki and Yoshitsune, although its manifestation is not uniform. In the majority, however, their rivalry is crystallized in a disagreement over strategy that occurs as Yoshitsune prepares to cross the straits and rout the Taira. This incident is referred to as the "reverse oars" (*sakaro*) controversy.

The "reverse oars" controversy appears in most variants of the *Heike*. In the Kakuichibon, it is the first of two episodes describing hostility between Yoshitsune and Kagetoki. "Reverse Oars" (11.1) opens with a long lyrical lament for the Taira, who have been scattered to the edges of the realm. Next, the narrative turns to Yoshitsune, who departs the capital to finally subdue the Taira; the officials of all the great shrines and temples pray for the "safe return of the sovereign (Antoku) and the Three Sacred Regalia."[29] The debate between Yoshitsune and Kagetoki takes place after the troops have arrived at Watanabe and are planning their attack on Yashima, across the straits in Shikoku:

> The Genji made ready to loose the hawsers of the vessels they had been
> preparing at Watanabe and Kanzaki. But a violent north wind blew up,

whipping the limbs off trees, and huge breakers damaged the boats so that they could not set out. The attackers stayed in port that day to effect repairs.

At Watanabe, the great and small landholders assembled in council. "We have had no experience in naval combat. How should we go about it?" they debated.

Kajiwara Kagetoki spoke up. "I suggest that we tell our men to put reverse oars on the boats for this battle."

"What are reverse oars?" Yoshitsune asked.

"When a man gallops forward, it is easy to turn his mount with the left or right hand," Kagetoki said, "but it is no small task to make a swift reversal in a boat's course. I say we should install oars at both the prow and the stern, with rudders on the side: then it will be simple to direct a boat wherever we please."

"Men usually retreat when the tide turns against them, even if they have resolved not to yield an inch. What good can come of anticipating flight all along? This is inauspicious talk for the start of an attack. The rest of you can fit out your boats with a hundred or a thousand 'reverse oars' or 'retreat oars' if you want to. I will be content with the usual equipment," Yoshitsune said.

"A good Commander-in-Chief gallops forward when he ought to and draws back when he ought to. Saving himself to destroy the enemy is the mark of an able leader. A rigid man is called a 'wild boar warrior'; people do not think much of him," Kagetoki said.

"I don't know anything about boars and deer. In battle what I like is to attack flat out and win," Yoshitsune said. Although the samurai did not dare laugh in Kagetoki's face, they showed one another their amusement through significant glances and grimaces. It looked as though Yoshitsune and Kagetoki might come to blows, they whispered among themselves.[30]

In most variants, their disagreement is picked up again several episodes later, when they nearly come to blows at the beginning of the battle of Dan-no-ura. Tomikura notes that the texts containing this two-part description of the acrimony between the men belong to the recited lineage. In the read-lineage texts, by comparison, the two men argue openly only regarding the issue of "reverse oars." In the Enkyōbon description of the "reverse oars" controversy, Kagetoki criticizes Yoshitsune for his lack of greater vision and for not conducting his strategic planning meeting well.[31] He claims that Yoshitsune's unwillingness to listen reflects disloyalty (fuchū) to Yoritomo; when the two draw their swords, other prominent retainers restrain them. The passage ends with the comment that this was a source of deep resentment (fukaki ikon) for Kagetoki. The Jōsuiki account likewise notes that the event becomes the source of resentment for Kagetoki.[32] The altercation is not included in the *Gikeiki*. Tomikura suggests that the recited-lineage texts reflect a lengthening of the (presumably earlier) story from the read-lineage texts; he further asserts that the actual debate may represent a narrative dramatization of the animosity toward Yoshitsune manifest in Kagetoki's letters from the front to Yoritomo.[33]

Tomikura's assertion raises the important issues of source material and its reliability. What actually occurred is difficult to ascertain, despite the use of patterns of narration that claim historicity—prophetic dreams, divinations, and embedded documents. The inclusion of such elements helped to construct a believable historical narrative for medieval readers and audiences, although, as we have seen, these traditional tropes were undergoing a reassignment of meaning within these very texts. In the case of dream interpretation and other sorts of divination, it is easy for modern scholars to treat their use as "proof" as a narrative device. Doing so in the case of documents is trickier, since documents are so vitally important for authenticating past events within our own practice of history. The impossibility of composing a completely objective document, of course, leaves their reliability as proof open to question. In the case of the documents considered here, their evidentiary value is further undermined by the likelihood that they were composed or embellished sometime after the war. The one consistent record we have of Kagetoki's battlefield correspondence, for example, is the *Azuma kagami,* the pseudo-historical text compiled nearly a century after the war and reliant on other sources, including the war tales themselves, for descriptions of wartime events. In other words, the existence of such letters is highly suspect, and their inclusion in works like the *Azuma kagami* most likely is a product of the need post-factum to create a rancorous relationship between Yoshitsune and Kagetoki. This record is discussed in more detail below.

The *Azuma kagami* provides an interesting complement to the rest of the variants. As a "history," it follows the form of earlier works of that genre and is arranged chronologically with dated entries. For the dates immediately surrounding that attributed to the reverse oars debate, nothing specific is mentioned regarding a conflict between the two men, but there is an entry for 1185/4/21 (the battle of Dan-no-ura was fought 3/24) recording a letter sent from Kagetoki. The *Azuma kagami* notes, "It recorded the events of the battle, and then the disloyalty of Yoshitsune. It said: . . ."[34] Under a dated entry a comment on the day's events includes what appears to be an excerpt from a report sent from Kagetoki to Yoritomo. Kagetoki's missive is not an embedded document per se, but the text strongly suggests the presence of an original letter through repeated use of the quotative "it said" (*to unun*).

The two items included in the excerpt here are both of interest. In the first Kagetoki reports that the victory at Dan-no-ura had been predicted in a dream one of his men had before the battle. In the dream, a man dressed in the white robes of a shrine attendant presented the dreamer with a formal letter (*tatebumi*). The man appeared to be a messenger from Iwashimizu Hachimangū. The letter said that the Taira would be destroyed on the day of the sheep, and so battle plans were made accordingly. Moreover, though the Genji forces were not great, they mysteriously appeared to be tens of thousands to the enemy. In the second passage he notes that the battle at Nagato two years earlier, a sea turtle appeared in the water, then climbed onto the shore. The fisherfolk brought the turtle before Noriyori, who, remembering an earlier dream, marked the shell of the turtle and returned it to the ocean. During the battle at Dan-no-ura, the turtle reappeared at the bow of the Genji boats. Then two white doves appeared over the cabins of the Genji ships; this occurred just as the Taira were drowning. Additionally, at the ensuing battle at Suō, white standards appeared in the sky, fluttered briefly before the eyes of the Genji, then disappeared into the clouds.[35]

These passages are significant for their overlap with earlier themes and symbols we have encountered—the prophetic dream, the messenger from Hachiman, the white doves and white standards. The narrative of the dream message is of particular interest: it is delivered in the form of an official and ornate *tatebumi*—it is inscribed, but, interestingly, within the context of the dream world. Inscription, so central to Yoshinaka's Petition and also, as we shall see, to the Koshigoe narrative, here moves in the opposite direction. The letter comes from the realm of the gods to the human world; written correspondence, it seems, moves both ways. The presentation of the *tatebumi*, moreover, highlights the materiality of this ethereal transmission of information—the realms of the ordinary and the divine are inseparable, and communication within the matrix of the dream world incorporates the kinds of formal missive found in everyday life. The focus on the meaningfulness of inscription is also apparent in the account of marking the turtle's shell; the turtle is recognizable during the battle of Dan-no-ura because of the writing on its back.

The chief thematic function of this episode is to assert divine sanction for the Minamoto victory, and the importance of correct interpretation of that sanction is critical for ensuring victory. The day of the battle was planned in accordance with the dream, and Noriyori's prohibition on killing the turtle in accordance with another dream allows it to reappear to herald the defeat of the Taira. The signs of Hachiman (the doves and the white standards) further support Kagetoki's assertion that the battles were fought well and that their outcome had the god's approval. The attribution of correct interpretation here, where given, is to Noriyori; Yoshitsune is not mentioned at all. Notably, this *tatebumi* is presented side-by-side with other manifestations of divine will—the sea turtle and the now-familiar white doves.

The *Azuma kagami* juxtaposes this passage concerning felicitation and success with Kagetoki's complaint against Yoshitsune. Again, it is prefaced by a quotative, "and then it said" (*mata iwaku*). Kagetoki does not mention the "reverse oars" debate per se, but he does complain about the insolence and rashness of Yoshitsune and his men. He notes that Yoshitsune's victory was accomplished only with the efforts of many; Yoshitsune's arrogance has been so intolerable that the men are obsequious to him and fearful of his censure. Kagetoki's greatest concern, however, is Yoshitsune's lack of respect for Kagetoki and others of his rank, men who are directly indebted and accountable to Yoritomo. He further notes that Yoritomo should consider Yoshitsune a potential enemy (*ada*) and asks that he, Kagetoki, be relieved from service to Yoshitsune and permitted to return to Kamakura. The entry concludes with the narratorial comment that Yoshitsune's actions have caused many people's resentment (*hitobito urami wo nasu*). Resentment is a sentiment that will prove central in the ensuing struggle between the two men at Koshigoe.[36]

This episode in all accounts performs the important function of defining a serious conflict between Yoshitsune and Kagetoki and characterizing each of the adversaries. Yoshitsune advocates action, while Kagetoki is more temperate, urging caution. Yoshitsune disparages Kagetoki's reticence by substituting "retreat oars" for "reverse oars," equating caution with cowardice. Although he eventually gets the last word and apparently the tacit support of his men, the rift is left unmended. Yoshitsune emerges victorious primarily because his attitude is acceptable on the field of battle; it does not, however, reflect a thoughtful understanding of the broader context of the war. In contrast to Kagetoki, who repeatedly communicates with Yoritomo and whom we see in the *Azuma kagami* actively involved in interpreting his surroundings, Yoshitsune is acting on his own, uninterested in the implications of his actions.

Koshigoe: Triangulation and Miscommunication

Shortly after the battle of Dan-no-ura, Yoshitsune and his men are ordered back to the capital; while there, he is praised by the retired sovereign and promoted to Fifth Rank. Yoshitsune then proceeds with his prisoners of war—Munemori and Kiyomune—towards Kamakura. In all narratives except the Enkyōbon and *Jōsuiki*, he is ordered to halt at Koshigoe, a stop along the Tōkaidō at the edge of Kamakura, and he releases his prisoners to a representative from Yoritomo, who has become suspicious of his brother's intentions. The stand-off ends with Yoshitsune composing the Koshigoe petition, a long missive protesting his innocence and proclaiming his loyalty to his brother. Yoritomo does not receive it favorably, and Yoshitsune returns to the capital empty-handed, having been denied the right to meet with Yoritomo. Within a few months, Yoritomo's complete censure compels Yoshitsune to flee the capital, and he remains a wanted man until his death. The Koshigoe narrative thus represents the turning point in the relationship between the two brothers, and a moment of extreme anxiety from the historical point of view. How are the tensions underlying the account of the brothers' relationship narrated? How is this story authorized, and what legitimizes it as history?

The representative texts of the Koshigoe narrative are taken from a broad and mostly familiar range of sources, including the Kakuichibon *Heike*, the Enkyōbon *Heike*, the *Jōsuiki*, the *kōwakamai* "Koshigoe," and the *Azuma kagami*. Since the read-lineage Enkyōbon and *Jōsuiki* present an alternative version to the better-known story of Yoshitsune's Petition, I will begin with a discussion of them. It is significant that the Enkyōbon is the oldest text considered here; the possibility that the tale it tells might be more accurate should be borne in mind.

The Enkyōbon account of the Koshigoe episode is included in chapter 6, parts 30 through 32. It opens with a melancholic *michiyuki* (road-going) sequence describing Yoshitsune's journey with Munemori and Kiyomune from the capital to Kamakura. This is, of course, a death journey. Munemori is well aware that it will be his last, and he lingers over each poetically familiar site as he moves farther and farther away from the capital. The passage is long and lyrical and is shared in all versions. The party first passes the Ōsaka barrier[37] and then Kagamiyama, where Munemori composes poems that reflect his understanding of the finality of his journey. He begs Yoshitsune to intervene with Yoritomo on his behalf, and Yoshitsune promises to exchange his anticipated awards (*kunkō*) for Munemori's life. The irony of Yoshitsune's words would not be lost on an audience familiar with his story. There will be no rewards, of course, and there will be no going back to a harmonious relationship with Yoritomo. Although Yoshitsune does not seem to recognize it—a further indication of his inability to correctly interpret the wider implications of his situation—this *michiyuki* is as much his own last journey as it is Munemori's.

Yoshitsune's first act upon his arrival at Kamakura is to return keepsakes of the drowned sovereign to his mother, Kenreimon'in, who is being held there. Yoshitsune then appears before Yoritomo, eager to be praised and awarded for his military victories. Obviously expecting a warm reception and the opportunity to relate his battlefield heroics ("Yoritomo will ask about what happened at those many battles, and he will be pleased"),[38] he is instead greeted by a brusque, guarded (*uchitoketaru keshiki mo naku*) elder brother who allows him to rest after his journey, but has no desire to discuss matters with him. Their brief exchange ends with Yoritomo's order that Yoshitsune remove himself to Kanearaizawa, another locale close to Koshigoe, on the periphery of Kamakura. Incensed, Yoshitsune withdraws.

Yoritomo's retainers who witness this exchange comment that Yoshitsune is indeed a fearsome person (*oroshiki mono nari*), around whom one ought to remain guarded (*uchitokubeki mono ni arazu*).[39]

The audience (*taimen*) between the brothers starkly contrasts the longer and far more genteel interviews that precede and follow it—the former between Yoshitsune and Kenreimon'in, the latter between Yoritomo and Munemori—which further emphasizes the jarring discord between these two brothers and former allies. Yoshitsune is appalled to be kept at Kanearaizawa, and the section concludes with the statement that "he was not permitted to enter Kamakura (*Kamakura e irerarezu*)."[40] Here the meeting is brief and Yoritomo's hostility clear. Although the retainers comment on Yoshitsune's unreliability *after* the meeting has occurred, Yoritomo's reaction to his brother seems to be his own. Moreover, no specific retainer is blamed for causing his distrust of Yoshitsune; the conflict between the brothers seems to be just that—a rivalry within the family, observed and commented upon, but not choreographed, by outsiders.

The *Jōsuiki* includes the episode of the brothers' falling out in the first two episodes of chapter 45. This version opens with the long lyrical *michiyuki*, containing eleven *waka* to the Enkyōbon's two. Included is an exchange at Ikeda station between Munemori and Jijū, a scene reminiscent of the famous encounter between Taira Shigehira and Senju-no-mae slightly earlier in the narrative.[41] Here too, Yoshitsune offers to trade his anticipated awards (*kunkō no shō*) in return for Munemori's life. After passing through the stations to the east of Kamakura,[42] including Koshigoe, they arrive in Kamakura. Of the brothers' encounter, the text notes that a meeting (*taimen*) took place with Yoritomo, but there were few words (*ito kotoba sukuna ni te*) and Yoritomo remained guarded (*uchitoketaru keshiki nashi*). Yoshitsune could not believe this incongruous response, and he did not get to relate tales of the battlefield.[43]

The similarity of the descriptions in these two texts is striking. Yet it is difficult to conceptualize the conflict between the brothers as one in which there is a clear-cut protagonist and an equally identifiable antagonist. In the *Jōsuiki*, however, there is also the first hint of what is developed into an important thematic element in the other variants of the narrative: in the third episode of chapter 46, Yoritomo decides to have one of his men kill Yoshitsune, citing a number of reasons including "his appointment to Fifth Rank (*goi*) in the ninth month of last year."[44] The text also remarks that Kagetoki, bearing Yoshitsune deep enmity (*fukaku ikon to omoikereba*) over the "reverse oars" episode (*sakaro no kuron*), has slandered him repeatedly (*oriori zansu*) to Yoritomo. This integration of the "reverse oars" story and Kagetoki's enmity provide important insight into the direction later texts will take.

In recitational *Heike biwa* practice the Koshigoe episode (11.17) is classified as a *yomimono*, a "document piece." This means that it, like Yoshinaka's Petition, thematically centers on a document, and the highlight of the performance is the recitation of that document. *Yomimono* constitute a special category in the *Heike biwa* repertoire; they are separated from the main repertoire in the *Heike mabushi*, the late eighteenth-century libretto for sighted amateur performers.[45] Musically, *yomimono* are patterned differently from the main body of episodes; they are among the last group of pieces a master performer would learn.

The Kakuichibon account also begins with a *michiyuki* describing Yoshitsune's trip down the Tōkaidō with Munemori and Kiyomune, but it is interrupted by the announcement that Kagetoki has arrived in Kamakura ahead of Yoshitsune and has insinuated to Yoritomo that Yoshitsune should be considered an enemy (*onkataki*) for his belligerent behavior during the campaign against the Heike.[46] Yoritomo agrees, has his men relieve Yoshitsune of his prisoners at Kanearaizawa, and sends him to wait at Koshigoe. Yoritomo remarks that Yoshitsune is a tricky fellow (*susudoki otoko*) and warns his men to stay on alert because he may try to enter Kamakura (*Kamakura e irunaru ni ono ono yōishitamae*).[47]

In a narrative shared in large part by the remainder of the texts (the Kakuichibon, *Gikeiki*, and the *kōwakamai* "Koshigoe"), Yoshitsune laments his fate, noting that he not only punished Yoshinaka and defeated the Taira, but also returned the box containing the two remaining Sacred Regalia, the mirror and the bead strand, to the palace (*naishidokoro, shirushi no onbako, kotoyuenaku kaeshiiretotematsuri*). He complains that the only award for his trouble has been the governorship of Iyo, and he further states that he and Yoshinaka are solely responsible for bringing peace to the realm of Nippon (*Nippongoku*).[48] This comment, intentionally or inadvertently, draws attention to the important parallels between Yoshitsune and his cousin: both are great generals, and both are doomed by their inability to place themselves in relation to Yoritomo. Yoshitsune remarks that the way Yoritomo has chased him away from Kamakura is cause for enmity (*ikon no shidai*). He writes a number of fealty oaths, but under the influence of Kagetoki's slander (*Kagetoki no zangen ni yotte*), Yoritomo does not accept them. This sort of petitioning is reminiscent of Kanetō's fealty oaths discussed in Chapter Three; here, however, they are not successful. This is a textual marker (absent in the Enkyōbon and the *Jōsuiki*) that a fundamental breakdown in communication has occurred.

Yoshitsune's final recourse in these texts is to compose the Koshigoe petition, which is inserted into the narrative at this point. As with other documents considered above, it is dated, formally addressed and signed, and set off from the surrounding text. Depending on the manuscript, the degree of *kanbun* with which it is composed differs slightly.

The petition is a defensive testament to Yoshitsune's loyalty, and it is filled with references to his identity as a warrior, and more importantly, a member of the Minamoto lineage. He complains that instead of receiving accolades (*kunshō okonawaru beki tokoro ni*), he has been undone by pernicious slander (*kokō no zangen*). Yoritomo's unwillingness to weigh the veracity of a slanderer's claim (*zansha no jippu wo tadasarezu*) has prevented him from entering Kamakura (*Kamakurajū ni irerarezaru*). Yoshitsune fears that the blood bond between the brothers has expired, and he laments that no one will comfort him in his sorrow unless the spirit of their deceased father should be reborn. He says that he has not enjoyed peace since his father's death, and goes on to remind Yoritomo that it was he, Yoshitsune, who defeated Yoshinaka and destroyed the Taira. His willingness to take armor as his pillow and live by the way of the arrow, he claims, stemmed solely from his desire to comfort their dead ancestors. He defends his promotion to Fifth Rank (*goi no suke ni funin no jō*) as a family honor (*tōke no jūshoku*) and claims that he has written numerous oaths on the backs of ox-head talismen (*goō-hōin*) from the various shrines and temples as further evidence of his sincerity. The document ends with an appeal to Ōe Hiromoto, the functionary through whom the petition is sent to Yoritomo, to act on Yoshitsune's behalf.[49]

The language of the petition further develops themes raised in the surrounding narrative: slander as the cause of discord, the fundamental importance of the brothers' blood relationship, the illustriousness of their shared ancestry, and Yoshitsune's deservedness of awards. It also mentions his two failures—accepting rank from the retired sovereign without Yoritomo's permission and the loss of the sword Kusanagi. He presents both of these as accomplishments—the first is a family honor, the second displaces the loss of the sword by emphasizing the safe recovery of the mirror and bead strand. He mentions as well the other written oaths he has sworn, to the point, perhaps, of protesting too much; the sudden inundation of documents seems a last-ditch effort to establish a paper trail of sincerity that, as his defense of his promotion suggests, does not harmonize with his actions.

The *Gikeiki* and *kōwakamai* variants add a few important flourishes. In the *Gikeiki*, the Koshigoe story is positioned immediately after a long account of the brothers' first meeting at the beginning of the Genpei War.[50] In that episode, the brothers pledge their good will toward each other. Yoritomo invokes their blood bond, their mutual descent from Yoshiie, and his pleasure at being reunited. He treats Yoshitsune as kin, placing him above other retainers, and, based on that kinship, he appoints Yoshitsune commander-in-chief of his forces. The initial meeting between the brothers, therefore, reiterates the familiar themes of brotherhood, shared ancestry, and family unity. This version elides the *michiyuki* sequence, noting simply that Yoshitsune journeyed as far as Koshigoe with his prisoners. In effect, this shifts attention away from the pathos of the Taira defeat and toward Yoshitsune's situation. One of the important differences between the *Gikeiki* and other Genpei narratives is evident in the *Gikeiki*'s focus on a single life altered, but not circumscribed and contained, by the Genpei War; the events of the war itself only merit several lines. The pathos of the fallen Taira is beyond its purview. What is most salient in its account of the war is Kagetoki, who slanders Yoshitsune more vehemently than in the Kakuichibon, finally advising Yoritomo not to allow Yoshitsune to enter Kamakura (*Kamakurajū e iremairasetamaite onza sorowan koto ibuseku sōrō*)[51] because he is dangerous.

In the *Gikeiki* Yoritomo responds rationally at first by deciding to allow each man to have a fair chance to present his case, because hearing only one side would be unjust. His retainers comment among themselves that since Yoshitsune is innocent, he normally should have nothing to fear. But Kagetoki's enmity (*ikon*) over the "reverse oars debate" (*sakaro taten to no ron*) may be cause for concern, since this enmity has led to slander (*zangen*), which is clearly damaging. Kagetoki at this point composes his own fealty oath to Yoritomo, which persuades Yoritomo that he need not hear Yoshitsune's side.[52]

When he is relieved of his prisoners at Koshigoe, Yoshitsune immediately discerns that it is "that wretch Kagetoki's slander" (*Kajiwara me ga zangen)* that lies behind his detention, and he remarks that his participation in the war was not only to cleanse their ancestor's shame and comfort the spirits of the dead, but also to please Yoritomo. He regrets allowing Kagetoki to live, after having had the chance to kill him in the West, only to find him behaving now as an enemy.[53]

At this point, Yoritomo decides to have Yoshitsune killed at Koshigoe. He unsuccessfully tries to summon potential assassins from among his men. Hatakeyama Shigetada even rebukes Yoritomo, reminding him of Hachiman's vow (*Hachiman bosatsu no on chigai*) to protect the clan, and contrasting the relationship between brothers to that between Yoritomo and the outsider (*tanin*) Kagetoki:

> It is more important to care for your own rather than an outsider. An outsider does not compare at all to family. Kagetoki is a temporary tool for you to use. Disregarding your brother's years of loyalty because of Kajiwara's slander [is unthinkable]. Even if you bear him enmity, grant him Kyūshū, grant him an audience.[54]

Yoshitsune first swears fealty oaths and oaths on ox-head talismans, then resorts to the petition. In this variant, Yoritomo is brought to tears when he receives the petition. He decides that Yoshitsune should be appointed warden of the capital. As autumn deepens, however, Kagetoki continues to relentlessly slander (*shikiri ni zangen mōshi*) Yoshitsune, and Yoritomo's thoughts again turn to murder.[55] This characterization in the relatively recent *Gikeiki* reflects the historical imperative to create an acceptable explanation for the actions that follow. Blame is displaced completely onto a non-Minamoto meddler as the theme is rearticulated in texts further separated in time from the events they describe.

In the *kōwakamai*, this characterization of Kagetoki as a villain is even clearer.[56] "Koshigoe" opens with praise for Yoshitsune, who has "defeated the proud Heike" and returned *all three* Sacred Regalia safely to the capital (*sanju* [sic] *no jingi kotoyuenakufutatabi teito ni osame*).[57] People laud him as a fine general. Having taken possession of Munemori and Kiyomune, Yoshitsune then decides to present them to Yoritomo, because "they are not only enemies of the sovereign, but also of our clan."[58] In preparation for their embarkation for Kamakura, Yoshitsune visits the Iwashimizu Hachimangū at Otokoyama, where he seeks the blessing of the clan's tutelary god, "a blessed deity."[59] Note here Yoshitsune's volition, but also the strong assertion he makes about Minamoto family identity; he acts as a loyal younger brother, placing the interests of the family and his elder brother first. The ensuing *michiyuki* resembles that in the Enkyōbon. Once the party reaches Sakawa, Yoshitsune summons Musashibō Benkei, who then dispatches Ise Saburō to Kamakura to announce their arrival.

Yoritomo is at first elated: "Yoshitsune has arrived at Sakawa, has he? Wonderful!"[60] He orders trees to be felled and a proper reception hall to be constructed so he can receive Yoshitsune appropriately. Kagetoki ruminates, "Here in Kamakura, everything from government to rites to people's comportment is determined by Yoritomo."[61] He is concerned that, should Yoritomo learn of the enmity he harbors over the "reverse oars" incident, he, Kagetoki, and his progeny will surely be killed after being dragged to Yuigahama, Kamakura's execution grounds. To avert this tragedy for his own clan, Kagetoki plans to present repeated slanderous charges (*oriori zanso wo tsukamatsuri*) to Yoritomo to make him suspicious of Yoshitsune's intentions. He warns his lord that Yoshitsune may represent an assurance of peace in the capital, but he will be a threat to Yoritomo if he is allowed to remain in Kamakura. Yoritomo finds this argument reasonable, and has Kagetoki direct Doi Sanehira to relieve Yoshitsune of the prisoners and send him back to the capital.[62]

Yoshitsune flies into a rage, "This is not Yoritomo's answer, it is that Kagetoki coming between us. I should push my way into Kamakura right now and kill him and his sons!"[63] Sanehira counsels caution, however, and urges Yoshitsune rather to wait and send pledges (*sosho wo sorawaba*), while he, Sanehira, tries to smooth things over. These efforts are again thwarted by Kagetoki's interference (*Kajiwara ga chū ni te kokoroe*).[64]

Kagetoki tells Ise Saburō (who is acting as Yoshitsune's messenger) that Yoshitsune will be appointed as governor of Iyo. If his loyalty is proven, he may also be appointed representative to Kyūshū. Ise Saburō returns with this message, which further infuriates Yoshitsune. He recounts his victories and his safe retrieval of the Three Sacred Regalia, asserting, "[under the influence of] slanderous retainer or no, he (Yoritomo) ought to at least meet with me once." The text then comments, "thinking about it, he knew this was all due to Kagetoki's slanderous heart, and Yoshitsune bore Yoritomo no resentment" (*koremo omoeba, Kagetoki ga zanshin ni yoru nareba, Yoritomo ni urami sarani nashi*).[65] Yoshitsune then swears his fidelity in writing on the back of a series of ox-head talismans, but these, too, are rejected because of Kagetoki's slander (*Kajiwara ga zanso*).[66] Yoshitsune next has Benkei compose the Koshigoe petition, which Benkei does with calligraphic skill reminiscent of Kakumei's. Although the text does not dwell on his dress and history, immediately before the petition appears, it contains the remark that "he mixed the ink, dipped his brush, and without even making a draft, wrote [the petition] perfectly in one stroke."[67] The petition itself is nearly identical to that of the other versions, and it is followed by the comment that Benkei's calligraphy received praise from everyone (*Ka no Benkei ga hissei, homenu hito koso nakari keri*);[68] this is another aspect in which this *kōwakamai* resonates with Yoshinaka's Petition.

The *kōwakamai* is the newest piece considered here, and it varies from the other works in ways that reveal important developments in the cultural consciousness about both the Koshigoe incident and Yoshitsune's life more generally. Yoshitsune has become not only blameless but also charmingly innocent, as has Yoritomo. Kagetoki, on the other hand, is scheming and self-interested, more concerned about himself and his progeny than the stability of the warrior family at the top of the sociopolitical hierarchy. The rivalry established here, in other words, is one between (rather than within) families, leaving intact a projection of idealized family unity we will return to below.

In both the *Gikeiki* and the *kōwakamai*, we encounter the juxtaposition of Kagetoki's successful oath-writing with Yoshitsune's failure, which hints at each man's relative competence at gauging his situation. The general arena in which their rivalry is played out reflects an interesting staging of the semiotic, a communication about communication. Actor/reciters recount a tale of retainers carrying missives back and forth between the primary characters, each of whom then expresses his rage, fear, or desire out of range of his adversary. The setting suggests judicial give-and-take, much like that we saw in Yoshinaka's situation. Importantly, Kagetoki proves the better litigator. As they take turns presenting their arguments, he consistently captures Yoritomo's attention, both when he writes and when he speaks; Yoshitsune, on the other hand, is unable to successfully communicate with his brother, which in effect seals his fate. Interpretation and communication are of paramount concern, and, as with Yoshinaka's Petition, we see a movement toward highlighting the act of communication (the movement of the messengers, the materiality of the document, the act of composition, the foregrounding of the composer) and the positioning of the primary characters one degree removed from the action and one step closer to the role of observer/audience, for whom they model the act of interpretation.

A further layer of meaning is added to the story because of its inclusion in the *Azuma kagami*. In adhering to the style of the history, the *Azuma kagami* contains shorter narratives arranged by date; this breaks up the story, creating a more fragmented account than the other versions. Following Kagetoki's missive to Yoritomo from the front described above are several other remarks implicating Yoshitsune. The first reports that Yoritomo relieved Kagetoki of his assignment to Yoshitsune.[69] The following day's entry includes an edict from Yoritomo condemning Yoshitsune for forcefully assuming control over Kyūshū.[70] On the ninth of the same month, Yoshitsune sends a fealty oath.[71] This action, the recorder notes, served to fuel rather than assuage Yoritomo's ire.[72]

A week later (1185/5/15),[73] a messenger arrives in Kamakura announcing Yoshitsune's imminent arrival. Yoritomo arranges for Hōjō Tokimasa to relieve him of the prisoners and instruct him to not enter Kamakura (*Kamakura ni sanzubekarazu*).[74] The party reaches Kamakura the following day, but no mention is made of Yoshitsune. The entry for the twenty-fourth day, however, includes the Koshigoe petition, recorded in a form virtually identical to that found in the *Heike* variants. On the ninth of the following month, the prisoners are returned to Yoshitsune, and he is instructed to leave for the capital. His resentment reaches a deeper level than ever before (*kono urami yori mo fukashi*).[75]

This account merits several general comments. First, it shares with the other texts the formal presence of the petition itself. And clearly Kagetoki has a hand in the general ill-will between the two brothers. Yet we see as well enmity between the brothers as a function of their own behaviors (and not Kagetoki's). Yoshitsune has provoked Yoritomo by acting in a way that validates Kagetoki's reports, and Yoritomo has angered Yoshitsune by being unwilling to confirm awards for him. The *Azuma kagami*, then, serves as a pivotal component complicating the more well-known variants of the narrative. It endorses the characterization of a legitimate conflict between Yoritomo and Yoshitsune we saw in the Enkyōbon and *Jōsuiki*, while simultaneously highlighting Kagetoki's meddling in their affairs. And as a "history," it exhibits an air of reportage that gives it a stronger flavor of veracity than the other texts considered.

These texts together, then, comprise a global narrative that is far more contentious than those treated in the preceding chapters. The actual degree of enmity between the brothers is the core problem posed for succeeding generations of readers and viewers, and each version handles it somewhat differently. Yet all versions revolve around the fundamental problems of communication and interpretation. How are these issues articulated within the general framework of proving one's rectitude? And what are the roles of bearing witness and presenting documentary evidence in this context? How these problems are articulated within a more general concern with presentations of proof is therefore an essential issue in our consideration of the story told in this narrative.

The Koshigoe Narrative in Context: Making Meaning

One of the fundamental preoccupations in this grouping of narratives is Kagetoki's slander. Where it is present, it moves the story forward, and it is so fundamentally a part of most versions of the tale that its absence in the Enkyōbon and *Jōsuiki* is particularly striking. Kagetoki is so specifically and constantly described as a slanderer that the association seems to function much like the fixed epithet.[76] How is this attribution used to shape the story according to recognizable tropes, and how does the narration of his conflict with Yoshitsune reframe the context for those tropes?

Kagetoki's slander is always described in terms that use the *kanji* "*zan*" (slander).[77] This *kanji* implies lying or misrepresentation intended to cause harm to someone. It is a particularly strong term, found frequently in the litigious rhetoric of jurisprudence or records of political affairs. In the Koshigoe narrative, we find it in a number of combinations that further cement this characterization. Most often, it appears in the term *zangen*, conventionally translated as "slander," and comprised of the two characters *zan* and *gen* (speech act, or to speak). In addition to *zangen*, other terms formed from *zan* include *zansha* (a person who slanders); *zanso* (a slanderous claim or petition, particularly in a formal judicial arena); *zanshin* (slanderous heart); *zanshin*[a] (slanderous retainer); and the verb *zansu* (to slander).

Binomes including *zan* are prevalent in the narratives; a diachronic evaluation reveals that they increase over time, with the late *kōwakamai* containing far more occurrences than any of the earlier texts. And slander as an act is tied specifically to Kagetoki, who uses it against Yoshitsune in the *Jōsuiki*, the *Gikeiki*, and the *kōwakamai*. Moreover, slander is implicated as the cause of the brothers' discord: "because of dangerous slander, I have not received great reward," Yoshitsune complains in all versions of the petition; "because of Kagetoki's slanderous petition," Yoshitsune's oaths are ignored in every variant but the *kōwakamai*. In addition to characterizing Kagetoki as evil, the focus on (public) slander also places the conflict within the judicial sphere. We can see the creation of such a context as yet another way in which Yoritomo's system of justice is anachronistically embedded in this story of its inception.

Other textual cues bring the scapegoating of Kagetoki into relief in all the variants, and particularly in those where the specific connection between slander and Kagetoki is not drawn. The most obvious of these is the frequent appearance in the texts of enmity (*ikon*, literally "lingering resentment") and resentment (*urami*). Although the same character is used to write *urami* and the -*kon* of *ikon*, the lexical relationship between them is, of course, only evident when the words are read, not spoken. That several different *kanji* can be used to write *urami* further obfuscates this connection.

The term *urami* is a variably nuanced word meaning, in its substantive form, anything from "loathing" to "grudge" or "resentment." *Urami* in the sense of resentment (as it is most commonly encountered in the Koshigoe narrative) usually stems from a cause, frequently abandonment by a lover (as in the *nō* play *Nonomiya*) or a political intrigue, most notably Genji's (in the fictional world of the *Genji monogatari*) or Michizane's.[78] One term for the kind of "vengeful spirit" that Michizane becomes is *onryō*; "vengeful" is written with a *kanji* that can be read *urami*. In highlighting the slippage of meaning associated with the term, I do not seek to give it a deconstructionist turn. Rather, these various associations unify and add breadth and depth to ideas like "resentment" here: *urami* and *ikon* are weighted with historical meaning.

Ikon and *urami* are used to triangulate the relationships in the Koshigoe episodes, and they almost inevitably tie Yoshitsune's problems at Koshigoe to the "reverse oars" debate. They appear increasingly in the other variants, and are most often used to describe the relationship between Yoshitsune and Kagetoki. Both men experience the feeling, although as time goes by, it is always Kagetoki's unjust behavior that provokes it in Yoshitsune. Notably, they are absent from the Enkyōbon, despite the open hostility between Yoritomo and Yoshitsune in that account.

Situating the "reverse oars" debate in causal relationship to the slander that undoes Yoshitsune is important in defining his relationship with Yoritomo. The thematization of the outsider who seeks to unbalance the brothers' inherently harmonious relationship intensifies and becomes more consistent over time. Kagetoki is an easy target as a man who, historically, went on to become an enemy of the Kamakura government after Yoritomo's death—and, what is more, as the result of again slandering an innocent. As an ultimately unfavored historical figure for the period beyond Yoritomo's time, he is expendable, though the degree to which the characterization of him as slanderer, meddler, and nefarious advisor to Yoritomo is accurate in the Koshigoe incident remains open to question.

The narrativization of disharmony between Kagetoki and Yoshitsune is articulated against an idealized Minamoto clan, epitomized by harmony and a strong sense of identity. It is precisely at the moment of

falling out between Yoritomo and Yoshitsune that this narrative idealization becomes necessary. This is most evident in the Enkyōbon and the *Jōsuiki*, which characterize the Minamoto familial relationship in negative
terms. In the Enkyōbon, Yoritomo is "guarded" (*uchitoketaru keshiki mo
naku*)—literally, he is unwilling to loosen his reserve. Yoshitsune for his
part is "not a person with whom to let down one's guard" (*uchitoku beki
mono ni arazu*); he is also fearsome (*osoroshiki*).[79] In the *Jōsuiki*, the characterization is identical. The conflict configured here diverges significantly
from that described in the narratives involving Kagetoki and represents a
fundamental version whose problems may underlie the attempts to overwrite it—to repeat it "with a difference" in the other versions.[80]

The texts including the Koshigoe petition figure the relationship in
strikingly different terms. In those versions, Yoshitsune's missive draws attention to the brothers' shared blood lineage, as we have seen. This focus
on lineage and family identity is reflected as well in his characterization of
the war as a battle between the Minamoto and the Taira, another analo-
gous clan (*ichizoku*, and, occasionally, Heike). The construction of the two
great clans further builds on the idea of the illustrious Minamoto history
of which Yoshiie is the progenitor and the brothers are the current manifestation, a theme further highlighted in Hatakeyama's reprimand about
family versus outsiders in the *Gikeiki*: Kagetoki is an outsider (*tanin*), while
Yoshitsune is kin. This configuration is in turn connected to Hachiman,
whose presence is felt even more strongly in the *kōwakamai* when Yoshitsune stops at the Iwashimizu Hachimangū as he leaves the capital. The
thematic framework is familiar, and its mobilization here seems particularly closely linked to protecting what the Enkyōbon and *Jōsuiki* suggest
was actually a precarious alliance between Yoshitsune and Yoritomo.

Why is so much attention given to sanitizing the relationship, and,
more importantly, to rendering Yoshitsune blameless? To begin with,
Yoshitsune, as the victorious general who is eventually killed by his brother,
is a culturally conventional object of sympathy. Although the widely used
term "*hōgan biiki*" (literally "sympathy for the lieutenant [Yoshitsune]"
and more broadly the "sympathy for the underdog") refers specifically to
Yoshitsune, the idea of sympathy for the underdog existed as a central
cultural tenet long before Yoshitsune's time. Sugawara Michizane, the
hero of *Ise monogatari*, and Genji are but a few prominent early examples
of men in the historical and fictional record whose stories successfully
use this trope. Yoshitsune appears historically at a time when there were
already discourses on failed heroes and exiles into which he could easily
be placed.

What makes the heroicization of Yoshitsune problematic is that his
persecutor was not only his brother but also an important power holder.[81]
As the first shōgun and the man through whom following generations of

warrior rulers claimed their authority, Yoritomo is not often the object of criticism. As we saw in Chapter Two, he is characterized rather in terms similar to that of the sovereign, and this deference is, interestingly, propagated and shaped in widely circulated legendary materials—even the *Heike* variants most strongly implicated in eulogizing the fallen Taira portray him as having the sanction of the gods, as rising to right what the Taira had made wrong.[82]

That these two men were brothers who challenged each other in a variety of arenas creates a problem for narration because, first, both are necessarily valorized in important cultural discourses and, second, their falling out points to the very real problem of intra-clan rivalry. Competition between close family members was in fact endemic into the early Kamakura period and not considered unusual.[83] By the late Kamakura and Muromachi periods, however, the need for unity grew as the clan became an increasingly important political and economic unit.[84] The best way to mobilize a family's resources under these circumstances was to designate a primary heir under whom strict hierarchical relationships were maintained.[85] This system relied upon submission of secondary sons and all daughters to the primary heir, a situation which created resentment and contributed to the numerous lawsuits brought against siblings over inheritance in the Kamakura courts. The portrayal in medieval narratives of the Minamoto family as fundamentally harmonious and loyal thus represents an attempt to shore up the primary heir system by anachronistically attributing something similar to the first generation of warrior leaders.

In this milieu, Yoshitsune's historically contentious relationship with Yoritomo presents a serious problem. In point of fact, Yoshitsune did not willingly submit to his older brother's authority, and Yoritomo in turn chose to solve their disagreement by having Yoshitsune killed—the two neither adhered to an idealized concept of family nor operated within the legal system to resolve their differences. By displacing blame for this particular familial falling out on an outsider, the later versions of the Koshigoe story maintain the ideal of cohesion for the Minamoto main line. The evident efforts of the creators and compilers of these works to vilify Kagetoki and portray the brothers sympathetically points to a nostalgic desire in later, more fractious medieval society to see fraternal harmony as a foundational characteristic of its own cultural identity.

That said, it is difficult to completely smooth over a past that includes a degree of fraternal contention that leads to forced suicide. In the Koshigoe grouping, both the presence of conflicting versions and the evident concern over historical time with sanitizing the relationship between Yoritomo and Yoshitsune highlight the points at which the contestation occurs, namely, Yoshitsune's rewards, his appointment to Fifth Rank, and his return of the Sacred Regalia to the capital.

Of these, the matter of rewards is the most pervasive across the variants. In the Enkyōbon, Yoshitsune wants to tell Yoritomo of his battles, and in the *Jōsuiki*, he regrets that he does not get the chance to do so. He is not permitted to speak in either account. In other words, he is not granted the right to recount the battles in a way that will demonstrate his worthiness for reward. His silencing here is significant, particularly given the medium through which the tale is conveyed; on a metatextual level, the denial of his right to tell his story to Yoritomo contrasts markedly with the act of telling by the tale's performer or narrator. Yoshitsune does not have the chance to bring his story to life, and therefore he is an unsuccessful author of his fate. In a text that stages the production and interpretation of texts as arenas of truth-knowing, this suppression of speech stands out.

Moreover, where his story is told in the remaining variants, it is not effective: though his valor is recounted by Yoshitsune himself, by the narrator, and even by Kagetoki, his rewards are meager. This result contrasts markedly with Yoshitsune's expectations—in later variants, he assumes that they will be available to barter for Munemori's life, and he then complains about the insufficiency of his rewards in every version of the petition. In the *Gikeiki*, the issue arises somewhat obliquely in Hatakeyama's reprimand, when he advises Yoritomo to grant Yoshitsune Kyūshū and to make him Kamakura's representative in the capital. In the *kōwakamai*, it is Kagetoki who decides that Yoshitsune's award will be the undesirable Iyo and hints that if he proves loyal, Kyūshū might follow. Underlying this problem, of course, is the award Yoshitsune did receive, rank and title from an authority other than Yoritomo, an issue raised in tandem with his complaints about rewards. Yoshitsune is proud of his promotion, and his subsequent defense of accepting it without Yoritomo's approval bears the mark of challenge to Yoritomo as surely as it marks proof of his interest in the family's overall prestige.

The final issue repeated throughout Yoshitsune's defense is the loss of the sword Kusanagi. Although it certainly cannot be seen as Yoshitsune's fault, its disappearance reflects a particularly worrisome historical development: one of the markers of divine sanction is gone as a result not only of Taira arrogance but implicitly also the Minamoto failure to avert its sinking to the bottom of the sea. In the *kōwakamai*, this narrative aporia is overwritten: Yoshitsune returns all of the Three Sacred Regalia safely to the capital. Although this version does not actually erase the history of the sword—an elaborate narrative explaining its return to the Dragon King at the bottom of the sea represents an important medieval narrative thread—the need here to present an alternative account indicates the significance of its disappearance. And at some level, this loss is part of Yoshitsune's fate. Because the sword has not been recovered, total order has not been restored, and there is a need for compensatory narration of the ending of the war. Swords and their significance for the Minamoto will be discussed in Chapter Five; here, however, we must register a nagging concern about the loss of this most vitally significant blade.

Writing Matters: Oaths, Petitions, and Other Evidence

Like Yoshinaka's Petition, Koshigoe is a *yomimono*, an episode centered on a document. Unlike Yoshinaka's story, however, there are versions of this tale that do not include the embedded petition, and this omission provokes further inquiry into the very idea of the document as part of this narrative. What is the meaning of the petition, and what of its absence? What can it tell us about the narration of Yoshitsune's falling out with Yoritomo?

In the variants containing the Koshigoe petition, the missive's form consistently contrasts with the narrative in which it is embedded. It is dated and signed, written either exclusively or primarily in *kanbun*, and set off physically from the surrounding text. The materiality of the document in written variants is echoed in performance. As a *yomimono*, it is performed using patterned melodic formulae conventionally used to evoke document reading. In the *kōwakamai*, the document is the grand finale; the piece ends, as does Yoshinaka's Petition, with a comment on the scribe's calligraphic skill. Moreover, although this document is the only one quoted in the episode, the narrative mentions numerous others, particularly Yoshitsune's fealty oaths and his oaths on the backs of ox-head talismans. In the context of medieval Japanese culture, and warrior culture in particular, these evidentiary texts make powerful claims—they are avowals of sincerity and veracity sworn before both earthly and heavenly authorities, committed permanently as records of the oath-taker's accountability to divine as well as political will.

Perhaps the strongest assertion made for the importance of the petition itself is its inclusion in the *Azuma kagami*, the Kamakura government's auto-history. This context asserts its historicity more profoundly than the *Heike* accounts: it is one of many written records collected and collated to create an allegedly accurate and contemporary picture of the period it documents. Items (notes on the weather, reports of Yoritomo's activities, the progress of construction projects, letters, decrees, etc.) are presented under dated entries. Quotations and summaries of written communiqués from the battlefield, such as Kagetoki's, in fact, comprise the heart of this work's record of the war—the *Azuma kagami* is a collection of contemporaneous information, from the quotidian to the significant.

The list-like, non-narrative frame and the seemingly uncensored inclusion of information simply for its own sake lends the *Azuma kagami* an air of objectivity, a resistance to shaping stories in favor of simply providing information. That some of the factual information, including individual documents, found in it is extant in original form or in contemporaneous records further contributes to the work's apparent neutrality. Of course, the impossibility of any objective history has been pointed out by Paul Ricouer, Hayden White and others, and it is clear from even the brief accounting here that not only is the *Azuma kagami* shaping a story about the falling out between the brothers, it is shaping it to validate the story told in the war tales.[86] Yet both in medieval times and today, the lure of "factual evidence" remains tantalizing, and it is easy to assume the facticity of pieces like the Koshigoe petition simply because of their inclusion in histories like the *Azuma kagami*. Yet numerous documents embedded in the war tales and the *Azuma kagami* yet not found anywhere else, such as the Koshigoe petition, Yoshinaka's petition, and indeed Yoritomo's pardon, are in fact most likely products of the history constructed in the war tales, rather than verifiable contemporary material evidence.

Importantly, the Koshigoe petition's presence within the recited variants assures a permanent place for it as part of cultural history outside the realm of the official record. An essentially circular process of textual influence codifies the Koshigoe narrative: the teller of a tale includes a document in his telling, and it is replicated in other traditional tellings of the tale. It is incorporated into the historical record, which in turn is cited as confirmation of the actuality of the object (the petition) itself. For a document that cannot be located in any document collection or contemporary record, the Koshigoe petition enjoys a materiality, and by extension historicity, that many actual documents do not. A visit to Manpukuji, a temple established at Koshigoe, even allows the modern tourist to view the "original document" in Benkei's hand.[87]

The document itself, in turn, lends an air of veracity to the Koshigoe story and also to Yoshitsune's innocence. The poignancy of his rejection is even more justifiable in light of his earnest written plea. The veracity of his claim and sincerity of his motivations are formally etched into Genpei narrative, and his blamelessness becomes a central tenet of his characterization both here and throughout narrativizations of his life in the medieval through modern periods.[88] Yet this theme is not the only possible one given voice in the narratives. The Enkyōbon and *Jōsuiki* indeed tell an alternative story, one in which Kagetoki plays little or no role; when the brothers meet, their conflict is clearly internecine and motivated by varieties of self-interest that we hesitate to attribute to heroes—self-aggrandizement through awards and promotions, and competition between brothers who should be working harmoniously.

Interpretation, Communication, and Authorizing History

As we have seen in earlier chapters, two of the most pervasive problems set up in these narratives are interpretation and communication. These are concerns of import both within the narratives themselves and on a metatextual level, since they at once guide characters within the stories and audiences hearing or reading them through the subtleties and difficulties of potentially tense historical moments. In the Koshigoe episode, we encounter perhaps the most troublesome spot in Minamoto family history and the accompanying breakdown in communication. How do the texts handle this moment, and what do they tell us about how we can interpret what happens at Koshigoe?

As described above, the factors contributing to the friction between Yoritomo and Yoshitsune are varied and numerous. On the one hand, the very real issues of Yoshitsune's promotion, his disappointment with his rewards, and the loss of the sword Kusanagi are present in all accounts. Yet in the works that include the Koshigoe petition, they take second place to the rivalry between Kagetoki and Yoshitsune that resulted from the "reverse oars" controversy. The petition suggests a situation somewhat similar to Yoshinaka's: Yoshitsune must prove his sincerity, and he is dependent on interpreters to make sure that he presents his case appropriately. Within the parameters shared between the stories, we can see Yoshitsune's problems immediately. He does not maintain proper communication with Yoritomo from the battlefield (*Azuma kagami*); he acts in ways that reflect his poor understanding of propriety; and he incorrectly assumes a familiarity with Yoritomo that will allow him to trade on his awards and maintain control over large and important areas of the country. When he is slandered by an outsider who has Yoritomo's ear, he loses his chance to express his sentiments directly to his brother and must rely on go-betweens. While many of these mediators are powerful and reliable (Hatakeyama and Doi, for example), they are no match for Kagetoki, who is powerful and dangerous. Communication is cut between the brothers and, as a result, Yoshitsune is unable to achieve his goals. Significantly, Yoshitsune's last-ditch attempt to work through a scribe here is unsuccessful—perhaps Benkei lacks Kakumei's sophistication, despite other accounts of his erudition (including the story of his youth in the *Gikeiki*).

The key to Yoshitsune's problems with communication is his mode of presentation; because he is unable to plead his case orally, he is forced to write a document. Because Kagetoki interprets Yoshitsune's position wrongly to Yoritomo, the document is insufficient. Certainly, Yoshitsune's sincerity is embedded in the document, much as Kanetō's and Yoshinaka's were earlier; the act of deliberate misinterpretation by Kagetoki is required to undermine it. Only the willful act of someone trying to disrupt the workings of the judicial system so symbolic of Yoritomo's rule could cause this kind of breakdown. Because Yoshitsune is unable to present his case directly to Yoritomo, he can only muster a half defense; because even that is intercepted by Kagetoki, it becomes subject to doubt. The full force of his incapacitation is driven home in another *kōwakamai*, "The Inserted Letter," which recounts Yoshitsune's death and the presentation of his head to Yoritomo. When the Kamakura Lord examines the head, he finds, rolled in Yoshitsune's mouth, a missive pleading his innocence and accusing Kagetoki of slander. This document, placed in the mouth of the severed head, is perhaps the most eloquent illustration of the broader significance of communication. Yoritomo eventually gets Yoshitsune's side of the story, but only after it is too late.

What does this mean for the Enkyōbon and *Jōsuiki* texts, where Yoshitsune does not compose a letter, and where animosity only grows when the brothers do in fact meet? Their encounter is marked by a paucity of words (*kotoba sukunaka*), even where there is an opportunity for unmediated communication. The breakdown here is solely the fault of the communicators and their unwillingness to talk with each other. This version is problematic for a narrative of the rise of the Minamoto, because it clearly demonstrates exactly the sorts of issues the other versions hide—murderous intent between brothers and a direct competition for power.

This rendering is perhaps a more accurate portrayal of the relationships between the brothers. It represents at the very least one viable story, and it appears to be the story that the others strive to re-write, to overgo, to erase. Yet even in the sanitized later versions, its trouble spots do not completely disappear, since the tensions between the brothers never entirely drop out of sight. Although the new versions are reinscribed over older ones, they do not completely erase the problem points, and it is ultimately the contradictory and many-tiered story told by all the variants together that defines the arena of interpretation for the Koshigoe narrative.[89]

Interpretation, then, is a problem for the characters in the tale, and it is an even bigger problem for audiences and readers trying to make sense of what seems like an abrupt change in the relationship between Yoritomo and Yoshitsune. On one hand, we are given familiar interpretive schemes and stories to negotiate this moment in Minamoto history— documents are written and oaths are sworn. Yet the ultimate failure of these very "proofs" to bring about a harmonious and fair result leaves us with nagging concerns about some of the underlying stories, particularly that of Minamoto harmony and unity.

The end of the war was a difficult moment. The social and political orders needed to be stabilized and the unspeakable losses—the drowning of the sovereign, the loss of the sword—had to be woven into a narrative that would not leave the community entirely bereft of its foundations. And so, we find here repeated attempts to shore up the new order with accounts of the rectitude of the Minamoto, their worthiness as protectors of the throne, and the ability of Yoritomo to conduct warrior affairs well. The story of the falling out between the brothers comes to be told in ways that accord with these paradigms; it necessarily engages an evil and self-aggrandizing lesser man to destroy the just Yoshitsune. The story is never quite completely believable, however—not only do contesting versions exist, but their most important elements make their way into even sanitized versions of the story, pointing to unnegotiable aporia in the narrative. Embedded in these stories so fundamentally focused on interpretation, in other words, is a deep-seated anxiety about the very consequences of interpretation. Narratives like Koshigoe and Yoshinaka's Petition, born of the pressing and ongoing need to rebuild the past out of events that do not meet cultural expectations, are repeated and reworked to allay these anxieties. Their reincarnation across works and genres points to the open-endedness of this project: only through repeated engagements with the subject matter can anxieties about it be put to rest, and then only provisionally.

Chapter Five

The Soga Brothers

Swords and Lineage

O n the twenty-eighth day of the fifth month of 1193, two brothers, Soga
Jūrō and Soga Gorō, stole into a hunt hosted by the Kamakura Lord,
Minamoto Yoritomo, and killed their kinsman, Kudō Suketsune.[1] The
brothers thus fulfilled a seventeen-year-long vow to avenge the death of
their father, Kawazu Sukeyasu, who had been murdered in an ambush by
Suketsune's men on a hunt hosted by Sukeyasu's father, Sukechika.[2] Jūrō
was slain in the ensuing melee, and Gorō was captured as he attempted to
enter Yoritomo's tent and murder him. He was executed a day later.[3] The
brothers' long-standing dedication to the goal of punishing their father's
killer earned them wide acclaim at the time and in subsequent generations. Their story is the basis for not only the *Soga monogatari*, a long narrative specifically about their lives, but also numerous pieces from the
kōwakamai and later *kabuki* and *bunraku* repertoires, which places the two
among the most beloved tragic heroes in the Japanese cultural canon.
Legend has it that the swords they used to enact the vendetta were Minamoto family heirlooms that had, a generation earlier, belonged to Kiso
Yoshinaka and Minamoto Yoshitsune. With the brothers' deaths, the
swords returned to the Minamoto shōgun, thus concluding their meandering circuit through generations of heroes tied to the family.

The backdrop for the brothers' vendetta is the newly emergent Kamakura era. Aristocrats had been replaced by warriors as power holders, and
the locus of power itself was being reconstituted in Yoritomo's capital at
Kamakura. The first years of the Kamakura era were marked by growth, as
the hamlet expanded into the center for warrior affairs. Commerce increased steadily between it and the capital, and the administration of warrior appointments, including the new positions of *jitō* and *shugo*,[4] came
under the purview of the fledgling non-central government.

Although in actuality Yoritomo's regime represented slow and subtle growth of the state[5] rather than a radical overturning of the earlier order, it nevertheless inevitably came to be seen as something new. Certain kinds of power emanated from Kamakura rather than the capital, and warriors under Yoritomo received rewards for their loyalty that, in turn, were recognized by the center in the form of officially sanctioned titles. In the retrospective gaze of later generations whose histories unfolded in the shadow of this shift, the "Kamakura period" came to represent a cultural and political turning point. Kamakura had become a site on the cultural map of Japan, and the warriors who populated and visited it became the subjects whose actions infused that space with historical, political, and narrative meaning.

The histories of the swords used to enact the brothers' vendetta represent a narrative strand found in three major texts: the *rufubon* version of the *Soga monogatari*, the *kōwakamai* "Praise of the Swords" (*Tsurugi sandan*),[6] and the secret *Heike biwa* text "Chapter of the Swords" (*Tsurugi no maki*).[7] As we shall see, these three very similar accounts delineate powerful and specific symbolic and instrumental roles for the blades as they move through the Minamoto family, then to the Soga, and then back to the Minamoto. As symbols of the Minamoto line, they embody both fractiousness and continuity within the family. By their passage into the hands of the Soga and then back to the Minamoto hegemon, Yoritomo, they dramatize the refiguring of Yoritomo as warrior lord and government head after the war.

Swords, *Heike biwa*, and the Performative Act

The sword is an old and powerful image. It is at once a weapon—a tool for exercising power—and a symbol of that power. Although more devastating technologies of warfare have superseded the sword in recent centuries, its symbolism resonates even today, as one can see, for instance, in the mass media images of both Manuel Noriega and Saddam Hussein brandishing swords on the eve of U.S. invasions. And the sword's romanticized, symbolic meaning retains emphatic value even within the most aggressively high-tech military milieus: it remains a part of the dress uniforms for all branches of the U.S. military.[8]

The sword endures as a powerful symbol of not only might, but of masculinity as well, and it is used by men in the conventionally masculine context of making war.[9] It is also an important sign of patrimony. In the Icelandic sagas, swords, often bearing names of their own, are traditionally bequeathed from father to son; in Greek mythology, Aegeus recognizes Theseus as his son by the sword he carries. Recuperation of patrimony via the reconstitution of a sword is the basis for the character Siegfried in the

Nibelungenleid and Wagner's opera based on it; Sigurd of *Volsunga Saga* becomes a hero when he fights with Gram, the reassembled sword of his father.

Whether historical, literary, or mythological, these examples are all the stuff of legend, of the stories that endure as time passes. The epic tradition has long recognized the direct relationship between wielding a sword and immortalization in song. From the *Iliad* to the *Chanson de Roland* to the *Heike monogatari*, men draw their swords in battle thinking to make a name for themselves and to be remembered. They enter the legendary record because they meet victory or defeat in history-making battles that in turn come to define their culture's own continuous identity. The sword that has passed from father to son and been raised in battle is storied, and the legend of the sword defines lineage. Through these heirs the victor's story continues. The vanquished is cut down, and his story must end or change direction. The sword and the story it generates are double-edged: they confer an identity that is always subject to a test in battle. Identity is then maintained through defeating others, be they individuals, families, or nations.

SWORD MAKING AND STORY MAKING

The potency of the image of the sword derives not only from the symbolics of weaponry, but also from the productive act implicit in sword making in particular and ironworking more generally. Mastery of the process of transforming ore into iron tools defines for moderns entry into the iron age. In iron-age cultures we find the importance of ironworking reflected in beliefs about iron's magical as well as practical value; swords were thought to offer talismanic protection against otherworldly beings such as fairies, monsters, and sprites (including *kappa* and snakes in Japan) in both European and Asian traditions. In addition to swords, needles, equally weighted with symbolic meaning, were also thought to ward off these creatures.[10] The magical significance of iron products stems from the transformation that occurs when ore is heated and shaped—that it can be made into something other than what it appears to be is miraculous in itself; that it can be polished to the point of reflectivity and fashioned into a deadly weapon only amplifies the wondrousness of this process. Although this practice is not alchemy per se, conceptually the ideas are related, and the magic surrounding alchemy to an extent adheres to the lore of ironworking worldwide.

The significance of the sword maker in the Japanese context reaches an important peak in the early medieval period. By the thirteenth century Japanese sword making had attained a level that much of the rest of the world would only achieve centuries later.[11] The techniques used by Japanese sword makers involved folding and hammering layers of high- and low-carbon steel during forging, creating a weapon that retained its sharpness without breaking. The process was time-consuming and complex; a good blade was both a work of art and a lethal weapon that would last for generations. The swordsmith was thus an important figure for sword lore: he mediated with great skill and patience between the raw materials and the processes that turned them into something both greater and fundamentally different.

Sword making was an esoteric practice; it was one of the many arts that, by the Tokugawa period, had been designated a "way" (*michi* or *dō*). Swordsmiths traced elaborate genealogies to specific ancestors, and their practices were kept secret, protected from outsiders.[12] Transmission of sword-making skills was, broadly speaking, "oral"; apprentices learned at their master's side without the benefit of texts. The mode of transmission involved imitation of the master's art—the apprentice learned by watching and by being corrected. The "orality" of this practice, like so many other arts (including the recitation of tales), thus refers not simply to listening rather than reading, but also to the exercise of the senses and a wide range of physical training. It was never merely connected to words, either written or spoken.[13] This does not imply the unimportance of texts for the tradition, however. Sword making, like other crafts, acquired official sanction through a multi-tiered validation process closely tied to writing; bladesmithing might be transmitted directly (without texts) and secretly, but the art's history, its progenitors, and its famous patrons were recorded in origin legends and other documents used to validate the art's historical authenticity.[14] Documentation of this sort grew out of a larger medieval practice of writing down histories and specific techniques of individual schools within arts as a means of asserting the legitimacy of their line and competing with collaterals; we see this happening with poetry, calligraphy, and ceramics.[15] Documentation became even more important during the Tokugawa period, however, as artisans like swordsmiths perceived the economic and political need to legitimize their art—the Tokugawa government strictly regulated the practice of artisans, and the ability to demonstrate the long history and illustrious origins of an art was useful in attaining official government sanction.

In this respect, sword making closely mirrors another art central to this tale, that of *Heike biwa*. For the guild of the *Heike biwa* performers, transmission of the art's practice was oral, but an intricate paper trail of authentication stretching back to the early fourteenth century recorded its history, its connections to an esteemed progenitor, a ritual calendar, and texts of the tale.[16] This pattern of asserting legitimacy will be discussed in more depth below, but it is helpful to note from the outset the contradictory methods involved in both arts. They maintained their status by being simultaneously secret and orally transmitted on one hand, and public and documented on the other. A central unifying element in both types of legitimation, of course, is lineage: arts are passed from master to disciple, and the written records tracing this back to a high-ranking founder (often a prince) are among the most important.[17] The tracing of the Minamoto kin group within these tales can be viewed as echoing the legitimizing function of such pedigrees for the arts of sword making and storytelling—the crafts that engender this narrative's central theme (the sword) and shape and transmit it as narrative (*Heike biwa*).

Given the abundance of special meanings attached to them, it is perhaps not surprising to find that swords were attributed with magical characteristics.[18] They could animate themselves and cut without human help, seeming often to have volition of their own.[19] This in turn makes them something like an individual character. They are furthermore among those special objects that in the Japanese context receive individual names, a practice in the *Heike* narrative tradition reserved for select and telling kinds of items—musical instruments, writing implements, and weapons figure most prominently. In this context, names most importantly imply lineages. Thus we find, for example, the history of Atsumori's flute, Tsunemasa's *biwa*, Hōnen's inkstone and, here, heirloom blades. As we shall see, these named swords endure for generations, being passed from one male to the next. In their movement and use over time, they both make history and, in so doing, acquire histories of their own.

Swords, Names, Lineage

The story of the Soga brothers' swords sheds light on the narratives we have been considering because it helps solidify the connections between an arguably new set of character types and themes within the Genpei War narratives. It thus provides both an endpoint for the war and a starting point for the age of the samurai within the cultural landscape described in Japanese narrative and drama. The brothers' revenge is most often recognized as the prototype for later vendettas by loyal retainers (most notably that of the forty-seven *rōnin*) that would become a mainstay of medieval and early modern popular culture. Yet it is also inextricably linked with the cycles of revenge connected to the war, through not only the themes of parricide and patrimony, but also a complex of relationships connecting the brothers to Yoritomo.

The boys' father Sukeyasu was the son of Itō Sukechika, whom we encountered in Chapter Two—it was Sukechika who ordered the drowning of Yoritomo's first child, Senzuru, because he did not approve of his daughter's liaison with the exile. Both Sukechika and Suketsune were putative descendents of Itō Suketaka: Sukechika was the eldest son of Suketaka's eldest son (Sukeie), while Suketsune was the grandson of Suketaka's stepdaughter. Suketaka had designated the stepdaughter's son (and

Suketsune's father), Itō Suketsugu, as his heir, which enraged the disen-franchised Sukechika. To complicate matters, the *Soga monogatari* states that Suketsugu had been "born of [Suketaka's] secret visits to his step-daughter's quarters," an assertion corroborated by the *Sonpi bunmyaku*.[20] Thus Suketsugu and Sukechika were either putatively cousins or actually nephew and uncle, a close relationship either way. Sukechika resented his grandfather's choice of Suketsugu as primary heir, and, after Suketsugu's death in 1160, Sukechika acquired the family holdings by appointing him-self guardian of Suketsugu's young son Suketsune and then marrying the boy to one of his own daughters.[21]

When Suketsune reached maturity and realized that he had been duped, he took the matter to the judicial court in the capital, but Sukechika's position as an important Taira retainer (he was, we remem-ber, one of Yoritomo's appointed guardians in Izu) enabled the elder man to retain possession of the land. In response to Suketsune's suit, Sukechika withdrew his daughter from Suketsune and married her to another man, then petitioned to be granted full control over the Itō family holdings. Suketsune responded by attacking him in a hunt Sukechika hosted in 1176. Although Sukechika was only mildly injured, his son and heir Suke-yasu was killed. When Sukechika insisted that Sukeyasu's widow remarry, to Sukeyasu's cousin, Soga Sukenobu, she took with her Sukeyasu's two sons, Jūrō and Gorō.[22] During the Genpei War, Suketsune sided with the triumphant Yoritomo, while Sukechika supported the Taira—in the end, Suketsune emerged victorious and was granted the Itō family holdings by Yoritomo.[23] Sukechika, who had aggrieved Yoritomo so deeply by killing Senzuru, was completely destroyed.[24]

The Soga brothers' story thus brings the larger cultural narrative of Yoritomo's rise to its conclusion. The Kamakura Lord had overcome the devastating blow dealt by Sukechika during Yoritomo's time in exile, brought the Taira and contentious Minamoto rivals under control, and, with the deaths of Jūrō and Gorō, avenged the death of his son, Senzuru. Thus although on one hand, the Soga brothers' revenge represents a new milieu both politically and narratively, it also provides an important sense of closure to the rounds of parricide and vendetta that brought the Kama-kura polity into existence.[25]

The Swords Narrative

What I will refer to as the Swords narrative is in all cases separate from the larger narratives in which it appears. Because of the complexity and the continuity of each individual narrative, I deal with each separately in the remainder of this section.

In the *Soga monogatari*, the Swords narrative occurs in an episode entitled "The Farewell Visit to Hakone,"[26] which recounts the last of the brothers' leave-takings as they prepare for their vendetta, from which neither intends to return. The brothers visit the intendant Gyōjitsu, who served as Gorō's teacher and surrogate parent during his stay at Hakone Shrine in his youth. Gorō seeks from his former mentor forgiveness for abandoning his religious training (which he did in favor of pursuing the vendetta). The intendant receives the brothers kindly, brings forth two swords, and says, "I would like to give you something as parting gifts."[27]

To Jūrō, he presents a dagger (*sayamaki*) and then recounts its origin story (*iware*):

> This sword is one of three heirlooms that had been passed down for three generations to Kiso Yoshinaka. The first of these was a broad sword forged by the Dragon King, the second was a long sword called Kumo-otoshi (Defeater of the Spider), and the third was this one. Its name is Mijin (Crusher),[28] because there is nothing it cannot cut through. These three swords were kept as treasures. Kiso's son Shimizu no Onzōshi was given to the Kamakura Lord (Yoritomo) as his son-in-law,[29] and when Kiso heard that the boy was sent out down the sea route as a great general of the land, he donated this sword to Hakone Shrine as a prayer.[30]

The intendant admonishes Jūrō to make a name for himself (*kōmeishi-tamae*) when he uses it. Next, he gives a long sword with a Hyōgo chain[31] (*Hyōgogusari no tachi*) to Gorō and recounts its more complicated origin story.

This sword was forged by a Chinese smith named Wu Ting, who had been summoned by Raikō (Minamoto Yorimitsu).[32] After three months of forging and another month of polishing, the two-*shaku* eight-*sun*-long sword[33] was presented to Raikō, who "treasured it above all other possessions." One day, "when he had placed two swords above his pillow, a sudden storm wind came up. Blown by the wind, this sword began to quiver, cutting three books at his bedside—seventy pages of paper—and Raikō dubbed it (*na zukete*) Chōka, 'Book Cutter.'"[34]

Raikō passed the sword to his brother, Yorinobu.[35] When Yorinobu drew the sword, it miraculously (*fushigi ni*) cut the wings off insects in all four directions, so Yorinobu called the sword Mushibami, "Insect Devourer" (*mushibami to zo tsukerarekeru*).[36] Next it passed to Yoriyoshi at a time when the world was plagued by earthquakes. When Yoriyoshi placed the blade by his pillow, it miraculously (*fushigi ni*) unsheathed itself and plunged one *jō*[37] into the earth. It cut the sixty-foot-long snake that had been causing the disturbances into four pieces, thus stopping the earthquakes. Yoriyoshi asked after the origin of the sword, learned of its miraculous (*fushigi*) past, and dubbed it "Poisonous Snake" (Dokuhebi).[38]

Next, the sword was given to Yoriyoshi's son, Lord Hachiman (Yoshiie).[39] The sword performed another miraculous feat when its new owner took it with him to confront Hashihime (the maiden of the bridge), a supernatural being who had been wreaking havoc at Uji.[40] When she attacked him, the sword unsheathed itself and cut off her hand. She then jumped into the river, and the disturbances that had been plaguing the area stopped. The blade therefore was dubbed Himekiri "Maiden Slasher" (*Himekiri to nazukete*).

From Yoshiie, the sword was passed to Tameyoshi. Strangely (*kitoku ni*), when Tameyoshi placed a sword six *sun* longer next to it, the two swords fought. They continued to engage each other for five nights, and on the sixth night, perhaps because it was uneasy that the other was longer, the shorter sword cut the extra five *sun* from its opponent[41] and gained the name Tomogiri, "Companion Slasher" (*Tomogiri to nazukete*).

The next owner of the sword was Yoshitomo, the hapless father of Yoritomo and Yoshitsune. He received the sword from his father, but under the worst possible circumstances. As the renegade son of the Minamoto house that otherwise supported the losing side in the Hōgen Uprising (1156), Yoshitomo was forced to execute his father and brothers to prove his loyalty to the throne. Yoshitomo made an offering of the sword to Bishamon at Kurama-in, but because he had killed his father in the earlier battle, his offering was rejected, and he was defeated in the Heiji Uprising.

For a time, the narrative states, there was no one to inherit the sword. But Yoshitsune, living as a youth at Kurama-in, had learned of the sword's existence and prayed to Bishamon, "Please give me a glimpse of the sword as a remembrance of [my] father."[42] Bishamon then appeared to him in a dream and gave him the sword; when Yoshitsune awoke, he ran to the temple, opened the gate and found the sword awaiting him. After running away from the temple, Yoshitsune went to Ōshū, where he won the support of Fujiwara Hidehira. Hearing of his brother's revolt, he then went to Kamakura to join Yoritomo. As he set out for battle, he stopped at Hakone Shrine and left the sword as a prayer for success in the impending war.

Upon completing the story of the sword's history, the intendant bids the brothers farewell. They take their leave and head toward Yoritomo's hunt, where they will kill Suketsune.

In its sequence of diverting—and always potentially diverging—narratives, this tale begins to elucidate one fundamental juxtaposition underlying the sword image. The blades (particularly Gorō's) are closely linked to male warrior identity, and they are objects of sufficient import to be passed from father to eldest son. As family heirlooms, they mark each succeeding recipient as recognized head of the family line. The sword is at once a clear sign of the father, the actual patrimony itself, and the instrument with which its passage (and its story) is ensured. As patrimony, it carries tales of the greatness of each passing generation, which the inheritor is implicitly expected to match or surpass, as demonstrated by the foregrounding of the sword's onomastics, a topic we shall consider in detail below. The content of these stories is the very literal cutting off of possible threats (to the sword, its bearer, or society at large); the storied sword establishes proper descent through the main line at the expense of peripheral contenders and in support of the established order.

At the same time, however, the sword generates potentially disruptive counter-narratives: without the stories of opponents, it has no story of its own to tell. The counter-narratives reveal tensions that underline the adversarial relationship between inheritor and challenger: Tomogiri's anxiety over his companion's greater length, or the dramatic legitimizing act embodied by Bishamon's rejection of Yoshitomo and bequeathal to Yoshitsune. And to destroy rivals and erase collaterals, the narrative must incarnate these foes as characters with stories worth telling. The "line" in the lineage tale, the notion of linear teleological continuity, in other words, is open to question. It cannot exist without also producing alternative stories that have the potential to become the dominant narrative themselves. It is important to remember that the swords' owners immediately prior to the Soga brothers were Yoshinaka and Yoshitsune, Yoritomo's two most worrisome rivals.

Of what significance is the placement of this assertive yet equivocating narrative within the longer *Soga monogatari*? Obviously, the passage of such powerful swords to Jūrō and Gorō elevates them as heroes, making them formal inheritors of the symbols of power formerly held by the great Minamoto generals, most specifically Yoshinaka and Yoshitsune. As recipients of the blades, the brothers are assured success when setting out to complete their shared final act. As dispossessed and poverty-stricken orphans, bequeathal of such treasures is a particularly powerful indication of the worthiness of their goal, and the blades come to represent the kind of patrimony from which they have been cut off. But it is an ambivalent patrimony: the two former owners died tragically, and this same future is inscribed in the passage of the swords to the brothers as well. Inserting the Swords narrative in the *Soga* at this juncture thus amplifies the heroic personalities of the brothers and imbues their actions with a degree of grandeur and tragedy derived in part from the larger-than-life former owners of the blades.

The duality implicit in the sword as symbol—while generating fractious narratives that threaten to dissipate the identity of the clan, it simultaneously stands for and serves as an instrument to insure continuity and cohesion of that identity—is also doubled at the extradiegetic level. The sword not only creates stories as it moves through the lineage, but the Swords narrative itself spawns alternative versions as it circulates in medieval Japan. Of these, the *kōwakamai* piece "Praise of the Swords"[43] provides the one variant in which the Swords narrative comprises the entire text. *Kōwakamai*, as discussed earlier, is a genre dedicated to celebration of warrior society, but particularly shōgunal rule.[44] "Praise of the Swords" is conventionally categorized as a *Soga-mono*,[45] meaning that it derives from the *Soga monogatari*. In the *Mai no hon* it is placed between "Kosode Soga" (based on the brothers' farewell visit to their mother, chapter 7 in the *Soga*) and "Youchi Soga" (the attack on Suketsune, chapter 8 in the *Soga*).

"Praise of the Swords" opens with a contextualizing tale about the brothers' trip to Hakone Shrine. As in the *Soga*, the intendant greets them with warmth and sympathy and brings out two swords as parting gifts. To Jūrō he presents a dagger with black-lacquered hilt and sheath (*kurosayamaki*); to Gorō, a Hyōgo-style long sword (*Hyōgozukuri no tachi*).[46] He then recounts the origin story of each sword.

The intendant remarks of Jūrō's dagger, "This sword . . . has been the possession of the Kiso clan for many generations. No true desire of the one who possesses this sword will go unachieved."[47] A long and colorful origin story for Gorō's blade follows, exhibiting some important variances with the *Soga* rendition. The narrative begins with the sword's forging in Tenchiku (the Indian subcontinent), where there was a waterfall with round deposits of iron in it;[48] these deposits were coveted far and wide. A man named Shōrifumu had made an eight-*shaku* broad sword (*naginata*) from this ore, which was stolen, taken first to Tang (*Tō*), and then to Japan (*Nippon*). The Nara Sovereign[49] ordered that it be made into two long swords (*tachi*). He summoned two expert smiths, Mōfusa of Ōshū and Kokaji of Sanjō,[50] gave each of them exactly half of the broad sword, and ordered both to make him a blade. After three years, Mōfusa presented the sovereign with a three-*shaku*-long sword, and Kokaji presented him with one that was two *shaku*, seven *sun* long (or three *sun* shorter than its companion) three months later. Believing he had been robbed of three *sun* of metal by Kokaji, the sovereign threw the smith in prison.

Here the naming begins. Mōfusa's sword was given the name (*nazuke*) Makuragami, or "Above the Pillow,"[51] and put in the place of honor. Kokaji's sword was given the name (*nazuke*) Sunnashi, or "A Little Short," and placed below Makuragami. The distraught Kokaji prayed from his cell to the myriad guardian deities of the forge[52] to manifest a sign revealing his innocence, and in response Sunnashi unsheathed itself and began to pursue Makuragami. Makuragami, also made of the magic iron, unsheathed itself as well, and the two began to parry.

The palace was in an uproar as the nobles and emperor watched the two swords fight. Sunnashi, on the offensive, cornered Makuragami, and "resentful . . . stood along side [Makuragami] to compare their lengths, cut off the three extra *sun* from the tip [of its companion], and then resheathed itself."[53] The sovereign, upon seeing this, granted Sunnashi the title Tomogiri, or "Companion Slasher," (*tomogiri ni kan to naru*) and released Kokaji from prison.

After this, the two swords passed to Tada Manjū (Minamoto Mistunaka),[54] who used Tomogiri to execute a criminal. Because the sword cut through the man's neck so quickly that it also cut through his beard, the sword was given the title Higekiri, "Beard Slasher" (*higekiri ni kan to naru*). Makuragami slashed through another criminal so quickly that the man's knees were cut off, and the sword was dubbed Hizakiri, "Knee Slasher" (*hizakiri ni kan to naru*). The swords then passed to Yorimitsu. Higekiri cut off the hand of a demon, and was dubbed Onikiri, "Demon Slasher" (*onikiri ni kan to naru*); Hizakiri was used to kill a supernatural spider, and was dubbed Chichugiri, "Spider Slasher" (*chichugiri ni kan to naru*). The swords were both passed to Lord Hachiman Yoshiie and then to Tameyoshi.

The narrative then digresses slightly from the tale of the swords to recount the situation that precipitated the next generation of owners. Tameyoshi's daughter Tazuhara-hime was sent to Kumano after Retired Sovereign Go-Shirakawa, during a pilgrimage to Kumano, appointed a shrine menial to fill the vacant spot of intendant and then declared that Tazuhara-hime should be the intendant's wife. Tameyoshi was heartbroken, since he had hoped to take a scion of the Minamoto or Taira, someone who could wield bow and arrows, as son-in-law. Tameyoshi subsequently disinherited the intendant.

Some time later, a disturbance requiring the attention of warriors occurred in the capital, and the intendant decided, "Even though I have been disinherited, my duty is to my father-in-law, so I will go see what I can do."[55] He set out for the capital, gathering mountain ascetics along the way and finally putting together a force at the Yodo Hachiman Shrine. When Tameyoshi spotted the large force he asked the identity of its leader and was told that the troops were led by his son-in-law.

Tameyoshi next asked after the intendant's ancestors, and was told that he was the last son of the Captain Sanekata. Upon learning of this lineage (which allegedly had royal antecedents), Tameyoshi decided that he was in fact a worthy son-in-law and arranged for a meeting with him. He then bequeathed Higekiri to Yoshitomo and Hizakiri to the intendant, who returned with it to Kumano.

At the time of the Genpei War, the intendant gave the sword to Yoshitsune. The narrative concludes:

> Because of the special qualities of this sword, [Yoshitsune] destroyed the proud Heike, returned the Three Sacred Regalia safely to the capital, and

went to the Kantō. Kajiwara slandered him, and he was forced to return
again to the capital from Sakawa [without entering Kamakura]. He
climbed this mountain and offered the sword as a prayer to the avatar for
peace between the brothers [Yoshitsune and Yoritomo].[56]

The Hakone Intendant tells the brothers that the sword is destined to kill
Suketsune, and the brothers take their leave.

There is significant variation in detail between this story and that in
the *Soga*, but the differences serve to amplify the scope and power of the
narrative. The "Tomogiri" story is placed in a context that adds to the
blade's symbolic potency: the sword belonged to the sovereign, and the ore
used to make it came from a mystical waterfall on the subcontinent.

Naming the smiths summoned to forge these swords also activates
the more general context of the genealogies of famous ironworkers and
their craft. The identification here of swordsmiths by name—especially
the legendary Kokaji, who moreover conjures the support of the gods of
the forge in his defense—points to their significance and also their potential power. In this latter respect, Kokaji fits one traditional interpretation of men who transform raw ore into magical weapons as possessors of
a particular, seemingly miraculous skill; these men are treated with deference (and suspicion) and are frequently portrayed as "other." Moreover,
Kokaji is able to communicate with the world beyond to bear witness to
his art. The swordsmith is a liminal figure,[57] operating between this world
and the underworld of mining, in touch with the gods, and distinguished
from all earthly others by his unique craft.

Another important aspect of this narrative is its framing as an *iware*,
or origin story, a characteristic it shares with the *Soga monogatari*. The very
idea of tracing lineages, of course, is closely connected to the concerns of
the blade's origin story, in which the explanation of creation and continuity gives the sword substance and meaning in connection to the Minamoto
clan. But this story also speaks to the position of the clan within a greater
cosmological order. The sword was initially granted to the Seiwa Genji by
their royal ancestor, and this connection is an important assertion of the
special place of the Minamoto name within hierarchies of power.

We find genealogical lineage also emphasized in the embedded narrative of the Kumano Intendant's history. The son-in-law is initially
shunned for not being of good warrior stock, then accepted and integrated into the Seiwa Genji after proving his military mettle and filial piety.
What finally makes him worthy as an adopted son-in-law, however, is his
revelation of his own lineage—he himself is the inheritor of a prestigious
name. He becomes integrated into the tale through a validation process
tied to lineage, both his own and his father-in-law's, for which he shows respect and eventually proves his own worthiness.

Possession of a name is vitally important for the Soga brothers as well. The Hakone Intendant urges them to use the swords to make names for themselves, to restore meaning to this paternal signifier in the context of their own dispossession. Further, the Kumano Intendant within the tale parallels the Hakone Intendant who tells it—he is an outsider and religious cleric with whom the symbol of lineage (the sword) has been vouchsafed until it can be taken up by an heir worthy of fulfilling its destiny. Note that the tale ends with a bequeathal by Yoshitsune that is intended to clear up his discord with Yoritomo; the Hakone Intendant enters the narrative to hold the blade-as-patrimony while it is in dispute. In this role, he may be understood as the textual double of the performer(s) of the *kōwaka-mai* piece; or, conversely, the cleric finds his double in the performer of the piece. For these swords are nothing if not storied: their potency may be defined by their capacity to generate narrative, and the cleric conveys these stories as he confers each sword on its new possessor. Performing the Swords narrative means telling the story of tellings of stories about the swords.

The "Chapter of the Swords"[58] moves us into the realm in which the voice of the performer is particularly important: recitational *Heike biwa*. Most significantly, it is a secret piece and stands as a discrete chapter. It shares this distinction with two other pieces, "The Initiate's Chapter"[59] (*Kanjō no maki*) and "The Chapter of the Mirror" (*Kagami no maki*), which constitute the "major secret pieces" (*daihiji*) of the *Heike biwa* tradition. It additionally is found as a selection (*nukigaki*) in the Yashirobon *Heike monogatari* and the *Genpei jōsuiki*, and it is also included (as a secret piece) in the *Heike mabushi*. The *Taiheiki* also includes a "Chapter of the Swords" very similar to the one considered here. All versions trace the histories of important heirloom swords, including, importantly, the blade Kusanagi, whose loss is narrated in the framing story of the Minamoto clan swords.

The independent version seems to have its closest antecedent within the Hyakunijukkubon *Heike monogatari*, whose eleventh chapter contains a two-part "Chapter of the Swords." Yamada Yoshio asserted that a version of this work existed in the late Kamakura period, a contention that is accepted by current scholars.[60] In other recited-lineage texts including the Kakuichibon variant, there is no discrete chapter dedicated to swords, but there is an episode in chapter 11 entitled "Swords" that briefly traces the history of Kusanagi; this episode is considered a relative of the "Chapter of the Swords."[61]

As a secret piece in the *Heike biwa* tradition, the "Chapter of the Swords" may be said not just to tell, but also to enact the Swords narrative in certain important respects. Its keeping and transmission mimic the practices associated with the swords. It is not available for all to read;

rather, it is conferred only to the elect, down the line from master to disciple, and it must be performed for its new possessor to validate the identity its possession bestows. Even more fundamentally, *Heike biwa* is a specifically eulogistic and placatory art, dedicated to simultaneously bringing the important historical moment of the Genpei War to life and putting it to rest. Although this duality is implicit in any historical narration, *Heike biwa* clearly acknowledges this two-sidedness as inextricably linked to, and the fundament goal of, performing the text. The significance of the "Chapter of the Swords" derives from its contents, which articulate extremely difficult problems connected to the Genpei War—specifically, the loss of the sacred sword at sea and the justification of Minamoto hegemony—through recollecting the epic histories of swords.

The *Heike biwa* narrative of the Minamoto swords is close to "Praise of the Swords," and in fact probably provided much of the material for the *kōwakamai* piece.[62] After introducing the important swords of Japan, the "Chapter of the Swords" begins by relating the origin (*yurai*) of two swords bearing striking similarities to those in the "Praise of the Swords" narrative, Hizamaru[63] and Higekiri. The narrative opens by describing the founding of the Seiwa Genji by Mitsunaka, grandson of the sovereign Seiwa. Mitsunaka, a stalwart defender of the realm, decided he would need a long sword. He acquired iron, but could not find a smith to forge a worthy blade for him.[64] He summoned a smith from another land (*ikoku*) living in Chikuzen (present-day Fukuoka Prefecture); again the text emphasizes the connection between the royal house and a foreign smith. The smith forged many swords, but none captured Mitsunaka's heart, so he was dismissed. Distraught at his failure, the smith presented a petition to Hachiman, who gave him iron from which to forge two swords, a task he accomplished in sixty days.[65] One was two *shaku*, seven *sun* long, and the other was three *shaku* long. Mitsunaka was thrilled to receive the blades, and he used them to execute criminals. Mitsunaka then named them (*nazuke*) Higekiri and Hizamaru and passed them to his heir Yorimitsu (Raikō).

In Yorimitsu's generation, miraculous things (*fushigi ari shidai*) happened. First, Higekiri was used to cut off the hand of Hashihime,[66] whom we encountered in the *Soga* version. This task was undertaken by one of Yorimitsu's "four heavenly kings" (*shitennō*), Tsuna, after which the blade's name was changed (*kaimyō su*) to Onimaru, "Demon Slayer." Later, Yorimitsu was stricken with illness and seemed on the verge of death. After a month of suffering, on a night while his four heavenly kings were keeping watch outside his room, he spotted a giant shadow outside and slashed at it with Hizamaru. The four kings rushed to his aid, found a trail of blood outside the door, and followed it to a mound, where they discovered a four-*shaku*-long mountain spider (*yamagumo*). Because of this miraculous (*fushigi*) event, the sword was named (*gōsu*) Kumokiri, "Spider Slasher."[67]

At this point, the narrative digresses to explain the unusual bestowal that has been simply glossed over before: Yorimitsu was ordered to give the swords to Yoriyoshi, heir of Yorimitsu's younger brother Yorinobu, for use in his campaign against the Abe in Ōshū. Yorimitsu's son, Yoritomo, willingly relinquished them, noting that they would protect Yoriyoshi because they were treasures held for three generations from Mitsunaka's time. Yoriyoshi then defeated the Abe in the Former Nine Years' War. The two swords next passed to Yoriyoshi's heir Hachiman Tarō Yoshiie, who defeated Fujiwara Munehira in the Latter Three Years' War. Yoshiie's heir had been killed in the fighting, and so the swords were entrusted to his fourth son, Tameyoshi.

Tameyoshi had many children, including a daughter who was given to the Kumano Intendant as a wife (and the story proceeds similarly here to the "Praise of the Swords" rendition). During Tameyoshi's tenure as their owner, the two swords began to make noises at night. Because Onimaru sounded like a lion, it was given the name (*kaimyō shi*) Shishi no ko, "Lion Cub," and because Kumokiri sounded like a snake's cry, it was named (*gōshi*) Hoemaru, "Screamer." After his reconciliation with the intendant, Tameyoshi gave him Hoemaru. Tameyoshi had another sword exactly like Shishi no ko made, and he named it (*nazukeru*) Kogarasu, "Little Crow." It is these two swords—Kogarasu and Shishi no ko—that animated themselves to fight; Shishi no ko cut the end off of Kogarasu and was renamed (*kaimyō shite*) Tomogiri. Both swords were then entrusted to Tameyoshi's heir, Yoshitomo.

Yoshitomo would subsequently kill most of his brothers and his father in the Hōgen Uprising. When he in turn was nearing his end in the Heiji Uprising, he presented a prayer of enmity to the Great Bodhisattva Hachiman, complaining that the god, from whom Hachiman Tarō Yoshiie had taken his name, had deserted his children. The deity appeared to Yoshitomo in a dream, stating that he had not forsaken Yoshitomo, but that the heirloom sword had weakened because it has been renamed so many times.[68] Yoshitomo awoke from his dream and reinstated the sword's original name, Higekiri.

The sword was next passed to Yoritomo, who used it to fend off many attackers in the Heiji Uprising. As his capture loomed closer, however, he feared the generations-old Genji heirloom would fall into Taira hands, and to forestall such a fate, he dedicated it to the Atsuta Shrine.[69] Yoritomo was exiled to Izu, the Genpei War began, and Yoshitsune was sent to punish Yoshinaka. The narrative reminds us at this juncture that the sword formerly known as Hizamaru and Kumokiri, and now known as Hoemaru, a generations-old Genji heirloom,[70] had been given to the Kumano Intendant by Tameyoshi, and dedicated to the Kumano deity. The intendant presented the blade to Yoshitsune, who in great joy changed its name (*na o aratametaru*) to Usumidori, "Light Green," after the color of the mountains in spring. The narrative continues through the Genpei War, and when it reaches the battle of Dan-no-ura and the loss of Kusanagi, it relates that sword's origin story.[71]

The narrative then returns to the Genji sword origin story:

> Because of Kajiwara Kagetoki's slander, when Yoshitsune took the Heike prisoners to Kamakura, he was sent to Koshigoe and not permitted to enter Kamakura. He then composed fealty oaths protesting his innocence and sent them to Kamakura to no avail. On his way back to the capital, his efforts unsuccessful, he dedicated the sword Usumidori to the Hakone deity hoping for an easing of the tensions between the brothers.[72]

The narrative comments that the sword Soga Gorō received from the Hakone Intendant to complete his vendetta was that dedicated by Yoshitsune and the one formerly known as Hizamaru. It continues: "After that, Hizamaru was given to the Kamakura lord. Both Hizamaru and Higekiri had been granted by the Bodhisattva Hachiman. Even though [their passage] had been discontinued for a while, they were Genji heirlooms passed down through many generations. They had wandered about and then come together at this place; how marvelous that they arrived at Kamakura!"[73] The "Chapter of the Swords" ends its meandering here.

As part of the *Heike* repertoire, the "Chapter of the Swords," focuses on a different aspect of the larger narrative of the Genpei period than the other two pieces: it is concerned with tying up several narrative loose ends from the Genpei War, principally the clash between the Taira and the Minamoto. Yet bringing the pre-1185 past to a conclusion also meant wrapping up Yoritomo's feud with Sukechika, which ends only with the deaths of Jūrō and Gorō. With the execution of Gorō, Yoritomo not only brings the brothers' revenge story to an end, but also the others interwoven with it: the destruction of the Taira and the loss of Kusanagi, but as well as Yoritomo's elimination of his kin-group rivals and his vengeance on the descendants of his son's killer. The Swords narrative thus provides an endpoint for the rounds of parricide and revenge that brought the Kamakura polity into existence. The "Chapter of the Swords," more than the other texts, is singly focused on resolving the cycle of violence. As a secret placatory piece, bringing closure through memorialization is its primary function. It foregrounds narrative strands regarding family conflict as a way of explaining and resolving these troubling stories.

In terms of narrative structure, all the component texts of the Swords story provide resolution through the use of a kind of repetition compulsion, to borrow from Freud and Brooks. On the one hand, the need to revisit and reenact the parricides upon which Yoritomo's rule was built is regressive, "an obsessive circular return to a traumatic past,"[74] ever threatening to derail the master narrative. This tendency is further manifest in the general centripetal impulse of the narratives, which seem constantly on the verge of collapsing back on the past. In each variant, however, despite the plot's circuitous route, its ultimate destination remains clear. The stories transport the swords toward a time and an owner, the new shōgun, who will endow their metonymic potential with telos, making them symbols of his sovereignty over warrior affairs and his protection of the throne. The most complete elucidation of the connection between royal power and shōgunal protection occurs in the "Chapter of the Swords." There the story of Kusanagi is folded into that of the Minamoto blades, the narrative's endpoint. The recuperation of the Minamoto heirloom swords here compensates for the loss of Kusanagi; this repetition refigures and reverses the past, creating a new version with a viable conclusion. It further brings to conclusion other tension-ridden stories connected to the war and the Minamoto kin group: Yoshitomo's execution of his father and brothers after the Heiji Uprising, Sukechika's drowning of Senzuru, and Yoritomo's killing of both Yoshinaka and Yoshitsune.

The Swords narratives engage these issues on a number of levels. Every use of the sword in all the variants *is* a story, and as such the sword represents a powerful and promiscuous metonymic potentiality that constantly risks derailing the master narrative. At the same time, each sword is an heirloom holding the generations together and anchoring the narrative's symbolic dimension. In a sense, the sword becomes emblematic of the paradoxical narrative structure we have been discussing, whereby a symbolic order is reconstituted by recounting and reworking chaos. This ritualistic function of the narrative in turn is enacted in the performance tradition of the *Heike biwa* raconteur.

What's in a Name: Lineage and Inheritance

As an instrument of lineage-making and a symbol of the lineage itself, swords move from father to "primary heir" (*chakushi*); the bestowal of the family name and an heirloom sword confers also an identity inextricably linked with an originary ancestor. In each case, the heir's worthiness is then certified by a miraculous achievement of the sword, in honor of which the sword is renamed. To be more precise, swords are given names (*na (o) tsukeru / gō su*); they are titled (*kan to naru*); and their names are changed or renewed (*kaimyōsu / na o aratamu*). For the most part, these expressions are used synonymously; this is even the case with the curious *kan to naru*, which appears only in "Praise of the Swords." *Na o aratamu* occurs only once, when Yoshitsune renames the sword Usumidori, the only name given to a sword unrelated to its exploits or specific characteristics. Notably, it is bestowed at the important moment of the Minamoto reversal in fortunes, perhaps emphasizing that the renewal (*aratameru*) is motivated by the family's immediate past, specifically, Yoshitomo's devastating murders of his father and brothers.

New names are inevitably inspired by mysterious (*fushigi* or *kitoku*) or otherworldly activity, as when the swords become animate and/or perform superhuman feats. In each new act they outstrip their given names, and the current owner must create a new one. Significantly, in the "Chapter of the Swords" this practice is questioned by Hachiman, who asserts that the constant renaming of swords—though a tribute to their miraculous feats—in fact weakens them. Hachiman recognizes the risk of name change leading to identity change; a renamed sword is one for which discontinuity has won out over continuity. The sequence of renamings has so alienated the sword from its own origins and the lineage it stands for that retaining a connection to them becomes impossible. The chain of stories we find in the Swords narrative likewise subverts narrative continuity, hinting at a dangerous potential within the narrative process. The narrative's meditation on the dangers implicit in the onomastic act becomes a kind of metapoetics that comments on the ambivalent nature of narrative. It intimates the difficulties enmeshed in a story that on one hand addresses a lengthy series of fundamental changes in a family and a larger political entity, and on the other seeks to reassert that family's originary identity and continuous lineage.

In all variants of the Swords narrative, the names of the swords are announced in their origin stories (*iware* and, once, *yurai*). In the *Soga* and "Praise of the Swords," origin stories are recounted by the Hakone Intendant to the Soga brothers (and indirectly to the audience), and in the "Chapter of the Swords" by the reciter directly to the audience. In the latter two tales, we further are told the origin story (*iware*) of Tameyoshi's daughter's marriage to the Kumano Intendant. The term *iware* is foregrounded in all cases; in no narrative is an origin story presented without being introduced specifically *as* an origin story. The originary status signaled by the term draws special attention to each tale it introduces, and the repetition of this gesture accentuates the broad centrality of origins in the Swords narrative.

The two-edged sword of many names and one essence, which generates the line by cutting off collaterals, thus symbolizes the Minamoto at a time when its future was uncertain. Further, the sword gives rise to complex narrative histories reflecting a tension between the narrative need to validate a continued line and explain its seemingly irreconcilable, internecine violence, particularly within that specific generational group. The "undoing" of this discord is enacted through narrative repetition at two levels. Yoshinaka and Yoshitsune are reintegrated into the clan as recipients of the swords, and they themselves are refigured in the Soga brothers, who are the next in line.

Engendering the Hero:
The *Soga monogatari* and the Minamoto Line

Once Yoshinaka and Yoshitsune are seen as refigured in the Soga brothers, other parallels become meaningful as well. Gorō trains at and then es-
capes from Hakone, mirroring Yoshitsune's experiences at Kuramadera.
There is long-standing animosity between Gorō and Kajiwara Kagesue,
which reanimates the old rivalry between Yoshitsune and Kagesue's father,
Kajiwara Kagetoki; here, Kagesue is a frequent antagonist and romantic
rival of Gorō.[75] And if we need further reminders of the Yoshitsune/Kage-
toki feud, Kagetoki's slander of Yoshitsune at Koshigoe is explicitly cited as
the impetus for the sword's arrival at Hakone Shrine in both "Praise of the
Swords" and the "Chapter of the Swords." The support shown by Yoritomo's retainers Hatakeyama Shigetada and Wada Yoshimori for the
brothers repeats their backing of Yoshitsune; the role of Jūrō's lover Tora
in praying for the repose of the brothers' spirits and telling their tale resembles that of Yoshinaka's companion Tomoe in the *Heike* or Yoshitsune's lover Shizuka in the *Gikeiki*. The Swords narrative can productively
be seen as an echo of the other Genpei narratives considered in earlier
chapters.

Such strong allusive connections between the Soga brothers and
Yoshinaka and Yoshitsune launches a repetition that reverses a difficult
past; the narrative progression to a time beyond the war and external to
the Minamoto family struggles also diminishes some of the power of the
earlier heroes. The Soga brothers' revenge is enacted during one of Yoritomo's grand hunts; it is a much-reduced stage, far less significant or potentially dangerous than the war that enabled the consolidation of
Kamakura rule. This particular repetition achieves but a qualified resolution, and that only through a diminution in significance of the arena in
which it is carried out. The Soga brothers were politically peripheral.
They did not own land, and they had no position in the new order. They
had no troops supporting them and no desire to establish themselves as
rulers. They carried out their vendetta in a setting where their wrath was
narrow in scope and intensely personal. Although their rebellion con-
tested shōgunal authority, it was clearly manageable.

By superimposing the Minamoto heroes onto the Soga brothers,
therefore, the narrative diffuses some of Yoshinaka and Yoshitsune's
boundless disorderly energies by releasing them in a less publicly significant context. Notably, this refiguring also prescribes a framework of fraternal harmony for the heroic ideal: the Soga brothers acted together,
choosing to forego opportunities to kill their enemy alone in favor of joint
action. The Minamoto kin, behind whose heroics always lurked treachery
toward one another, are thus recast as loyal brothers who act as one.

The Great Adjudicator: Minamoto Yoritomo

In both the *Soga monogatari* and the "Chapter of the Swords," the travels of the swords come to an end with the capture of Gorō and the presentation of his blade to Yoritomo. The Kamakura Lord immediately recognizes it as a Minamoto heirloom. In the *Soga monogatari*, the sword becomes "his most valuable treasure, for it was said to have been handed down through many generations."[76] In both texts, this juncture formally marks the moment when the sword ceases its meandering circuit and endless name changes once in the hands of the Minamoto lord.

The general problem of sibling rivalry over inheritance that plagued the Itō would face many provincial warrior families throughout the medieval age. Possessions and prerogatives of a set of parents needed to be distributed among sibling groups that could often be large. In the opening years of the Kamakura rule, however (and particularly while Yoritomo was still alive), disputes within sibling groups about inheritance often surfaced shortly after the death of the previous generation's patriarch, as we see here. Jeffrey Mass argues that the sibling unit was the site of the most rancorous and suspicious relationships at this time—donors far preferred making bequests to their children rather than to their siblings.[77] Thus competition among brothers and sisters of the children's generation was the norm, and families often split into separate collaterals at this relatively close level. Although hierarchies led back to the unit of "clan" (*ichimon*), cousins and uncles were not close kin. As in the case of the Soga brothers, they were potential rivals in lingering generations-old disputes.

In this potentially volatile context, it was important for Yoritomo to create an environment in which disputes could be resolved fairly and, more importantly, peacefully. The early warrior government thus adopted and elaborated the Heian period judicial system, which they dedicated to adjudicating conflicts between housemen appointed by Yoritomo, as well as disputes between them and officials appointed by the central government. Although its jurisdiction expanded over time to include a broader range of legatees and types of claim, throughout the Kamakura period, the idea of a judicial body to which grievances could be presented and from which a careful judgment could be expected remained the hallmark of Yoritomo's government.[78] To keep the precarious peace, decisions had to be considered well reasoned and fair; to assure a corresponding level of objectivity, the court required proof, both in the form of evidentiary documentation and testimony by the parties in question. As a result, records of the frequent inheritance disputes from this period are filled with wills, judgments, and accords.[79]

As an important arena for recounting family identity and lineage, the Kamakura court and the general judiciary processes associated with it represent one model for articulating acceptable histories. The pervasive thematic concerns of interpretation and justification that we have encountered in earlier chapters occur, too, in connection with the Soga brothers and further their rhetorical function as (at least in part) stand-ins for Yoshitsune and Yoshinaka. The significance of petitioning the authorities, for example, appears throughout the *Soga* in the repeated suits brought before the judiciary powers in the capital and, later, in Kamakura. In Kamakura we encounter Yoritomo's more even-handed judgments, including his generous bestowal of lands to retainers who perform exceptional or meritorious deeds.[80] Yoritomo hears cases and composes edicts, bequeathing land and title to the deserving, including the brothers' mother. The omnipotent Kamakura Lord's attentive adjudication provides a stark contrast to the rash military acts taken up by the brothers. Yoritomo's arena of action is strongly delineated as a judicial milieu, in which cases are heard, documents presented, and decisions handed down. Even more than in those narratives considered in earlier chapters, this setting requires action to be consonant with the rule of law; and unruly (if heroic) action will ultimately be stamped out by the regulations of the judicial system.

Kamakura warrior rule, symbolized by the now-quiet swords, created a new set of boundaries for future action (or narrative). Internecine conflict had been domesticated with the emergence of a new definition of correct family (and social) relations that would remain a vital theme in literary and dramatic discourse for the next several hundred years.[81] And it is at this level that a more conventional sort of "repeating-to-reverse" occurs: Yoritomo is reconfigured not only as victor, but more significantly as a judge of, rather than participant in, the kinds of internecine struggles that brought him to power. By being set apart as adjudicator—audience to the drama in which the Soga brothers are the actors—he is removed from the central narrative, a shift that effectively renders him external to the cycles of violence at its heart. The Soga—as re-workings of the politically and historically peripheral and, more importantly, collateral Minamoto—come under Yoritomo's control, where they can be observed and judged.

This is a much safer position from which to consider the Kamakura Lord. There is now a clear hierarchy into which potential contenders for his position can be integrated beneath him. The characterization of Yoritomo as fair-minded judge suggests that his rise represents the triumph of reason; from now on, disputes will be of a more private and civil nature and judged by the sympathetic but ultimately impartial warrior government. Where the Soga brothers represent a repetition of the characters of Yoshinaka and Yoshitsune, Yoritomo embodies a successful overwriting of the unjust Taira control of the realm. As the fair judge of a family vendetta whose heroes are clearly narrative refigurings of his own kin group rivals, he is effectively removed from the most damaging part of the narrative of his own history. This repetition and refiguring of the Minamoto past thus establishes a new cultural identity, in which the meandering and onomastically promiscuous heirloom swords are returned to their proper lineage, and then put away. Yoritomo's law replaces the war's violence, transforming the very metalanguage of culture.

Performance as Repetition, Repetition as Performance

The Swords narrative is an important site for explaining this incompatibility between warrior heroes and the peacetime world and for neutralizing it. The narrative moves action away from discrete moments in heroes' lives and onto the grander scale of cosmological time, reaching from the legendary pre-history of Susanō-o up to the present of the Soga brothers and Yoritomo. It incorporates the various elements that assert cultural authority—petitions to the gods, dream visions directing action, and ongoing dialogue between the Minamoto and their ancestors. It shrinks momentary problems within a trajectory that has diversions, but never abandons its ultimate destination. Much like the hunt that is the scene for the vendetta, the Swords narrative provides a frame for the volatile tales it recounts. It is thus as performance that the narrative comes into full force, opening old spiritual wounds and then soothing them through the act of vocalizing memory.

The act of placation necessarily involves an invocation of the dead. In performance, the mode of communication is direct—by calling forth events and people, by *naming* them, the performer makes a physical (rather than textual) entreaty to an invisible audience. Like the other invocations we have seen in these narratives, these performances hope for a response from the spirit world, albeit a quiet one. That the "Chapter of the Swords" is a secret piece points to the significance and sacrality of this act; only initiates can handle it.[82] This is not surprising, given its contents, namely the histories of supernatural swords associated with the royal and shōgunal houses, swords that were both lost (Kusanagi) and recovered (Hizamaru) in the course of the reshuffling of power during the Genpei War. Invoking their histories orally is a powerful act.

The special placatory status of this story is emphasized in its other variants, too. Although the *Soga* exists as a discrete and textualized story, it was part of a recited tradition, and it also contains characters who perform in a similar recitative function in the text, very much like what occurs in the *Heike*. Like Kenreimon'in of the *Heike*, Jūrō's beloved, Tora gozen, devotes her life to praying for the brothers' souls. And as in the recited *Heike* texts, this image of the praying female survivor brings the tale to a close. "Praise of the Swords," like other *kōwakamai*, performs the same placatory function in a slightly different context: it lauds the new order while celebrating the fallen who have brought that order into being. Each tale is quite literally a vocalized call not only to the audience but also to the spirits of the dead; performance in its various generic representations here becomes symptomatic of the repetition of the trauma that is the Genpei-period past. And in its repetition and wide dissemination, this trauma, limited historically to a small group of warriors at a specific moment, becomes the collective traumatic past —mastered—for an emerging popular culture in a land increasingly identified in its narrative histories as "Nippon."

But these narratives also were preserved from early on as *texts*. They were committed to paper to protect their integrity and as proof of their veracity. The idea of textualized voice, of course, is nothing new: Ō no Yasumaro's preface to the *Kojiki* claims that the work is a faithful record of the oral narration of Hieda no Are; the colophon's description of the Kakuichibon's production similarly describes the performer's voice being captured on the page. Textualization of such narratives performs the important role of preservation and containment, while vocalization animates them, if only for the duration of the performance.

Conclusion

Warrior Rule in Medieval Japan

> Depending on its circumstances and point in time, society repre-
> sents the past to itself in different ways: it modifies its conventions.
> As every one of its members accepts these conventions, they
> inflect their recollections in the same direction in which collective
> memory evolves.
>
> —M. Halbwachs, *On Collective Memory*

*T*he Genpei War was clearly a monumental event in the shared memory of medieval Japan. Although later conflicts like the Mongol invasions and the Ōnin War contributed more dramatically to the shaping of
warrior society, no other medieval military event has received anything resembling the narrative attention paid the clash between the Taira and the
Minamoto. And none has remained as salient in the national cultural
consciousness.[1]

The Minamoto Line in Medieval Narrative
and Performance Traditions

This volume has examined places in the larger narrative of the war and its
aftermath where actual fractiousness within the Minamoto line conflicted
with the general narrative trajectory of the closure brought by Yoritomo's
post-war rise to power as the leader of a coherent clan. We have seen how
these tensions were resolved or at least confronted in the multiply told war
narratives that proliferated, changed, and expanded as Japan's medieval
age wore on. So too did the audiences for historical narratives and drama
strive to accommodate the complexity of events in what increasingly came
to be seen as a shared past leading to their own present.

Situating the past in relation to the present is an ongoing task faced
by every society. As present realities change, so do relationships to the past;
we find that the ways narratives of the past are altered or refined to address
concerns of any given present indicate important preoccupations for
those involved in presenting and receiving that past. This inclination is
particularly evident in times when the present changes rapidly. The war

tales and their corollary genres, including *kōwakamai*, histories, and tales of heroic lives, are involved in this sort of historical project, particularly because of their subject matter—the civil conflict that gave rise to rule by warriors, who in turn came to be seen as the most powerful cultural symbols in Japan. Beyond relating their battlefield heroics, narratives of the Genpei period also take on the difficult project of interpretation. And this project was clearly a vital challenge for a society in which relationships to old social, political, and cosmological parameters were changing as provincial peoples and regions became politically more important, negotiating new or changing systems.

Throughout this volume, I have presented cases where interpretation became a central issue in the Minamoto rise. We have seen how Yoritomo's ascension is framed throughout medieval narrative by a body of interrelated tropes, both well established and newly emerging, that foreground the interpretive act. As time goes by and narratives are reworked in later texts, this concern becomes even more pronounced. Yoritomo's realm emerges as a place where any action's appropriateness is determined by a correct interpretation of the rules and norms governing that action. The Kamakura Lord's court becomes the prototypical arena for determining appropriateness; there petitions are presented, witness borne, and decisions made in a reasoned and fair manner. This general model of action mediated by interpretive processes applies to decisions in other areas as well, including strategy in battle or a prayer or oath made before the gods. It is the careful petitioner, acting through a superlative scribe, who becomes the model for correct and laudable behavior.

Each of the first three central chapters of the book examines one definitive event leading up to the acknowledgement of Yoritomo as Kamakura Lord: a prophesy of Yoritomo's rise from exile to shōgun; the beginning of Yoshinaka's successful campaign on the capital; and Yoritomo's falling out with Yoshitsune. These events represent turning points at which fortunes or ambitions of individuals present challenges to an idealized portrayal of the clan's history and unity. The negotiation between the untidy historical realities and an increasingly idealized interpretation of the past was a primary driving force in creating multiple versions of stories about those men.

My discussion of Yoritomo's exile highlighted interpretation through the traditional trope of the prophetic dream, in which the weight of divine will is brought to bear on Yoritomo's imminent rise to power. This narrative is found across a wide spectrum of texts, ranging from the *Heiji monogatari* to *Heike monogatari* variants, the *kōwakamai*, and the *Soga monogatari*. In all of them the prophetic dream is interpreted by a loyal retainer, and how those interpretations change—or do not—across variants and over time reveals much about the cultural milieux within which the tale is told and retold. The *Heiji monogatari,* in all likelihood the oldest version of the episode, places the event early in the narrative of Yoritomo's life, at the moment of his sojourn *into* exile. A work situated within a body of war tales chronicling the fall and rise of the Minamoto, it points to Yoritomo's elevation to Kamakura Lord as its final destination. This general narrative pattern is found in many recitational *Heike* variants as well; they terminate with the conclusion of the war and refer only obliquely to Kamakura rule once it is in place.

The *Hōgen monogatari, Heij monogatari,* and *Heike monogatari* constitute a cycle that begins with the fall in fortunes of the Minamoto and ends with its revival.[2] This narrative cycle is intimately connected to the concomitant rise and fall of the Taira, and its teleological movement is arrested at the moment the world is brought to peace after the battle of Dan-no-ura. Performances of these placatory tales thus represent a backward turn to an ongoing dialogue with the story of the fallen Taira.

This is not as obviously the case with *Heike* texts outside the central performance tradition or with works from other genres treating the war. These tend rather to move beyond the end of the war and celebrate Yoritomo's rule, as we see in the *Soga* and *kōwakamai* renditions of the Dream Interpretation narrative. In these variants, the Dream Interpretation episode occurs after Yoritomo has reached adulthood in exile in Izu, while he casts about for a way to reverse his fortunes. His first liaison with a daughter of one of his guardians, Itō Sukechika, results in the cruel and brutal loss of the male child born of that union when Sukechika is unwilling to accept an enemy of the court as a son-in-law. While still in exile and under guard, Yoritomo repeats this cycle of involvement with Hōjō Masako, a daughter of another of his guardians. The insertion of the Dream Interpretation sequence at this moment indicates that this liaison will bring a change in fortune. His initial marriage is overwritten by his second; the new pair's willful assertion of both their union and the inviolability of their progeny triggers the dream sequence foretelling Yoritomo's rise.

The *Soga monogatari* provides the fullest articulation of the Dream Interpretation sequence within the context of Yoritomo's youthful romantic affairs, and it demonstrates a general trend toward partnering Yoritomo's rise to power with this reanimation of his family line. The *Soga monogatari* was compiled after Yoritomo's death and the successful ascendancy of the Hōjō as shōgunal regents, so its emphasis on the Hōjō connection is not surprising. But this focus also plays into another crucial concern for the *Soga monogatari*: the specific cycle of revenge initiated with Itō Sukechika's drowning of Senzuru. This cycle is juxtaposed with the retribution by Sukechika's grandsons, the Soga brothers, on a kinsman for killing their father; with their deaths, in turn, Yoritomo effectively has exacted his revenge on Sukechika's descendents.

That the *kōwakamai* foregrounds the dream episode in Yoritomo's exile indicates the importance of dream interpretation in this genre intently focused on eulogizing Yoritomo.[3] What is more, the far wider presence of the Dream Interpretation narrative—imparted in fairly consistent form across various works in various genres—indicates the important role of both the dream vision and the dream interpreter in the narrative justifying Yoritomo's rise.

Within the dream episode, we also find prefigurings of what kind of rule Yoritomo will establish. Yoritomo is attended by followers whom he evidently values. The harmonious relationship between the lord and his men is replicated in the *mise en scene* of the dream itself: the dream-world lord is waited upon by loyal retainers with whom he shares his good fortune; this characterization of Yoritomo is elaborated in the Swords narrative. The dream vision is explicitly attributed to Hachiman, the Minamoto clan tutelary deity, to whom Yoritomo has prayed earlier in the longer narratives of the Enkyōbon, the *Genpei tōjōroku*, the *Genpei jōsuiki* and the *Soga monogatari*. Hachiman promises Yoritomo's change in fortunes and assures that the Minamoto line will be avenged; this connection is actively strengthened by Yoritomo after the war, when he makes Hachiman's shrine the centerpiece of his new capital.

Above all, this tale makes a case for the vital role of interpretation: it is the interpreter and dreamer who actually are the central characters within the narrative. By emphasizing the centrality of the interpreter and the interpretive act, the narrative casts Yoritomo as audience, a role not dissimilar from that of adjudicator, which we see him fill in narratives set later in his career. And configuring the dream incarnation of Yoritomo as a figure writ large over a map of the realm asserts and sanctions the political dimension of his role in very explicit terms.

Chapters Three and Four address narratives that situate Yoritomo's two most serious kin-group rivals: his cousin, Yoshinaka, and his brother, Yoshitsune. The story of Yoshinaka's Petition provides a study in success. Yoshinaka, the first early threat to Yoritomo's hegemony, prepares for battle carefully, pausing to ask for information about the unknown terrain in which he finds himself and to order divinations when he is unsure of his next steps. Like Yoritomo in the Dream Interpretation narrative, Yoshinaka here is an audience for various acts of interpretation; he replicates precisely the behavior of the rightful lord enacted earlier by his cousin. In all versions of the story he seeks advice from an *annaisha*, someone who possesses the information he lacks and can discern the will of the gods; in both tactical matters and larger strategic maneuverings he makes sure he has divine favor before proceeding. His ability to abide by the signs is demonstrated most eloquently in the Enkyōbon, which contrasts his reverent approach to divination with the Taira's flagrant disregard for the signs they are shown.

Earlier representations of this narrative tend to focus more clearly than later ones on scenes of divination; later texts instead devote more attention and detail to the presentation of Yoshinaka's petition to Hachiman. The *kōwakamai*, the most recent text, even cuts out the final scene of the god's approval in favor of praising the skill of Yoshinaka's scribe, Kakumei. Thus later texts focus not only on the act of writing but also on the role of the scribe; Kakumei is praised throughout as a paragon of both martial and civil arts. He stands in his own right as a model for later generations, someone who knows how and when to wield the brush instead of the sword. In his capacity as scribe, he is also held up as an exemplary *annaisha*, thus further emphasizing the critical role of petitioning, and of doing so properly.

This interplay between divination and petitioning over time tends toward an increased reliance on petitions (and particularly, on well-written ones) as the means for communication with superior powers. To be sure, the power in question here resides in the god Hachiman; but the narrative emphasis on the act of preparing a document and the insertion of the document as such into the text point to the increasing importance of evidentiary documents in society. Although petitions had been used to communicate with the gods for centuries, their relative value rose, hand-in-hand with their new function as legal proof as the medieval period progressed. In the war tales, we find documents, such as Yoshinaka's petition, embedded in the narrative at numerous critical moments. Moreover, Yoshinaka's lapse in document writing later in his career signals the beginning of his decline in the *Heike monogatari*; it is only while petitioning the gods in this formal manner that his success is assured.

The story of the Koshigoe petition considered in Chapter Four foregrounds an act of petition writing under a very different set of circumstances. Yoritomo has become suspicious of Yoshitsune following the conclusion of the Genpei War; when Yoshitsune is not permitted to enter Kamakura with his prisoners to meet Yoritomo, he composes a petition pleading his innocence. The petition explains how his actions have been misinterpreted by his elder brother. For the audience, this petition also documents Yoshitsune's naïveté—unlike Yoshinaka before the battle of Kurikara, Yoshitsune has not been able to read the signs and interpret the will of either the gods or his brother. And precisely like Yoshinaka later in his career, Yoshitsune reveals that he has been unable to navigate the politics of life off the battlefield. This has made him an object of Yoritomo's wrath. Tellingly, he pleads his innocence from a station at the fringes of Kamakura: his physical location mirrors his political position. Moreover, Koshigoe is dangerously close to Yuigahama, Yoritomo's execution ground, which provides another ominous geographic indication of Yoshitsune's situation.

There is more variation in the handling of the Koshigoe petition story than in any other episode of the texts considered in this book. In the early Enkyōbon as well as the *Genpei jōsuiki*, the brothers do in fact meet and the animosity between them is palpable. In later versions, Yoshitsune is denied an audience and Kajiwara Kagetoki is increasingly turned into the scapegoat for the brothers' falling out: it is only the interference of an outsider, these narratives assert, that causes the bond between brothers to go so wrong. This rhetorical shift is required by the political and cultural ideology of a Minamoto lineage destined to rule the land; it contributes a new coherence to the story by effacing the fratricidal competition that threatens to undermine the very idea of family. The *kōwakamai* version of the Koshigoe story foregrounds the role of the scribe much like the narrative of Yoshinaka's Petition; the piece ends with praise of Benkei's calligraphy, a conclusion clearly echoing Kakumei's role *vis-à-vis* Yoshinaka. The emphasis on the composition of documents to be presented before earthly and divine authorities here again reflects the change in cultural mores as the medieval age progressed. Yoritomo's consolidation of power came to be seen as the origin of governance based on the rule of law and the peaceful settlement of disputes. Yoshitsune's failure to operate effectively in this system foreshadows his demise.

The more recent component texts in this study, the *kōwakamai*, the *Gikeiki*, and the *Soga monogatari*, although rooted in the Kamakura age, were circulating most prominently and being recorded in writing during the late Muromachi period, when rule of law was increasingly being disregarded in favor of military confrontation. Not surprisingly we find an added emphasis in all three texts not only on the glories of past warriors, but also on the ultimate authority and rectitude of Yoritomo as lawgiver. This characterization of Kamakura rule was progressively becoming a tenet central to the development of a number of lasting themes in the cultural memory of post-Genpei period: loyalty within lineage groups, divine sanction of military rule, and the court of law as the appropriate arena for resolving disputes. These themes represent ideals rather than actual history for both the period they describe and the period of their origin and circulation, but they became extremely powerful foundation myths that later generations mobilized in their understanding of the origins of warrior culture. By examining how the messy and contradictory events of this key moment in the development of warrior culture were subsequently turned into coherent narrative, we engage issues vital to the creation of what would become the Japanese identity.

The narratives at the center of this study—those focused specifically on matters of interpretation and adjudication—coexisted with and often were intimately connected to other stories of glorious, brave behavior on

the battlefield. Yet we find in the *kōwakamai* and in the war tale literature
an emphasis on the importance of bringing war to a close with the instate-
ment of fair civil law; bearing witness and presenting documents are to re-
place drawing swords and engaging the enemy. The irony of this situation
is that these order-centered works must explain the deaths of two popular
heroes of the war tales at the hands of Yoritomo, the giver of law and, more
importantly, a member of his victims' kin group. The problem of reconcil-
ing the need to impose law with the celebration of battlefield heroics by
men like Yoshinaka and Yoshitune gave rise to the overabundance of tales
in which we see a diachronic progression toward explaining this incompatibility. The narrative drive to continually reframe their stories, and the
constant retelling, rewriting, and reinterpretation only highlights the
grave difficulty of resolving the narrative and historical tensions in these
stories. This narrative exuberance, however, also points to the shifting
foundations of the society doing the reinterpreting. By the Muromachi
era, the realm had experienced two Mongol invasions, a split within the
royal house, and expanding internal violence that would come to a head
with the Ōnin War. The need to explain the past as a frame for an uncertain present required the creation of order where it was deteriorating.
This gave rise to a social and political origin story that provided clear an-
swers to the dilemmas faced by performers and audiences of these works
in the late Muromachi age. It is not surprising that the *kōwakamai* and tales
from the Genpei period were also favored by the late Sengoku and early
Tokugawa hegemons, since they too were deeply engrossed in asserting
their rights as inheritors of Yoritomo's government.[4]

The final narrative investigated here, the powerful story of the Minamoto heirloom swords, uses the tale of the Soga brothers to contain the
fractious stories of Yoshinaka and Yoshitsune. It returns to a realm well ordered under Yoritomo. The story of the Swords is closely tied to Yoritomo's own. It alludes very specifically to the larger narrative of Minamoto
supremacy as it brings to a conclusion the cycles of parricide that have
haunted all the stories considered thus far. The Swords narrative refracts
the problems created by the fractiousness of the Minamoto line, through
the noble revenge and sacrifice of the Soga brothers, onto an elaborate
narrative highlighting the continuity of generations of Minamoto, ending
finally at Yoritomo's feet. As symbols of the Minamoto line, the swords
bring into sharper focus the thematic concerns central to the other narratives. They stand for patrimony, for family name, and for the family's military might and connection to the deity Hachiman.

Although not concentrated on the juridical arena per se, the story
of the swords is framed by the narrative of the Itō family's court battles in
the capital, an ordeal so fraught with unfairness and enmity that it eventually erupted into a violent family feud. This unproductive engagement

with the royal court in Heian is then juxtaposed with Yoritomo's bureau of military affairs, whose fairness is emphasized in the *Soga monogatari* and the *kōwakamai* based on the brothers' story. The larger story of a fair system of law replacing the corrupt one that had spawned both the small-scale violence of the Itō family feud and the large-scale violence of the Genpei War sets the stage for the resolution achieved in the Swords narrative. That narrative metaphorically ends the cycles of murderous retribution by laying to rest the blades as they are returned to the Minamoto shōgun, who appropriates them as markers of his hegemony.

The swords in this narrative serve a number of functions in their capacity as symbols of the Minamoto patrimony. As they pass from hand to hand and acquire new names and stories with each generation, they give rise to new, potentially divergent narratives that constantly run the risk of derailing the master narrative, sending it off in radically new directions. As blades used to subdue enemies of both the worldly and otherworldly realms, they configure the master narrative by very literally cutting off potential contenders. Further, they help contain the fractiousness of Yoritomo's own generation by facilitating the recasting of the heroic figures of Yoshinaka and Yoshitsune. In representing the heroic legacy of the two slain Genpei heroes, the swords bring to life the bravery, valor, and loyalty of the warrior hero in the personalities of Soga Jūrō and Soga Gorō. When the swords are inherited by the Soga brothers together with other trappings of the Minamoto cousins (loyal courtesan lovers, rivalry with a Kajiwara, a peripheral position to the main line of the family, loss of a father), they play a role in a refigured clan feud that is both distanced from internal Minamoto contentions and displaced to a lesser stage. The brothers' behavior is easily contained. Their resistance to Yoritomo, a by-product of a credible dispute with their father's killer, can be framed as heroic, and their deaths as fully tragic. In asserting their undying devotion to their father's memory and to each other, they demonstrate that close, harmonious family relations have been restored with the quieting of the realm.

This narrative, like the others, filled a cultural need: the Soga brothers in fact bore Yoritomo personal malice for destroying their line, and he in turn saw them as inheritors of the wrath he felt toward their grandfather. How much this characterization of Mimamoto–Itō relations reflects actual historical fact and how much it relies on the narrativization of Yoritomo's rise *as a response to* historical fact is impossible to determine, but this cycle of retribution closely resembles patterns we see more broadly in characterizations of the Minamoto feud with the Taira as well as conflict within the Minamoto clan. Resolving these cycles of revenge allowed the establishment of Yoritomo's rule to function retroactively as an origin point for succeeding generations of warrior society in its numerous permutations from the late Kamakura through Tokugawa periods. The idea of bringing order to a disorderly period, of setting it up as a stable foundation for ever-changing warrior "presents," lies at the heart of the story of the Swords. Its numerous tellings and retellings—and in this case particularly, its inclusion as a secret *Heike biwa* piece—reveal and create the significance of this historical moment, shaping it in ways that met the needs of medieval audiences.

Dramatic Transformations:
Kōwakamai and Narrating the Minamoto Rise

Although the narratives considered in this book traverse textual and genre barriers, none of them have made their way into the *nō* canon; or at least we do not have extant canonical *nō* directly based on these stories.[5] Where they move into the realm of drama, they seem to enter the *kōwakamai* repertoire. Why is this preference so distinct, and what does it mean for our interpretation of each episode's status both as a discrete story and part of a larger genre or narrative?

The body of *kōwakamai* exceeds the episodes or even kinds of episodes studied here; moreover, some *kōwakamai* stories are in fact part of the *nō*, *kabuki*, and/or *jōruri* repertoires as well. However, one important difference between the *kōwakamai* and these other theatrical genres is its clear privileging of narrative. Although stories are performed in *kōwakamai*, what is performed is the telling of a story and, from what little we can actually discern about early *kōwakamai* performance, it may never have been a primarily mimetic form. As has been demonstrated in the preceding chapters, many pieces are in fact borrowed largely verbatim from the *Heike monogatari*, *Soga monogatari*, or *Gikeiki*, all identified as parts of narrative recitational traditions.[6]

Moreover, the *kōwakamai* themselves came to be strung together in a longer thread that tells the larger story of the rise of the warriors. All the episodes considered here are integrated into that narrative, much as their counterparts are integrated into the larger narratives of texts like the *Heike* variants, *Gikeiki*, *Soga monogatari*, or even the *Azuma kagami*. *Kōwakamai* have been characterized as praise pieces about the warrior class for an audience of members of that class, focused specifically on the rise of the Minamoto. This study certainly supports such a characterization. I would suggest further that the existence of *kōwakamai* reveals a sociopolitical need for the narrative it alone creates: a pared-down, Minamoto-centered story. The *kōwakamai* repetoire is one of the few performed or literary arts in which Yoritomo consistently appears as a character. And although he is prominently present, he is generally portrayed as being a step removed from the central action of the piece—in "The Dream Interpretation," he listens to his retainers tell and interpret auspicious dreams, and in "Koshigoe" and "Praise of the Swords," he simply adjudicates. Within the repertoire, he becomes the founding father of peaceful, law-driven rule by the warrior class.

Yoritomo's characterization as lawgiver certainly contributes to the centrality of evidentiary documents in a number of *kōwakamai*, another characteristic that distinguishes the *kōwakamai* from canonical *nō*—in both Yoshinaka's Petition and Koshigoe, a document is the focal point of the work. While the *nō Ataka* and the *kabuki Kanjinchō* also feature a document—the subscription roll—as their centerpiece, the drama of these pieces is dependent on the document's absence; it is Benkei's performance of "reading" the fictional document that creates drama in those other dramas. The actual text of a document does not figure there. However, the milieu of the *kōwakamai* specially favors the plot device of document presentation. In addition to the two included here, we also find "Togashi" (the *kōwakamai* version of the subscription roll story), "Mongaku" (about Mongaku's plea for subscriptions to build a hall at Jingoji), and "The Inserted Letter," a piece describing Yoshitsune's final, ultimately posthumous, plea of innocence.

What makes the *kōwakamai* a locus for document-centered pieces? One important element is the role of the diegetic reading of the document as metatextual commentary on the act of interpretation. In a context where the audience was composed of members of the warrior class, the foregrounding of a document as the appropriate proof of sincerity and legitimacy in disputes would have been particularly meaningful. This audience would have been composed of men whose families had risen to prominence as military supporters of successful campaigns beginning with the Genpei War, but who had to maintain that prominence by more peaceful means—at least, that is the ideal promoted in this genre. The presentation of documents before a judge had become the appropriate and usual means of proving one's rectitude in disputes, and so these scenes provide a version of reality that is at once prescriptive and descriptive for the post-Genpei warrior world.

Yet *kōwakamai*, although originating as early as the Kamakura period, came to the fore during the Muromachi and Sengoku ages, when a second shōgunate had been established and the balance of political control between the shōgunal house, the royal house, and powerful lords was becoming increasingly unstable.[7] The portrayal of a world brought under control by Yoritomo, in which he enjoyed a position of respect and the loyalty of his men, who were in turn justly rewarded, reflects a decidedly nostalgic view. In sequences of *kōwakamai* about Yoshinaka, Yoshitsune, or the Soga brothers—potentially disruptive forces in this idealized world—attention is given to the external factors that caused their fall, and the narratives glorifying them focus on the aspects of their behavior that align with protocol: Yoshinaka's respectful petition to the Minamoto tutelary deity, Yoshitsune's heartfelt plea for his brother's understanding of his intentions, and the Sogas' tragic inheritance of a feud that could only end with their deaths. To be sure, the war tales participate in the general trend toward portraying something like earthly apotheosis for Yoritomo,[8] which elsewhere occurs first with sovereigns and then also with certain shōguns.[9] But this picture of Yoritomo reaches a level of consistency only with the *kōwakamai*, where scenes like the Enkyōbon account of Yoshitsune's confrontation with Yoritomo simply do not happen.

The trope of documentation can therefore be seen as one essential part of a larger thematic characterization of the warrior world found throughout the *kōwakamai* repertoire. Unflinching bravery in battle, loyalty to one's lord or parent, and a celebration of warrior identity repeatedly appear in these works. The genre is the military class' own paean to itself and its idealized origins; it depicts the founding of the shōgunate in terms that embrace both the violence necessary to bring order and the peaceful adjudication of disputes required to ensure its continuation. Although this ideal reflects neither the actuality of the age it describes nor that in which it was created, it does manifest key values of the warrior community and the attempt to create a narrative about that community in which both battlefield bravery and level-headedness in governance could coexist.

The Genpei War in the Medieval Imagination

Who made up the community that supported, promoted, and developed the narrative and dramatic traditions from which these stories are taken? This is among the most debated questions in scholarship on the medieval texts, particularly on those falling outside the explicit purview of aristocratic patronage. Scholars of medieval popular culture, including Amino Yoshihiko, Gomi Fumihiko, Wakita Haruko, and Barbara Ruch have all offered provocative insights regarding the contributions of peripheral arts and peoples to what eventually came to be Japan's national identity. The picture of movement up the social ladder for marginal arts has therefore provided a useful and inviting model for exploring the popularization of Japanese culture during the medieval and early modern ages.

This sort of trajectory can be seen in the narratives considered here; certainly, local legends were picked up by compilers of the *Heike* variants, the *Gikeiki*, and the *Soga monogatari*, and in many instances, non-central, non-aristocratic narratives seem to be vital sources for the larger work. Yet central, aristocratic, and institutional Buddhist interests also clearly had a hand in compiling works about the Genpei period: clergy, temples, and shrines figure prominently in the stories; allusions to earlier elite texts are plentiful, and the musical framework for *Heike biwa* performance derives from *shōmyō* chanting, a practice of aristocratic priests. Tales of the Genpei period are an important site where the various dichotomies we associate with the creation of medieval works came into highly productive interactive play.

This interaction between elite arts and aesthetics and non-elite performance genres has long been recognized as fundamental in the development of several important literary and performance arts during the medieval period: hands from various social and geographical groups helped mold the *kōwakamai*, tale literature, and, of course, *nō* drama. That this trend is manifest in a body of narratives intimately connected to the historical past makes this expansion of collective consciousness even more meaningful. We find not only Ruch's shared body of characters and stories, but also the emerging idea of a common cultural history comprised of events, people, and relationships that has formed the basis for much of Japanese identity even up to the present day.

By looking at historical moments that appear in a number of works over an extended time span, we can begin to discern precisely what topics continued to be important and anxiety-producing enough to generate repeated reinterpretations. And, as the preceding chapters have demonstrated, it is not only the actual events but the act of interpretation itself that remains a primary concern for generation after generation of raconteurs and their audiences. What we see with the progression of retellings is a record of developing understandings of the vital narratives that bring interpretation and, by extension, narrative itself front and center in the creative process.

In our examination of stories that do recur over time, we witness the cumulative effects of retelling and the simultaneous presence of multiple, sometimes even contradictory accounts of the same historical event. Considered together, they verge on cacophony, but this polyvocal, variegated, and multivariant tale becomes one of the most potentially interesting sources for scholars of the medieval period, for it is here that we most specifically encounter the counternarratives, alternative histories, and under-represented voices that directly engage any hegemonic narrative. And the process by which those voices were winnowed out or brought into line over the course of Japan's medieval age facilitated the emergence of modern Japan, as a culture and a nation.

Appendix A

The Hōgen and Heiji Uprisings

B y the twelfth century, fighting men bearing the family names of Taira and Minamoto had become, if not indispensable, at least a significant asset for central power holders who employed them to ensure smooth operation of both provincial landholdings and the distribution networks needed for uninterrupted movement of goods produced there. This role of provincial enforcement from its inception tended to allow military men to act as private as well as public enforcers, and their usefulness in this role only increased over time. By the mid-twelfth century, two successive clan leaders of the Taira had, through their willingness and ability to enforce the will of the royal house against enemies including powerful religious institutions, attained aristocratic rank beyond that usually accorded men of their background. In 1131, Tadamori, the scion of the Taira house, was granted permission to enter the Courtiers' Hall, a significant step toward recognition as a member of the central community of powerful aristocrats.[1] Although he died in 1153, three years before the Hōgen Uprising, the presence of his provincial, military family in such proximity to central authority was a primary factor in the Hōgen and Heiji disturbances.

The *Hōgen monogatari* recounts events surrounding two concurrent succession disputes of the mid-1150s—one in the royal family, and the other in the Fujiwara house that normally supplied ministers of the highest rank. Within the royal house, the dispute erupted between the reigning Sovereign Go-Shirakawa and Retired Sovereign Sutoku, who had been forced by his father, Retired Sovereign Toba, to abdicate in favor of Konoe, the son of Toba's favorite consort, Bifukumon'in. Things came to a head when Konoe died, and Toba chose another son, Go-Shirakawa, to succeed Konoe. Sutoku was angered by his father's decision not to put his (Sutoku's) son on the throne. In the house then providing regents, the former regent Fujiwara Tadazane and his second son, Yorinaga, simultaneously were engaged in a dispute over clan leadership against

Tadamichi, Tadazane's first son. Tadazane was able to gain regental powers for Yorinaga through a number of maneuvers, but Toba interceded and returned power in both name and fact to Tadamichi.

Things came to a head in the first year of the Hōgen era (1156), when Toba died, and the disenfranchised Sutoku and Yorinaga joined to try to forcibly remove their kinsmen from positions they saw as rightfully theirs. Each side called upon the warriors of the Minamoto and Taira to protect their interests, and members of both houses responded, but not as unified forces: Taira Kiyomori, eldest son of Taira Tadamori, and Minamoto Yoshitomo, head of the Seiwa Genji, sided with Go-Shirakawa's faction. Kiyomori's uncle and Yoshitomo's father and younger brothers sided with Sutoku. Under the leadership of Yoshitomo, Go-Shirakawa's side won the one battle of the conflict following a successful night attack. Yorinaga was killed in battle, and, following the insurrection, Sutoku was exiled to Sanuki, where he died.[2]

In addition to representing the potential of devastating rifts within the upper aristocracy, the rebellion was also a tragedy for the Minamoto house. In his role as victorious general, Yoshitomo was ordered to execute his traitorous kin, which he did, although ostensibly only with extreme regret and guilt. This seemed even at the time to have gained him infamy, and from then on his fortunes waned, while Kiyomori received instead significant emoluments for his role in the victory, and his family prospered.

Fewer than four years later, in the first year of the Heiji era, yet another dispute broke out among the Fujiwara nobles. Fujiwara Nobuyori, resentful of the success of the Lay Priest Shinzei (Fujiwara Michinori), allied himself with Yoshitomo, and the two attempted to dispossess Kiyomori and Shinzei of their positions by kidnapping the now-retired Go-Shirakawa and the reigning Sovereign Nijō while Kiyomori was away from the capital on pilgrimage. Yoshitomo's forces were initially successful, destroying Shinzei's house and forcing him to commit suicide, but shortly thereafter Kiyomori and his sons and retainers returned and were able to crush them decisively. The defeated Minamoto fled to the east, where Yoshitomo was eventually betrayed by a retainer and killed. His adult sons all either died in battle or were executed, but his four youngest sons were spared. Yoritomo, the eldest at age twelve, was formally exiled to Izu Province, where he was placed under the supervision of the Hōjō and Itō families, hereditary retainers of the Taira. The younger boys were sent to temples to receive religious instruction.

Appendix B

Genealogical Charts of the Seiwa Genji and the Itō

The Seiwa Genji Lineage

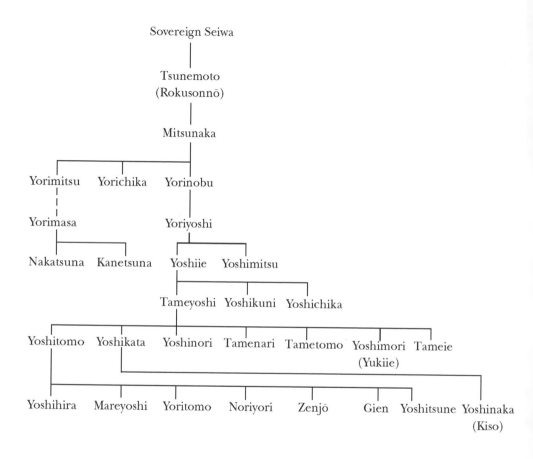

The Itō Lineage

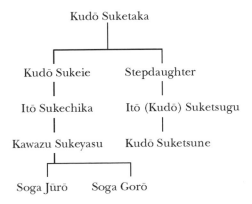

Appendix C

Texts and Genres

The following texts are considered in Chapters Two through Five. The variants of the *Heike monogatari*—and their names in Japanese—are arranged in rough chronological order, along with their approximate dates of compilation.

The *Heike monogatari* variants

Enkyōbon *Heike monogatari* 延慶本平家物語. Colophon of copy from 1419 cites original colophon dated 1309.

Genpei tōjōroku 源平闘諍録. Colophon dated 1337. Only five of original eight chapters extant.

Yashirobon *Heike monogatari* 屋代本平家物語. Oldest extant text is from Tokugawa period; thought to be compiled originally in the thirteenth or fourteenth century, but this is disputed among scholars.

Hyakunijukkubon *Heike monogatari* 百二十句本平家物語. Close relative of Yashirobon.

Kakuichibon *Heike monogatari* 覚一本平家物語. Colophon dated 1371.

Nagatobon *Heike monogatari* 長門本平家物語. Oldest extant text is from Tokugawa period; thought to be compiled originally in the Muromachi period.

Genpei jōsuiki 源平盛衰記. Oldest extant text is from Tokugawa period; thought to be compiled originally in the Muromachi period.

Other Works

Azuma kagami 吾妻鏡. Late thirteenth century. Pseudo-history compiled by the Kamakura government.

Heiji monogatari 平治物語. Ca. fourteenth to fifteenth century. Narrative about the Heiji Uprising (1159-60).

Gikeiki 義経記. Ca. fifteenth century. Narrative account of life of Minamoto Yoshitsune.

Soga monogatari 曾我物語. Ca. fifteenth century. Narrative account of the revenge of the Soga brothers.

Kōwakamai 幸若舞. Ca. fifteenth to sixteenth century. Collected in the *Mai no hon* 舞の本, ca. 1624-43. Pieces used in this study include:

"Yume awase" (The Dream Interpretation) 夢合わせ;
"Koshigoe" (Koshigoe) 腰越;
"Kiso no Ganjo" (Yoshinaka's Petition) 木曾の願書;
"Tsurugi sandan" (Praise of the Swords) 剣賛談.

Notes

Chapter 1: The *Heike monogatari* and Narrating the Genpei War

1. In English, see George Sansom, *A History of Japan to 1334* (Stanford, CA: Stanford University Press, 1958), pp. 264–338.

2. Asakawa Kan'ichi, *Documents of Iriki* (Tokyo: Society for the Promotion of Science, 1955), provides one early example.

3. William LaFleur's introduction to *The Karma of Words* (Berkeley, CA: University of California Press, 1983) outlines his conceptualization of a Buddhist worldview as a frame for medievality; for him, the medieval period begins when a consciousness of the decline of the Buddhist law emerges, locating it in the mid-Heian period; the Genpei War thus marks not the beginning of the period, but rather an important manifestation of its full flourishing.

4. See, for example, Jeffrey P. Mass, ed., *The Origins of Japan's Medieval Age* (Stanford, CA: Stanford University Press, 1997).

5. Sanctioned histories enjoyed a prominent place in Heian period historiography, as exemplified by the idea of the *Rikkokushi* (Six national histories). The *Rikkokushi* were all composed during the Nara (710–794) and Heian periods, and consist of the following: the *Nihon shoki* (Records of Japan, also *Nihongi*), in thirty books plus (not extant) genealogies covering mythical time to the early eighth century; the *Shoku Nihongi* (Nihongi, continued), in forty parts, covering 697–707; the *Nihon kōki* (Later records of Japan), in forty parts, covering 824–833; the *Shoku Nihon kōki* (Later records of Japan, continued), in twenty parts, covering 833–850; the *Nihon Montoku tennō jitsuroku* (Actual records of Sovereign Montoku of Japan), in ten parts, covering 850–858; and the *Nihon sandai jitsuroku* (Actual records of three reigns in Japan), in fifty parts, covering 858–887. All were written in *kanbun* and were contemporary to the eras they describe. They are collected in Saeki Ariyoshi, ed. *Zōho Rikkokushi* (Tokyo: Asahi shinbunsha, 1940–1941).

6. The mobility of texts and performance genres is addressed by Barbara Ruch in "Medieval Jongleurs and the Making of a National Literature," in John W. Hall and Takeshi Toyoda, eds., *Japan in the Muromachi Age* (Berkeley, CA: University of California Press, 1977), pp. 279–309, and "The Other Side of Culture

in Medieval Japan," in Yamamura Kōzō, ed., *Cambridge History of Japan*, vol. 3 (Cambridge, UK: Cambridge University Press, 1990), pp. 500–543.

7. There are three complete English translations of the *Heike monogatari*: Arthur Sadler, "The Heike Monogatari," *Transactions of the Asiatic Society of Japan* 46.2 (1918): 1–278 and 49.1 (1921): 1–354; Hiroshi Kitagawa and Bruce T. Tsuchida, *The Tale of the Heike* (Tokyo: Tokyo University Press, 1975); and Helen Craig McCullough, *The Tale of the Heike* (Stanford, CA: Stanford University Press, 1988). Additionally, portions can be found in A. L. Sadler, The Ten Foot Square Hut *and* Tales of the Heike*: Being two thirteenth-century Japanese classics, the "Hojoki" and selections from "The Heike Monogatari"* (Sydney: Angus & Robertson Limited, 1928). All citations in this study are from McCullough's translation unless otherwise noted.

8. The precise number of variants differs depending on the criteria used to define an individual line. In one recent study, Heike monogatari *wo yomu: seiritsu no nazo wo saguru* (Tokyo: Izumi shoin, 2000), p. 4, Hayakawa Kōichi identifies eighty. Each line is represented by a number of individual manuscripts, many of which exhibit small peculiarities.

9. The expression *chūsei*, a translation of the European term "medieval," was first applied to the Japanese milieu during the Meiji period, and its dates of initiation and disintegration, not to mention its applicability at all, have been debated ever since. See Thomas Keirstead, "The Gendering and Regendering of Medieval Japan," *U.S.-Japan Women's Journal*, English Supplement no. 9 (1995), p. 79. Throughout this study, I consider Japan's "medieval age" to span the Kamakura through Sengoku periods, or roughly the thirteenth through sixteenth centuries. Medievality in Japan, even more than in the West, is a contentious term, one that has been applied to periods as early as the Heian and as late as the Tokugawa (1603–1868), depending on the concerns of the specific study. This book, too, views the medieval period through a fairly focused lens: the period epitomized by widespread dissemination of narratives about the recent historical past. Most of the works considered here emerged and circulated broadly from the late Kamakura through early Muromachi periods. This segment of medieval culture, I contend, is fundamental to our understanding of how early modern and modern Japan configured "Japan" as a nation, and I see this long moment as a central step towards a sense of cultural and national identity that would profoundly influence the way Japanese nationality was presented as the modern nation came into social and political dialogue with Western interlocutors.

10. The Nanbokuchō refers to the period of divided courts which coincided with the early years of the Muromachi period, initiated when the Ashikaga shōgunal house established its headquarters in the Muromachi district of the capital. The Ashikaga replaced the Kamakura shōgunate, which had been inaugurated by Minamoto Yoritomo after the Genpei War and continued following the death of his last heir under the control of the shōgunal regency dominated by the Hōjō family. The end of the Kamakura period is usually thought to coincide with Go-Daigo's Kenmu Restoration (1333), in which the sovereign unsuccessfully attempted to wrest

power from the shōgunate. Although he personally failed, the Ashikaga took advantage of the situation and forced their way to power. Generally, histories assign the beginning of the Muromachi period either to the Kemmu Restoration or the official recognition of the Ashikaga shōgunate (1336); in some accounts, its beginning is instead located at the end of the Nanbokuchō (1392).

11. See Jeffrey P. Mass, "Black Holes in Japanese History," in his *Antiquity and Anachronism in Japanese History* (Stanford, CA: Stanford University Press, 1992), pp. 157–177.

12. For a brief discussion of royal succession rivalries and their influence on capital politics and insurrections at this time, see Appendix A. Paul Varley's *Warriors of Japan as Portrayed in the War Tales* (Honolulu: University of Hawai'i Press, 1994), pp. 46–77, provides a more complete treatment of the Hōgen and Heiji Uprisings.

13. 1104–1180. A distant relative of the Minamoto kin group comprising the center of this study (Yoritomo, Yoshitsune, and Yoshinaka). Yorimasa joined the winning side in the Hōgen Uprising, then during the Heiji Uprising switched from the losing to the winning side; allegedly, his resentment over Kiyomori's fortunes after the Heiji Uprising was the basis for his spurring to action of Mochihito in 1180. He died in battle defending Mochihito, along with his sons, including Yoshinaka's brother, whom Yorimasa had adopted after the boys' father's death.

14. Included in document form in the *Heike* variants, this edict in fact was probably fictional.

15. Yoshinaka was promoted to Junior Fifth Rank and was appointed Director of the Imperial Stables of the Left and awarded the governorship of Echigo Province on 1183/8/10. The *Heike* records that because he disliked Echigo, he was given Iyo instead. The appointment of rank and title is confirmed in the *Hyakuren-sho* and Kujō Kanezane's diary, the *Gyokuyō*; another assertion made in the *Heike*—that he was at this juncture appointed *Asahi no shōgun* (Morning Sun General)—is not (see Kuroita Katsumi, ed., *Hyakurensho*, vol. 9 of *Shintei zōho kokushi taikei* [Tokyo: Yoshikawa kōbunkan, 1977-]). For the *Gyokuyō*, see Fukuda Toyohiko, ed., *Shintei zōho kokushi taikei-bon* Azuma kagami, Gyokuyō (Tokyo: Yoshikawa kōbunkan, 1999). Further, the *Heike*'s recounting that two months later, on 1183/10/14, Yoritomo was appointed *Sei-i taishōgun* (Barbarian-Subduing Great General) is also wrong; he was granted that title in 1192. See Tomikura Tokujirō, Heike monogatari zenchūshaku, vol. 2, pp. 514–515. Cited hereafter as Tomikura, *Zenchūshaku*. The emphasis of the military title of general (*shōgun*) here marks a preoccupation in the war tales with the identity of the Minamoto as hegemons of a class that defined itself as military; the anachronistic construction of a clearly defined military identity is an important theme running through the following chapters.

16. Dates throughout are listed as: Gregorian calendar year/month/day.

17. Although the fates of Yoshitsune and Yoritomo are well known, the other brothers' destinies are usually not of general concern. I include them here because they are of interest in the general narrative of the Minamoto rise to power at the center of this study. Yoshikado, Yoshitomo's fourth son, died

young. Mareyoshi, the fifth son, was forced to commit suicide in exile when Yoritomo raised troops in 1180. Noriyori was exiled by Yoritomo in 1193 to Izu, where he was killed. Zenjō allied himself with Yoritomo, married the sister of Yoritomo's wife, and outlived all his brothers. He was killed during the Hiki Uprising in 1203. Gien joined Yoritomo's forces in 1180, fought under Yukiie, and was killed in battle in 1181. Yoshitsune was forced to commit suicide in 1189, after the falling out with Yoritomo investigated here. For a discussion of the postwar lives and deaths of Noriyori and Zenjō, see Komori Yoshiaki, *Kanagawa no rekishi to densetsu* (Tokyo: Akatsuki in shokan, 1977), pp. 103–117.

18. See Yamashita Hiroaki, *Ikusa monogatari no katari to hihyō* (Tokyo: Sekai shisōsha, 1998), pp. 132–161 and Hyōdō Hiromi, Taiheiki *"yomi" no kanōsei: rekishi to iu mongatari* (Tokyo: Kodansha, 1995), p. 31.

19. David Quint, *Epic and Empire: Politics and Generic Form from Virgil to Milton* (Princeton, NJ: Princeton University Press, 1993), p. 32, discusses this role of (epic) historical narrative, shared to an interesting extent by Genpei War accounts as well, as we shall see.

20. *Biwa* refers to the Japanese lute. Often translated as "priest," *hōshi* is a more general term for males, often of indeterminate rank, affiliated either specifically or loosely with religious institutions. For a recent discussion of spirit placation (*chinkon*) and *Heike* performance, see Hyōdō Hiromi, Heike monogatari: *katari no tekusuto* (Tokyo: Chikuma shinsho, 1998), pp. 110–126; 160–178. The *biwa hōshi* is one mode of the tale's transmission, but there are numerous others, as we shall see. The blind lute-playing male, however, is the stereotype, and can be found in the "Earless Hōichi" (Miminashi Hōichi) story popularized by Lafcadio Hearn and later in Kobayashi Masaki's film *Kwaidan*.

21. Apparently a historical figure active during the mid- to late fourteenth century. Kakuichi's performances are mentioned in contemporary journals, including Nakahara Moromori's *Moromoriki*.

22. The colophon states that it was written in Enkyō 2 (1309). The Enkyō period lasted from 1308 to 1311, during the reign of Hanazono (r. 1308–1318).

23. A particularly clear description of variant lines, individual variants, and the terminology used to discuss them in Japanese can be found in Saeki Shin'ichi, Heike monogatari *sogen* (Tokyo: Wakakusa shobō, 1996), pp. 13–36, in which the author lays out the general problems faced by scholars engaged in genetic studies of the *Heike* variants.

24. Suzuki Takatsune, "Heikyoku," in Kajihara Masaaki, ed., Heike monogatari *hikkei* (Tokyo: Gakutōsha, 1985), p. 204. In the performed *Heike* tradition, *kyokusetsu* are usually applied to sections within a *ku*, although they sometimes also refer to phrases within a section. The ordering of *kyokusetsu* within a *ku* is often dictated by syntactic rules: certain *kyokusetsu* follow certain others. Some can be stretched or condensed, while others cannot. Additionally, some have extra-musical associations. For example *hiroi* is used for heroic descriptions. I am indebted to Alison Tokita for these observations.

25. I am grateful to Steven G. Nelson for this descriptive English translation of the term *kyokusetsu*.

26. For a succinct description of the *kyokusetsu* and their musical and narrative significance, see Komoda Haruko, "Heikyoku no kyokusetsu to ongaku kōzō," in Kamisangō Yūkō, ed., *Heike biwa, katari to ongaku* (Kasube-shi: Hitsuji shobō, 1993), pp. 161–193.

27. Komoda, "Heikyoku no kyokusetsu to ongaku kōzō," especially pp. 161–163.

28. The Saiku Rekishi Hakubutsukan (Saiku History Museum, Ise, Mie Prefecture), for example, holds a three-scroll Edo-period illustrated scroll labeled *Genpei kassen emaki* (Genpei War picture scroll) whose general organization follows most closely that of the *Jōsuiki* (discussed below), but which also contains a number of episodes from the *Gikeiki* (also discussed below) not generally included in the *Heike* variants. The changes in the restructuring of the narrative derive from the basic modularity of episodes. This is just one of many variants epitomizing the movement across works and genres at the center of this study.

29. Texts associated with the "read lineage" (discussed below) are generally divided into chapters, but organization at the next level of specificity is more often designated by date than by episode (see the Enkyōbon, for example). Some texts, including the hard-to-classify *Genpei jōsuiki*, however, are divided into episodes rather than dated entries.

30. In Ozaki Masayoshi's (1755–1827) *Gunsho ichiran* of 1802, the *Heike* was included with *Ōkagami*, *Hōgen mongatari*, *Heiji monogatari*, *Genpei jōsuiki*, *Azuma kagami*, *Gukanshō*, *Jinno shotoki*, and *Taiheiki* under the category of "miscellaneous history" (*zatsushirui*). See Takagi Ichinosuke, Ozawa Masao, Atsumi Kaoru, and Kindaichi Haruhiko, eds., Heike monogatari *jō*, vol. 32 of *Nihon koten bungaku taikei* (Tokyo: Iwanami shoten, 1962), p. 19.

31. First translator of Darwin's *On the Origin of Species* into Japanese. His involvement with the project of categorizing literary works bears an interesting resemblance to the kind of scientific endeavor laid out in Darwin's study.

32. Takagi et al., Heike monogatari *jō*, p. 19.

33. Better known as a translator and social critic; his credits include a translation of Nietzsche's collected works.

34. Orikuchi saw the *Heike* as a manifestation of oral literature, and oral literature as the expression of the people. See "Kosho bungaku to bunsho bungaku to" (1935) in *Orikuchi Shinobu zenshū*, vol. 7 (Tokyo: Chuokoron sha, 1966), p. 431. Yanagita's influential opinion on the importance of holy men (*hijiri*) as transmitters of tales that eventually were compiled in the *Heike* is most famously outlined in "Ariō to Shunkan sōto," in *Teihon Yanagita Kunio shū*, vol. 7. (Tokyo: Chikuma shobo, 1967), pp. 66–79. This article was originally published in 1940.

35. McCullough, *The Tale of Heike* (Stanford, CA: Stanford University Press, 1988), p. 7; in Japanese, see Satake Akihiro and Kubota Jun, eds., *Hōjōki, Tsurezuregusa*, vol. 39 of *Shin Nihon koten bungaku taikei* (Tokyo: Iwanami shoten, 1989), p. 295.

36. Note the similarity of this title to that of the *Hōgen monogatari* and *Heiji monogatari*. All use the reign name plus "tale" (*monogatari*). From these similarities, it is adduced that the referent to "Jishō" here is to another military disturbance during the Jishō era (1177–1181) like that described in *Hōgen* and *Heiji*, which would suggest the Genpei War.

37. Yamashita (*Ikusa monogatari no katari to hihyō*, pp. 84–85) discusses the possibility of what this reference might mean. He concludes that it does indicate something like the *Heike*, possibly in a three-scroll version like the others.

38. There are several other early sources mentioning the *Heike* including the Jien's *Gukanshō* and several less prominent early Muromachi texts. For a summary of early sources, see Kajihara Masaaki, ed., Heike monogatari *hikkei* (Tokyo: Gakutōsha, 1998), pp. 144–164.

39. This is a model adopted, importantly, in Tomikura's Heike monogatari *zenchūshaku*, published in 1966–1968, perhaps the most detailed annotated edition of the *Heike* today.

40. The guild was an important organizational structure during the Tokugawa period for the blind; one important role supported by the government through the guild was performance of the *Heike* and other repertoires. Although the guild probably originated before the Tokugawa period, its official recognition and regulation by the Edo government allowed *Heike* recitational practice and transmission to be formalized and officially monitored. See Gerald Groemer, "The Guild of the Blind in Tokugawa Japan," *Monumenta Nipponica* 56.3 (2001): 349–380.

41. The *Tōdōyōshū* (Collection of Fundamentals of the Guild, ca. 1634), the most elaborate guild record, traces the history of the *biwa hōshi* to antiquity; external sources including the *Chūin ippon ki* suggest that the guild actually came into existence during the early fourteenth century. For pertinent guild documents, see Atsumi Kaoru, Maeda Mineko, and Ubukata Takashige, eds. *Omura-ke zō Tōdōza, Heike biwa shiryō* (Kyoto; Daigakudō shoten, 1984). For the *Tōdōyōshū*, see Kondō Heijō, ed., *Tōdōyōshū*, vol. 27 of *Kaitei shiseiki shūran* (Kyoto: Rinsen shoten, 1984).

42. See, for example, Shinkawa Tokio, *Kanji bunka no naritachi to tenkai* (Tokyo: Yamakawa tosho shuppan, 2002) in Japanese and Thomas LaMarre's *Uncovering Heian Japan* (Durham, NC: Duke University Press, 2000) for recent engagements with this issue.

43. LaMarre's book includes a provocative discussion of the modern framing and reframing of this dialectic in response to the various factors informing scholarship at important moments over the past century. See particularly his Introduction, pp. 1–10.

44. Shinkawa, *Kanji bunka no naritachi to tenkai*, pp. 20–22.

45. Shinkawa, *Kanji bunka no naritachi to tenkai*, especially pp. 36–47. This is also a position taken by LaMarre.

46. Recent innovative work on this topic was presented by David Lurie in a paper entitled, "Nara and Heian Reading/Writing Practices and the Foundations

of Japanese Culture," at the Association for Asian Studies Annual Meeting, March 28, 2003.

47. Mizuhara Hajime's work has brought the Enkyōbon to the fore; the text has recently been a popular topic of scholarly concern in Kokubungaku (national literature) departments of prominent universities.

48. Quint, *Epic and Empire*, especially pp. 45–46.

49. Benedict Anderson's description of premodern conception(s) of temporality, in which "cosmology and history were indistinguishable" attributes a similar model to the Western medieval world; it holds truer in the Japanese context, however, probably in large part due to the prevalence of Buddhist worldviews that privileged non-teleological conceptions of time and space (in the form of return and rebirth primarily, but also in the idea of modeling and repetition found in mandala, for example). See Benedict Anderson, *Imagined Communities: Reflections on the Origin and Spread of Nationalism* (London and New York: Verso, 1991), p. 36.

50. Konishi Jin'ichi, in *"Heike monogatari no gentai to kado keitai: honmon hihan no kihonteki taido,"* in Hyōdō Hiromi, ed., Heike monogatari *katari to gentai* (Tokyo: Yūseidō, 1987), pp. 64–79, proposes dividing the texts into *tōdōkei* (guild-lineage) and *hitōdōkei* (non-guild-lineage) to emphasize the organized performativity associated with the *biwa hōshi* guild. Significantly, this nomenclature is adopted by Yamashita Hiroaki in his discussion of *Heike* variants and their genealogy in the *Nihon koten bungaku daijiten* and other general reference texts. Another rubric employed is the *ryakuhon* (abbreviated) versus *kōhon* (expanded) text lines. This categorization is generally used within one of the other two frameworks to discuss variants in each.

51. Kitahara Yasuo and Okawa Eiichi, eds., *Enkyōbon* Heike monogatari *honmonhen* (Tokyo: Bensei shuppan, 1996–1999), provides a complete annotated translation in two volumes and a comprehensive index, also in two volumes. Quotations from the Enkyōbon in this study are taken from this edition unless otherwise noted. Cited hereafter as Kitahara and Okawa, Enkyōbon.

52. See David T. Bialock, "Peripheries of Power: Voice, History and the Construction of Imperial and Sacred Space in *The Tale of the Heike* and Other Medieval and Heian Historical Texts," Ph.D. diss., Columbia University, 1997.

53. Sadler translated the *rufubon* in "The Heike Monogatari" and *The Ten Foot Square Hut* and *Tales of the Heike*.

54. Various manuscripts of the Kakuichibon as the primary base text for the *Heike monogatari* volumes are included in Takagi Ichinosuke et al., eds., *Nihon koten bungaku taikei*, vols. 32–33 (Tokyo: Iwanami shoten, 1958–1959); and Ichiko Teiji, ed., *Shinpen Nihon koten bungaku zenshū*, vols. 45–46 (Tokyo: Shogakkan, 1994). The text cited in this volume comes from Kajihara Masaaki and Yamashita Hiroaki, eds., *Shin Nihon koten bungaku taikei*, vols. 44–45 (Tokyo: Iwanami shoten, 1991–1993), hereafter cited as Kajihara and Yamashita, Kakuichibon.

55. See Kajihara and Yamashita, Kakuichibon.

56. The appellative Ōan is an era name during the reign of Go-Kōgon

(r. 1353–1371), fourth sovereign of the Northern Dynasty. The sovereign Chōkei was reigning concurrently for the Southern Dynasty.

57. The *Kanjō no maki*, translated as "The Initiates' Chapter" by McCullough, recounts the final destiny of Kenreimon'in, daughter of Kiyomori. She was also the mother of Sovereign Antoku, who drowned at the battle of Dan-no-ura. After the Genpei War, Kenreimon'in took the tonsure and retreated to Ōhara, where she prayed for the repose of her dead.

58. Kajihara and Yamashita, Kakuichibon, vol. 2, p. 409.

59. Hyōdō Hiromi, Heike monogatari *no rekishi to geinō* (Tokyo: Yoshikawa kobunkan, 2000), pp. 43–45.

60. See Hyōdō Hiromi, "Kakuichibon *Heike monogatari* no denrai o megutte," in *Heike biwa: katari to ongaku* (Tokyo: Hitsuji shobo, 1993), especially p. 58. This assertion is part of a larger argument that he makes about Ashikaga shogunal patronage of the Yasaka recitational line of *Heike biwa.* See also his *Heike monogatari no rekishi to bungei,* in which he constructs a lengthy argument about early patronage of the *biwa hōshi* by the Ashikaga shōguns.

61. The Minamoto (or Genji, written with the characters for "Minamoto" [*gen*] plus "clan" [*ji*]) descended from Sovereign Murakami. Likewise, the Seiwa Genji were descendents of Sovereign Seiwa. The "Heike," the clan portrayed as the sworn enemies of the Genji in the Genpei War, is a similarly sinicized reading of the characters for "Taira" (the family name) plus "house" [*ke*]. The Kanmu Heike are descendents of Sovereign Kanmu.

62. Michael G. Watson, "A Narrative Study of the Kakuichi-bon *Heike monogatari*" (Doctoral thesis, University of Oxford, 2003) is the most recent study on the text in English. A comprehensive evaluation of narrative structuring in the Kakuichibon variant, it is also an illustrative example of the usefulness of narratological approaches to the work.

63. Mizuhara Hajime, ed., *Shintei Genpei jōsuiki* (Tokyo: Shinjinbutsu ōraisha, 1988–1991), vols. 1–6. Cited hereafter as Mizuhara, *Jōsuiki.*

64. Yamashita Hiroaki, "Gen 'Heike' no omokage," in Kajiwara, Heike monogatari *no hikkei,* p. 16.

65. Nagazumi Yasuaki, *Hōgen monogatari, Heiji monogatari* (Tokyo: Kadokawa shoten, 1976), p. 16, cites a reference dated 1297 from the *Futsūshōdōshū* about the performance of all three.

66. Outlines of general textual issues pertaining to the *Hōgen monogatari* and *Heiji monogatari* can be found in Ichiko Teiji, ed., *Nihon koten bungaku daijiten* (Tokyo: Iwanami shoten, 1984), vol. 5, pp. 399–401 (*Heiji monogatari*) and pp. 424–426 (*Hōgen monogatari*). In English, see Varley, *Warriors of Japan as Portrayed in the War Tales,* pp. 50–53; 67–68.

67. Ichiko, *Nihon koten bungaku daijiten,* vol. 5, pp. 424–426; Varley, *Warriors of Japan as Portrayed in the War Tales,* p. 50.

68. Ichiko, *Nihon koten bungaku daijiten,* vol. 5, pp. 424–426; Varley, *Warriors of Japan as Portrayed in the War Tales,* p. 52.

69. Ichiko, *Nihon koten bungaku daijiten*, vol. 5, pp. 399–401; Varley, *Warriors of Japan as Portrayed in the War Tales*, p. 52.

70. Ichiko, *Nihon koten bungaku daijiten*, vol. 5, pp. 399–401; Varley, *Warriors of Japan as Portrayed in the War Tales*, p. 67.

71. In later texts, Kiyomori becomes a less heroic figure, suggesting the retrospective gaze of author/compilers active after the Genpei War. That he would be treated sympathetically in the apparently oldest text suggests the possibility that it was composed before the outcome of the Genpei War was clear. The subsequent foregrounding of Yoshihira, a Minamoto, similarly points to the sort of glorification of the Minamoto house that epitomizes the kinds of narratives included in this study.

72. There is one English translation of the *Gikeiki*: Helen C. McCullough, trans., *Yoshitsune: A Fifteenth-Century Japanese Chronicle* (Stanford, CA: Stanford University Press, 1971). Its introduction includes a comprehensive discussion of the relationships between individual episodes and shorter narratives within the *Gikeiki* to works in other genres. All English translations of the *Gikeiki* are from this text unless otherwise noted. Cited hereafter as McCullough, *Yoshitsune*.

73. Concise discussions of textual lineages for the *Gikeiki* can be found in the Ichiko, *Nihon koten bunkagu daijiten*, vol. 2, pp. 118–120, and in the introduction to McCullough's *Yoshitsune*, pp. 62–66.

74. See Ojima Yoshiyuki, "*Shintōshū* to *Soga monogatari* to no kankei," in Murakami Manabu, ed., *Nihon bungaku kenkyū taisei Gikeiki/Soga monogatari* (Tokyo: Kokusho kankō kai, 1993), p. 190.

75. For a discussion in English of *Soga* variants, see Thomas J. Cogan, trans., *The Tale of the Soga Brothers* (Tokyo: University of Tokyo Press, 1987), pp. xxxvi–xxxix.

76. See Tsukasaki Susumu, "*Soga monogatari* denshō ron," in Murakami, *Nihon bungaku kenkyū taisei Gikeiki/Soga monogatari*, p. 128.

77. The Taisekijibon is difficult to categorize. While on the one hand, it is linked closely to the Manabon through content and organization, the fact that it is written in *kana* connects it as well to the other *kana* texts. The problem in categorizing texts as either "*mana*" or "*kana*" (written or recited) is indicative of the inadequacies of compositional models based on simple bifurcations; further concerns this model raises for the *Soga* in particular are addressed more fully in Chapter Five.

78. See Murakami Manabu, "*Soga monogatari* no shohon," pp. 23–25. In Murakami Manabu, ed., *Nihon bungaku kenkyū taisei Gikeiki/Soga monogatari* (Tokyo: Kokusho kankō kai, 1993).

79. For a complete English translation with helpful additional materials and essays, see Cogan, *The Tale of the Soga Brothers*.

80. *Etoki bikuni* (picture-explaining nuns) and *nenbutsu hijiri* (itinerent priests who chanted the Amida buddha's name) were other wandering narrators (note again the overlap of what moderns would tend to separate into "entertainment" and "preaching"). The role of this sort of figure in the dissemination of popular narratives is the subject of Ruch's seminal article, cited above, as well as the work of

scholars in Japan including, prominently, Amino Fumihiko, in for example, *Umi to retto no chūsei* (Tokyo: Nihon edita sukuru shuppanbu, 1992), and Wakita Haruko in, for example, *Josei geinō no genryū* (Tokyo: Kadokawa shoten, 2001).

81. Murakami Manabu suggests that long, compact passages in the Manabon seem antithetical to performative art. See his entry for *Soga monogatari* in Ichiko, *Nihon koten bungaku daijiten*, vol. 4, pp. 39–41.

82. Murakami Manabu, entry for *Soga monogatari* in Ichiko, *Nihon koten bungaku daijiten*, p.40.

83. James Araki, *The Ballad-drama of Medieval Japan* (Berkeley: University of California Press, 1964) presents a study of the extant repertoire and translations of several pieces. In addition, a doctoral dissertation, "Reading the Kōwaka-mai as Medieval Myth: Story-Patterns, Traditional Reference, and Performance in Late Medieval Japan," by Todd A. Squires (Ohio State University, 2001) provides translations as well as a comprehensive treatment of five *kōwakamai*.

84. The characterization of *kōwakamai* as strictly a warrior theater is problematic within conventional paradigms for several reasons. First, it frequently features hints of "orality" generally associated with "popular performance." Second, the *kōwakamai* repertoire is not exclusively comprised of warrior narratives. Third, warrior narrative, as demonstrated by the wide dissemination of the *Heike*, the *Gikeiki*, *Soga monogatari*, and other tales of war and warriors, was hardly the exclusive possession of the warrior elite. While extant evidence does point to its popularity and patronage from within the warrior class, I would propose here that 1) we do not have proof that it was not performed for other audiences and 2) if *kōwakamai* was an artistic form solely controlled by warriors, this indicates that art supported by the ruling elite was not exclusively what Barbara Ruch calls the "canonical, participatory" style. Either way, *kōwakamai* presents an important challenge to established paradigms and represents a good reason to look beyond the written/oral and "canonical"/"repertory" divisions of medieval art. Ruch's argument is discussed in more detail in Chapter Two.

85. Araki, *The Ballad-drama of Medieval Japan*, pp. 8-9. Araki notes that, as in the *nō*, a third performer, when included, is referred to as the *tsure*. In modern performance, the medieval terms *waki* and *tsure* are replaced by *shite* and *waki* (p. 92).

86. Araki, *The Ballad-drama of Medieval Japan*, p. 92.

87. A journal entry from 1497 mentions a performance of two named pieces. This indicates to scholars that by this time, pieces were being titled, but before that they were performed as shorter units. See Muroki Yatarō's entry for *kōwakamai* in Ichiko, *Nihon koten bungaku daijiten*, vol. 2, p. 528.

88. See Kobayashi Kenji, "Eirihanpon 'Mai no hon' no sashie no keisei," in Fukuda Akira and Manabe Masahiro, eds., *Kōwaka bukyoku kenkyū*, vol. 10 (Tokyo: Miyai shoten, 1998), pp. 19–66.

89. Takehisa Takeshi, "Azuma kagami," in Kajihara, *Heike monogatari hikkei*, p. 165.

90. See Shinoda Minoru, *The Founding of the Kamakura Shogunate 1180–1185* (New York: Columbia University Press, 1960), p. 7.

91. Shinoda, *The Founding of the Kamakura Shogunate*, p. 8.

92. Takehisa, "Azuma kagami," in Kajihara, Heike monogatari *hikkei*, p. 165.

93. Shinoda, *The Founding of the Kamakura Shogunate*, p. 12.

94. Shinoda, *The Founding of the Kamakura Shogunate*, p. 10.

95. I use the word "chirographic" as defined by Walter Ong in his *Orality and Literacy: The Technologizing of the Word* (London: Methuen, 1982). He uses it identify cultures in which writing and reading play integral roles in the communication of meaning; this term, as opposed to "literate," is intended to remove the value judgment involved in the illiterate/literate paradigm while also more accurately describing the fundamental characteristics of a culture using a written language.

96. Brian Stock, *Listening for the Text: On the Uses of the Past* (Philadelphia: University of Pennsylvania Press, 1990), p. 146.

97. John M. Foley, *Immanent Art: From Structure to Meaning in Traditional Oral Epic* (Bloomington and Indianapolis: Indiana University Press, 1991), pp. 39–60. His model for referentiality in the oral setting is based on Wolfgang Iser's reader reception model. See Wolfgang Iser, *The Implied Reader: Patterns of Communication in Prose Fiction from Bunyan to Beckett* (Baltimore: Johns Hopkins University Press, 1974), especially pp. 16–17.

98. Foley, *Immanent Art*, p. 41.

99. Foley, *Immanent Art*, p. 59.

100. Ruch, "Medieval Jongleurs and the Making of a National Literature," p. 291.

101. Stock, *Listening for the Text*, p. 146. Originally conceptualized to describe marginal or heretical groups in medieval Europe, the term "textual communities," both in Stock's work and here, forms the basis for characterizing newly emerging audience groups as well.

Chapter 2: Minamoto Yoritomo

* Kitahara and Ogawa, Enkyōbon, vol. 2, pp. 549–550. All translations are by the author.

1. Okano Tomohiko, in his *Genji to Nihon kokuō* (Tokyo: Kōdansha gendai shinsho, 2003), argues for the untranslatability of the term "shōgun" into English (p. 166). One primary contention of his book is that the term was used by ensuing generations of shōguns to mean something like "king." This chapter tackles similar issues, particularly the idea of a special Minamoto identity linked to a military and political destiny tied to evolving ideas about the office of shōgun.

2. As will be discussed below, the term "shōgun" antedates Yoritomo by centuries, but it is in connection with Yoritomo that it takes on the political dimension we associate with it today.

3. Yoritomo was Yoshitomo's third son. The eldest, Yoshihira, is portrayed in

the *Heiji monogatari* as the loser-hero of the Heiji Uprising. Born in 1141, Yoshihira was executed following that rebellion in 1160. Tomonaga, the second son, was killed by Yoshitomo following a grievous injury that prevented his escape to the east country after their defeat in the Heiji Uprising.

4. Jeffrey P. Mass, in *Lordship and Inheritance in Early Medieval Japan* (Stanford, CA: Stanford University Press, 1989), argues that the war was in fact a series of private, local battles rather than the true war it is portrayed as in the war tales and the *Azuma kagami.* While his point that local concerns were of greater significance to many participants is well taken, the events of 1180–1185 came to be seen as a historically important moment as the medieval age progressed. It therefore does not contradict Mass to argue, as I do here, that certain events of those battles—the forcible removal of the sovereign and the Three Sacred Regalia from the capital, the loss of the sovereign and the sacred sword at sea during the war's final battle, and the attenuation of authority represented by Yoritomo's warrior government— were large-scale symbolic catastrophes that became mobilized in medieval narrative to help shape the epic struggle we know today as the Genpei War.

5. Presenting a particularly stark contrast with the Tōshōgu, Tokugawa Ieyasu's mausoleum at Nikkō.

6. Yamaji Aizan, *Minamoto no Yoritomo* (Tokyo: Heibonsha, 1987), p. 364.

7. Saeki Shin'ichi, in Heike monogatari *sogen* discusses the importance of his historical role as jurist in shaping those *Heike* variants strongly focused on glorifying the establishment of the Kamakura government. See particularly "Minamoto Yoritomo to gunki, setsuwa, monogatari," pp. 385–419.

8. Within the *Heike* repertoire, this characterization is stronger in the *yomihonkei* texts, whereas the *kataribonkei* texts tend to make him peripheral to their story. The bifurcation that scholars find between the two lineages is linked to this difference in narrative focus, as we shall see.

9. As marked by *genbuku*, the coming-of-age ceremony for boys, which usually occurs in their twelfth or thirteenth year.

10. The Ike Nun flourished in the late twelfth century. She was the wife of Tadamori, the stepmother of Kiyomori, and the mother of Yorimori. According to the *Heike*, following the Genpei War, Yorimori was spared and awarded holdings in recognition of his mother's intecession on behalf of the boys.

11. See Jeffrey P. Mass, *Warrior Government* (New Haven and London: Yale University Press, 1974), p. 59, on this issue.

12. Mass, *Warrior Government,* pp. 59–61.

13. Nagahara Keiji, *Minamoto no Yoritomo* (Tokyo: Iwanami shoten, 1995), p. 23.

14. All *Heike* variants of the Dream Interpretation narrative are considered to be constituents of the *yomihonkei.* In the *kataribonkei Heike* texts Yoritomo remains in exile for the opening chapters of the work, in which occasional references to him call him "the Izu Exile Minamoto no Yoritomo." His narrative absence and the frequent identification of him as an exile direct attention back

to his plight at the end of the Heiji Uprising and reinforce his displacement from the center and the key events of the closing years of the Heian period.

15. Nagahara, *Minamoto no Yoritomo*, p. 23.

16. Nagahara, *Minamoto no Yoritomo*, pp. 17–23. Sukechika's drastic action is a response to the daughter's liaison with an exile who is an enemy of the court and the Taira, not only the most powerful family at the time but also an important patron of the Itō. The infanticide is cited elsewhere in the legendary record as a primary cause for Yoritomo's animosity toward Sukechika's line, including the ill-fated Soga brothers. See Chapter Five.

17. The trope of the young noble in exile is prevalent enough that Orikuchi Shinobu labeled it *kishu ryūritan,* or "wandering noble" tale. See Orikuchi Shinobu, "Nihon bungaku no naiyō," in Orikuchi hakushi kinenkai, eds. *Orikuchi Shinobu zenshū,* vol. 7 (Tokyo: Chūō Kōronsha, 1965–1966). The wandering noble derives from mythological exiles like Susanō-o and Yamato-takeru, who are significant primarily as martial figures. Scholars recognize the transformation of the mythic hero into the amorous one in Heian works, in particular the *Ise monogatari* and *Genji monogatari;* see, for example, Norma Field, *The Splendor of Longing in the* Tale of Genji (Princeton, NJ: Princeton University Press, 1987), pp. 33–39; and Haruo Shirane, *The Bridge of Dreams: A Poetics of 'The Tale of Genji'* (Stanford, CA: Stanford University Press, 1987), pp. 3–4. Yoritomo here inherits qualities from both amorous and martial models—he reverses his status as an outcast by overcoming (political) obstacles, but this success is also closely linked to his romantic adventures with Sukechika's daughter and Masako.

18. Asahara Yoshiko and Kitahara Yasuo, eds., *Mai no hon,* vol. 59, *Shin Nihon koten bungaku taikei* (Tokyo: Iwanami shoten, 1994), pp. 138–143. Hereafter cited as Asahara and Kitahara, *Mai no hon.* All translations are my own.

19. Agō Torashin and Fukuda Akira, eds., *Kōwaka bukyoku kenkyū,* vol. 6 (Tokyo: Miyai shoten, 1991), pp. 229–246. Hereafter cited as Agō and Fukuda, *Kōwaka bukyoku kenkyū,* vol. 6. All translations are my own.

20. One mark of the *yomihonkei* lineage in the minds of contemporary scholars is its stronger focus on the victors. The *yomihonkei* is conventionally defined as those variants intended to be read as (historical) records of the Genpei War rather than performed as elegies for the Taira clan. Sorting out these differences and discerning whether their complexities allow such categorization is an ongoing scholarly project.

21. James Araki, *The Ballad-drama of Medieval Japan,* pp. 13–14. Although the present study is not focused specifically on the genre, I hope to provide some insight here about its relationship to other contemporary narratives and the important role it played as celebratory performance closely linked to one version of the history of the realm.

22. This episode appears at the conclusion of the *Heiji monogatari,* which ends following the disposition of rewards and punishments after the conflict. Thus although the *Heiji monogatari* version's placement of the episode in Yoritomo's life differs from that of the other texts, the very inclusion of the Dream Interpretation

narrative in the *Heiji monogatari* at all emphasizes its significance in all narratives re-counting Yoritomo's rise. Here, as elsewhere, it occurs when Yoritomo's fate seems grimmest.

23. The *Mai no hon*, a printed collection of *kōwakamai* libretti, more or less charts a chronology of the important Genpei-period stories. The result is some-thing like a long narrative of the rise of the Minamoto and the vendetta of the Soga brothers that occurred soon thereafter. The *Mai no hon* was circulated during the Tokugawa period; until that time, we think *kōwakamai* was strictly a performance genre, and each piece a discrete unit in itself. See Araki, *The Ballad-drama of Medieval Japan*, p. 4.

24. "Yume awase" follows "Ibuki," the story of Yoritomo's separation from his family at the end of the Heiji Uprising, and precedes "Uma-zoroe," which de-scribes his initial raising of troops.

25. In the *Heiji monogatari* identified as Adachi Moriyasu, who also serves as interpreter. The Tenri text identifies Morinaga as Moriyasu's son, but genealogies do not support this. Scholars believe this fabricated genealogy suggests that the composer/compiler was, consciously or not, accommodating the *Heiji monogatari* account. See Agō and Fukuda, *Kōwaka bukyoku kenkyū*, vol. 6, p. 231. According to the *Sonpi bunmyaku*, Morinaga was a Fujiwara descendent, son of Onoda Saburō Kanemori, but there are doubts about this attribution as well. He became husband to the daughter of Yoritomo's wet nurse. Following the Genpei War, he partici-pated in the subjugation of Ōshū in 1189, took the tonsure following Yoritomo's death in 1199, and served the shōgunal house until his death in 1200. See Asahara and Kitahara, *Mai no hon, furoku*, p. 7.

26. Descendent of the Kanmu Heike line, but a long-term resident of Sagami (*Mai no hon*, p. 138).

27. Mizuhara, *Jōsuiki*, vol. 2, p. 358. All translations are by the author.

28. Adachi Tō Kurō Morinaga. One of Yoritomo's closest retainers, he served in the capacity of the future shōgun's scribe. Morinaga's wife was the daughter of Yoritomo's wet nurse.

29. Mizuhara, *Jōsuiki*, vol. 2, pp. 358–359.

30. Tokimasa, Masako's father, went on to become one of Yoritomo's most important supporters. Following the death of Yoritomo, Tokimasa's descendants established themselves as shōgunal regents (*shikken*) and remained the most power-ful political figures in the shogunate throughout the Kamakura period. See Carl Steenstrup, *Hojo Shigetoki, 1198–1261, and His Role in the History of Political and Ethical Ideas in Japan* (London: Curzon Press, 1979), for a discussion of the Hōjō regency.

31. Kitahara and Ogawa, Enkyōbon, vol. 1, pp. 440–444. In this text, the Dream Interpretation episode is separated from Mongaku's visit to Yoritomo, which constitutes the opening episode of chapter 3.

32. Kitahara and Ogawa, Enkyōbon, vol. 1, p. 442. He requests that should he not be made shōgun, he be made lord of the eight provinces of the Bandō, and only short of that, master of Izu.

33. The sequence of episodes is: "The former commander of the right guards Yoritomo marries the third daughter of the Itō" (*Uhyōe no suke Yoritomo Itō no sanjo ni yome suru koto*); "The Death of Yoritomo's Son Senzuru" (*Yoritomo no shisoku Senzuru wo ushinawaruru koto*); "Yoritomo Marries the Eldest Daughter of the Hōjō" (*Yoritomo Hōjō chakujo ni yome suru koto*); and "The Story of Morinaga's Dream" (*Kurō Morinaga yume monogatari*). Found in Fukuda Toyohiko and Hattori Kōzō, eds., *Genpei tōjōroku: Bandō de umareta* Heike monogatari, vol. 1 (Tokyo: Kōdansha gakujitsu bunko, 1999–2000). The pertinent episodes are contained in pp. 160–191. Hereafter cited as Fukuda and Hattori, *Tōjōroku*. All translations are mine.

34. Fukuda and Hattori, *Tōjōroku*, p. 143.

35. In other texts, this role is fulfilled most frequently by Ono Naritstuna or Moritsuna; only here do we find Sadatsuna (Fukuda and Hattori, *Tōjōroku*, p. 141).

36. Fukuda and Hattori, *Tōjōroku*, p. 155.

37. Fukuda and Hattori, *Tōjōroku*, p. 164.

38. Fukuda and Hattori, *Tōjōroku*, p. 166.

39. A comparison of the third daughter of Itō to Wang Chao-chün is also included in the *Tōjōroku*, albeit not as a separate episode, which suggests that the *Soga monogatari* derives from the *Tōjōroku*.

40. See Cogan, *The Tale of the Soga Brothers*, p. 58. The narrative is also found in Mihashi Tokugen, Soga monogatari *chūkai* (Tokyo: Zoku gunshoruishō kanseikai, 1986), pp. 138–146. Hereafter cited as Mihashi, *Soga monogatari*. Translations are from Cogan except bracketed terms, which I have translated differently to maintain consistency of lexical items across narratives. This description is more elaborate than that found in the *Tōjōroku*, but contains the same sentiment and, at places, identical phrasing.

41. In the *Tōjōroku*, Sukezumi; according to the *Sonpi Bunmyaku*, his name was Suketada. Itō Sukechika's second son. Sukekiyo's role in the *Soga monogatari* is significant. He later adopts Ombō, the son of Itō Sukeyasu, born to the mother of the Soga brothers shortly after her husband's murder. The *Soga monogatari* relates that Yoritomo pardoned him for siding with the Taira against Yoritomo at Ishibashiyama because of the kindness we see Sukekiyo show the exiled Yoritomo here. Sukekiyo is later killed fighting for the Taira against Kiso Yoshinaka in the north; Ombō is then adopted by Minamoto Yoshinobu. See Cogan, *The Tale of the Soga Brothers*, pp. 42–43, 64–65.

42. Cogan, *The Tale of the Soga Brothers*, p. 52; Mihashi, *Soga monogatari*, p. 125.

43. The prominence of the "evil stepmother" trope in the *Soga monogatari* is unique among the variants considered here, but it appears frequently in Heian and medieval tale literature. Note that in the *Soga monogatari*, the evil stepmother provides a contrast with the good stepfather who later adopts the orphaned Jūrō and Gorō.

44. Cogan, *The Tale of the Soga Brothers*, p. 57; Mihashi, *Soga monogatari*, p. 138.

45. Ōba Heita Kageyoshi, a descendant of the Kanmu Heike, was a resident

of Sagami. He sided with Yoritomo at the beginning of the Genpei War and went on to become one of his most trusted advisors. Other more prominent members of his family were early enemies of Yoritomo: Ōba Kagechika was part of the original force with which Yoritomo clashed at Ishibashiyama. In the *Soga monogatari* account, we find this character identified as Heita Kagenobu, and scholars assume that the different name merely reflects a transcriptional or recitational error.

46. *Hyōe no suke*, or Assistant Commander of the Military Guards, was Yoritomo's court title prior to his exile following the Heiji Uprising. In most war tales, he is referred to as the Former Assistant Commander of the Military Guards and addressed as the Assistant Commander of the Military Guards. Here, as throughout the war tales, the title is used as a name; this occurs with not only Yoritomo but also most of the major characters in the works.

47. The Ippō Priest seems to have been a monk who was in attendance on Yoritomo during the period of exile. The identity of this man is unclear, but he is also mentioned elsewhere in the *Jōsuiki*. The appearance of the same name in the *Azuma kagami* is thought to be a reference to the same person. In the *Soga monogatari*, there is a young man identified as the Ippō Priest in attendance on Yoritomo on the night of the brothers' attack.

48. Ono Naritsuna. He seems to have been in attendance on Yoritomo throughout the latter's exile in Izu, and he was later awarded holdings in the east. In the *Jōsuiki*, he is in attendance at the time the dream occurs.

49. Mizuhara, *Jōsuiki*, vol. 2, pp. 359–360.

50. Mizuhara, *Jōsuiki*, vol. 2, p. 360.

51. The pardon is not part of the documentary record, a situation that will be repeated in equally important circumstances in Chapters Three and Four. The importance of documents generally speaking, however, is underlined by the frequency with which both real and fictional documents appear in the narrative record.

52. Kitahara and Ogawa, Enkyōbon, vol. 1, p. 443.

53. Saplings and other new greens are picked on the first day of the rat in the New Year and used in felicitous celebrations for the longevity of the realm.

54. In the *Jōsuiki* and "Yume awase" accounts, it is Kageyoshi who arrives.

55. Cogan, *The Tale of the Soga Brothers*, pp. 57–60; Mihashi, *Soga monogatari*, p. 138.

56. According to *Azuma kagami*, Sanechika was the younger brother of Ōmi Masamitsu. He served Yoritomo during the battle of Ishibashiyama and was rewarded as well for his service against the Ōshū Fujiwara.

57. Cogan, *The Tale of the Soga Brothers*, p. 57; Mihashi, *Soga monogatari*, pp. 138–139.

58. Cogan, *The Tale of the Soga Brothers*, pp. 59–60; Mihashi, *Soga monogatari*, p. 140.

59. Cogan, *The Tale of the Soga Brothers*, pp. 59–60; Mihashi, *Soga monogatari*, p. 142.

60. See annotation in Asahara and Kitahara, *Mai no hon*, p. 138. These categories are modern, but the possibility of a category dedicated to Yoritomo suggests a presence here that he does not have in other genres. This is due in large part to the general congratulatory nature of the *kōwakamai*, an issue explored throughout this study.

61. Asahara and Kitahara, *Mai no hon*, pp. 138–143.

62. For example, Yoritomo teases Morinaga for his pre-dawn visit by saying, "My goodness, Lord Adachi, you're up even earlier than usual this morning!" Morinaga's digression into the auspicious history of dreams elicits, "Yes, yes, that was certainly an auspicious dream. Now get on with it!" from Kagenobu.

63. The contents of this dream diverges somewhat from the more common "white elephant" dream attributed to the historical Buddha's mother, which also includes his birth from her sleeve.

64. Scholars are unsure about this toponym, but speculate that it refers to the eastern hills of Kyoto. See annotation in Asahara and Kitahara, *Mai no hon*, p. 140.

65. Attire often associated with the performance of court ritual.

66. In the Kan'ei variant, the second dream ends at this point, with the addition that Yoritomo takes seven steps in the four cardinal directions (interpreted as indicating that "the seven obstacles have been overcome;" Asahara and Kitahara, *Mai no hon*, p. 140). The remainder of the dream is recorded as a separate third dream.

67. Fukuda establishes a genealogy for an Ōba Kisō in the Tenri variant (see Agō and Fukuda, *Kōwaka bukyoku kenkyū*, vol. 6, pp. 235–236).

68. In legend, eating a nine-holed abalone assures long life. This motif is not mentioned in the dream interpretation.

69. Asahara and Kitahara, *Mai no hon*, p. 141.

70. Asahara and Kitahara, *Mai no hon*, p. 142.

71. Agō and Fukuda, *Kōwaka bukyoku kenkyū*, vol. 6, p. 237.

72. Asahara and Kitahara, *Mai no hon*, p. 142.

73. Asahara and Kitahara, *Mai no hon*, p. 143.

74. Tochigi Yoshitada et al., eds., *Hōgen monogatari, Heiji monogatari, Jōkyūki*, vol. 43, *Shin Nihon koten bungaku taikei* (Tokyo: Iwanami shoten, 1992), pp. 264–273. Hereafter cited as Tochigi, *Heiji monogatari*. All translations are by the author.

75. Tochigi, *Heiji monogatari*, p. 270. The Takebe Shrine within the narrative context is associated with the Minamoto. Note in Chapter Three that Kiso Yoshinaka is said to have had his coming-of-age ritual performed at Iwashimizu Hachimangū, a shrine famously connected to the Seiwa Genji.

76. At which Hachiman, patron deity of the Minamoto, is worshipped; it is located on the east bank of the Yodo River, south of Kyoto. Iwashimizu Hachimangū in fact became an important part of the Ashikaga shōguns' narrativization of their own authorial (Minamoto) identity. The investing of tropes like the Iwashimizu Hachimangū with narrative meaning for the Minamoto rise is emblematic of the narrative and historical processes I address here.

77. Tochigi, *Heiji monogatari*, pp. 270–271.

78. See Inui Yoshihisa, "*Heiji monogatari* no seiritsu—hito to toki to ba," in Tochigi Yoshitada et al., eds., Heiji monogatari *no seiritsu* (Tokyo: Kyūko shoin, 1998), pp. 180–201. Inui focuses specifically on the inclusion of the narrative of Yoritomo's rise as one lens through which development of the textual lines can be explored.

79. Sotonohama represents the northeastern edge of the realm. Hokkaidō, the northernmost of Japan's major islands, had not yet been assimilated into the realm at this time. Although colonization by the Japanese began during the Kamakura period, an outpost occupied by the Matsumae clan was not established on the Ōshima peninsula until the Edo period. Kikaigashima is a legendary island off Kyushu. For the Kakuichibon's description of it in relation to the Shishinotani exiles, see McCullough, *The Tale of the Heike*, pp. 82–100 and 110–115.

80. The term for jug, *heiji*, is subject of a well-known pun on the Taira family name found in the Shishigatani episode of the *Heike*: breaking the jug symbolizes crushing the Taira.

81. See "The Night Attack at the Courtiers' Hall" (1.2), in McCullough, *The Tale of the Heike*, p. 24; Kajiwara and Yamashita, Kakuichibon, vol. 2, p. 7.

82. Hachiman Tarō Yoshiie is cited as ancestor for the Minamoto in not only the *Heike*, but also the *Hōgen monogatari, Heiji monogatari*, and *Soga monogatari*, as well as in other genres celebrating the warrior class. On the one hand, he is the prototypical Minamoto, but on the other, he is also in many ways the cultural ancestor of the warrior class, and to a lesser degree non-aristocrats more generally, as his sphere of action was the provinces. That he was not properly supported by the throne following the Latter Three Years' War, and forced to reward his provincial supporters from his own coffers, further contributes to his characterization as a non-aristocratic hero.

83. Hyōdō Hiromi notes that the relationship between the early Ashikaga shōguns and performers of the *Heike* reflected a seemingly conscious play by the Ashikaga to co-opt the Genpei history recounted in the tale as a necessary and fortuitous step toward their own rise to power. Early shōguns actively patronized *Heike* reciters; a 1452 colophon of the Kakuichibon text in fact claims that it was commended to the Muromachi Lord (presumably Ashikaga Yoshimitsu). Both the Ashikaga and later the Tokugawa claimed and documented their places within the Minamoto lineage (Heike monogatari *no rekishi to geinō*, p. 15). This connection is somewhat problematic, as recitational texts tend not to idealize the Minamoto victors explicitly; Hyōdō's assertion does however suggest the fundamental link between the placatory and the laudatory. For other discussions of the links between the office of shōgun and the Seiwa Genji for later generations, see Yamashita Hiroaki, *Ikusa monogatari to Genji shōgun* (Tokyo: Miyai shoten, 2003), especially pp. 155–174; Okano, *Genji to Nihon kokuō*, pp. 166–208.

84. The process of dynastic shedding created numerous new "families" descended from a prince who was reduced to commoner status, given a family name

(the sovereign has none), and granted gubernatorial rights over outlying provincial areas. The Minamoto in question here are the descendants of the sovereign Seiwa (r. 858–876), while Taira Kiyomori descended from an offspring of the sovereign Kanmu (r. 781–806). The Minamoto name has particular cultural significance as that granted the hero of *Genji monogatari*, widely thought to be based on the historical Minamoto Takaakira, first-generation descendent of the sovereign Daigo. Although not a specific referent in Yoritomo's story, Takaakira represents another famous exile—framed by Fujiwara rivals, he was appointed to serve at Dazaifu, which effectively shattered his political aspirations. The link between Yoritomo and his royal antecedent is accentuated in Genpei narrative—in the Kakuichibon *Heike* the history of Seiwa, the progenitor of the line, constitutes most of an episode.

85. Karl Friday, *Hired Swords: The Rise of Private Warrior Power in Early Japan* (Stanford, CA: Stanford University Press, 1992), p. 91.

86. Varley, *Warriors of Japan as Portrayed in the War Tales*, pp. 46–77. Varley provides a concise description of each of these campaigns.

87. Mass, *Lordship and Inheritance*, pp. 37–38.

88. For the Kakuichibon account, see McCullough, *The Tale of the Heike*, pp. 172–173 and Kajiwara and Yamashita, Kakuichibon, vol. 1, pp. 275–279. For the *Jōsuiki* account, see Mizuhara, *Jōsuiki*, vol. 2, pp. 331–334.

89. A topic that will figure prominently in Chapter Five as well.

90. See Sacki Shin'ichi, "'Chōteki' izen" in *Kokugo to kokubungaku* 74.11 (November, 1997): 94–102. Saeki notes that the term *sei-i tai shōgun* is used in works as early as the *Nihon shoki* to identify the general entrusted with subduing the peripheries of the realm. In this early usage, the term designated a person as commander-in-chief for the duration of his engagement with the enemy.

91. Saeki, "'Chōteki' izen," pp. 94–97.

92. Jeffrey Mass ("Yoritomo and Feudalism" in *Antiquity and Anachronism*, pp. 70–91) discusses this issue.

93. Documents generally include the title of both the addressee (where appropriate) and the promulgator. In Yoritomo's case, he frequently signs documents he authors with "Utaishō." See Mass, *Antiquity and Anachronism*, p. 21.

94. The Hōjō went on to annihilate the Hiki in armed conflict in 1203. After the death of Yoritomo's final heir, Sanetomo (the third Kamakura Lord and shōgun), the position was filled by aristocrats brought from the capital. Although it may appear strange that, with the death of the last Minamoto heir, the Hōjō did not simply seize the position of control, they were apparently sufficiently empowered by the regent system that it served them best to leave the post of shōgun intact and separate from their own.

95. Mass, *Antiquity and Anachronism*, p. 77.

96. The exile system was codified in 724 by the sovereign Shōmu, who established a three-tiered system of near-, mid-, and distant exile (*konru*, *chūru*, and *onru*, respectively) that defined the terms delineating punishments and appropriate

banishment locations for each level. Six sites were demarcated for distant exile, including Tosa, Oki, Sado, Awa, Hitachi, and Izu.

97. I am grateful to Thomas R. Howell for this insight. He discusses both dream accounts in "Setsuwa, Knowledge, and the Culture of Reading and Writing in Medieval Japan" (Ph.D. dissertation, University of Pennsylvania, 2002).

98. For one of the most influential discussions of liminality, see Victor Turner, *Dramas, Fields, and Metaphors* (Ithaca, NY, and London: Cornell University Press, 1974), pp. 23–59; especially pp. 25–30. Turner's conceptualization of liminal individuals as actors who initiate shifts in cultural paradigms by tapping into the power of metaphor seems particularly appropriate here, as it is the marginality of Yoritomo's predicament that enables this re-writing of meaning.

99. The *kōwakamai*'s expanded borders probably reflect the relatively late date of the work's creation—such an interest in continental places most likely expresses a worldview postdating the Mongol invasion or even the conflicts that gave rise to the Sengoku period.

100. The term Nippongoku appears prominently in variants of the *Heike, Soga monogatari, Hōgen monogatari*, and *Heiji monogatari* as well as the *Taiheiki*.

101. Although the *Heiji monogatari* image is, as with the rest of the narrative, distinct from the other versions, it echoes the primary themes evoked in them.

102. The term *rokujūrokkagoku* is found in the *Heike* and other texts dating from the early Muromachi period.

103. The exception being the priest Gikei (former self of Yoshitsune, who would, of course, be reborn not as intimate retainer but rival brother).

104. In all versions of the *rokujūrokubu* origin story, some conflict is recorded between the former incarnations of Yoshitsune and Kagetoki. In one story, they are merely rival priests, and in another, Yoshitsune was formerly incarnated as a mouse that nibbled on Kagetoki's sutras.

105. This description resonates, of course, with the Izanagi/Izanami creation myth of stirring the yet-unformed world with the sword. It is difficult to assess the significance of this link, but the use of a similar motif might be read to imply the newness or creativity embodied in Yoritomo's rise, especially in his role as progenitor of the warrior world. That he stirs the purple eightfold clouds also nods to the Buddhist worldview, in which purple clouds signify the Western Paradise.

106. The "purple clouds" mentioned in this account are a conventional reference to the capital. Asahara and Kitahara, *Mai no hon*, p. 140.

107. Lady Nijō's dreams in *Towazugatari*, for example.

108. Norma Field's probing discussion of the role of prophecy broadly as representing a "sacred world of transcendental knowledge potent enough to govern human relativity" that becomes, in fiction (specifically the *Genji*), the motivation for transgressive action is instructive here. Although this study addresses a narrative with specific historical dimensions, prophesy as she describes it in the *Genji* operates similarly: it foretells a reality that is puzzling in the context in which it is revealed, thus providing the impetus for a transformative narrative. Although the contexts are very

different between the worlds of the *Genji* and Genpei historical tales, both generate their narratives through invocation of the prophesy trope; the significance of established traditions of fictional as well as historical narrative, therefore, is of vital importance for this study. See Norma Field, *The Splendor of Longing in the* Tale of Genji, p. 27.

109. For a discussion of dreams as prognosticators of political and military future events in the early Chinese context, see John Brennan, "Dreams, Divination, and Statecraft: The Politics of Dreams in Early Chinese History and Literature," in Carol Schreier Rupprecht, ed. *The Dream and the Text: Essays on Literature and Language* (Albany, NY: State University of New York Press, 1993), pp. 73–95. Brennan notes the public nature of political dreams, which could be dreamt by persons other than the sovereign, but prognosticate future events for the realm or the sovereign. They were seen, as they are here, as communications from the gods.

Chapter 3: Kiso Yoshinaka

1. For a discussion of the absence of a consistent characterization of the Minamoto as a coherent and unified unit in documents from this period, see Mass, *Antiquity and Anachronism*, pp. 52–53.

2. Saeki Shin'ichi, in discussing the characterization of Minamoto Yoritomo in the Enkyōbon, hints at something similar in his discussion of forged documents attributed to Yoritomo awarding land rights as reward for support in the campaign against the Taira. See Saeki, Heike monogatari *no sogen*, pp. 385–395.

3. In the post-Genpei medieval world this is perhaps not a surprising trend, since during this period court cases for members of all classes became a much more common event, and the tools of the court—oral witness, buttressed by written proof—were entering vernacular experience. For a discussion of early Kamakura judiciary policy, see Jeffrey P. Mass, *The Development of Kamakura Rule, 1180–1250* (Stanford, CA: Stanford University Press, 1979).

4. Although this is less true for *yomihonkei* texts (the Enkyōbon in particular), the introduction of Yoshinaka inevitably occurs as the worlds of the capital and the peripheries come into sustained contact with each other, as it is from this point that the insurgent Minamoto enter the capital and force the Taira to flee.

5. Prince Mochihito was a son of Retired Sovereign Go-Shirakawa by the daughter of the Kaga Major Counselor Suenari. He is significant historically for the call to arms discussed here. His actual degree of volition in the call to arms is a matter of historical debate: the Kakuichibon and most other *Heike* variants depict him as the somewhat reticent sponsor of a move urged by Minamoto Yorimasa (uncle of Yoritomo, Yoshinaka, and Yoshitsune). In other variants, however, he is a more aggressive participant (for example, the Enkyōbon). In the *Heike* texts, he is referred to by his more common appellative, Prince Takakura (*Takakura no miya*). In this study, I follow the convention in *Heike* scholarship by referring to him as Mochihito, to avoid confusion with his half-brother, the sovereign Takakura, who was also the father of the sovereign Antoku.

6. Exilic narratives within early Japanese writing tend to focus on the pathetic figure of the wronged (often slandered) good minister who is unjustly hounded from the capital. This is a trope that derives from Chinese narrative and becomes fully integrated into Japanese by the early Heian period. Narratives (and poetry) connected to Sugawara Michizane exhibit this tendency, and it is also an important feature in depictions of the protagonists of *Ise monogatari* and *Genji monogatari*. For a discussion of Michizane's life, see Robert Borgen, *Sugawara no Michizane and the Early Heian Court* (Honolulu: University of Hawai'i Press, 1994). The trope of the pathetic exile both in historical and fictional narrative continued to be a vital interpretive tool in medieval times as well—it is central not only to Genpei narrative, but also renderings of the lives of culturally significant exiles including Zeami, Nichiren, and Go-Daigo.

7. See, for example, Victor W. Turner, "Pilgrimages as Social Processes," in *Dramas, Fields, and Metaphors*, pp. 166–230, especially pp. 196–199.

8. For ease of reference in this discussion of the Kakuichibon narrative, English titles of episodes are followed by their location within the text by chapter and episode number. "The Sea Bass" (1.3) is in chapter 1, episode 3, for example.

9. One of the reasons cited for Mochihito's call to arms is a physiognomy reading that his "is the countenance of one who could ascend the throne. It would be a mistake for him to remove himself from public affairs" (McCullough, *The Tale of the Heike*, p. 138). This prediction, of course, was proven wrong, since Mochihito lost his life soon after he called the Minamoto to arms against the Taira.

10. The general narrative structuring of the other accounts will be taken up later in this chapter; one noteworthy point, however, is that omens and citing of precedent generally are important narrative frames in all cases. The de-centering of the capital as a locus of power, however, is handled differently elsewhere, particularly in the Enkyōbon and *Jōsuiki* texts, which emphasize peripheral activities earlier in the narrative. Although these differences mark important distinctions in narrative focus among the variants, in all cases the rise of the peripheries to challenge a corrupt center is a fundamental motif.

11. McCullough, *The Tale of the Heike*, p. 139.

12. Takakura is forced to abdicate on 1180/2/21 in favor of his son, Antoku, born to Kiyomori's daughter Tokushi (later Kenreimon'in).

13. For a discussion of Kiso's status in relation to other power holders, see Ōtsu Yūichi, "Yoshinaka kō" in *Nihon bungaku* 39.7 (1990): 35–44.

14. For a discussion of Yoshinaka's paradoxical character, see Mizuhara Hajime, *Enkyōbon* Heike monogatari *ronkō* (Tokyo: Katō Chūdōkan, 1979), p. 335–355.

15. Yoshinaka successfully navigates protocol through writing documents in the episodes considered in this chapter and also in "Kiso Yoshinaka's Letter to Enryakuji," (Kakuichibon 7.10) immediately preceding his entry into the capital. From that point on, however, he is unsuccessful. Beginning with "Nekoma" (Kakuichibon 8.6), in other words, he is no longer a master of communication—he

misreads his surroundings and ceases to author communiqués (at least within narrative accounts)—and he consequently is drummed out of the capital and killed.

16. McCullough, *The Tale of the Heike*, p. 207.

17. Despite the close ties to the capital enjoyed by members of the branches of the Seiwa Genji during the latter years of the Heian period, the Minamoto name is consciously and consistently attached to the eastern provinces in *Heike* narrative. The characterization of the Minamoto as provincial is a recurring theme in this study. See Mass, *Antiquity and Anachronism*, pp. 78–80. See also Jeffrey P. Mass, "The Missing Minamoto in the Twelfth-Century Kanto," *Journal of Japanese Studies* 19.1 (Winter 1993): 121–145.

18. Tomikura speculates that, due to the timing (immediately prior to the Hōgen Uprising), the dispute between Yoshihira and Yoshikata was about establishing Minamoto hegemony in the eastern provinces (Tomikura, *Zenchūshaku*, vol. 2, p. 202). This is generally corroborated in the historical record: see Kanagawa ken kiga chōsa kenshi henshū shitsu, ed., *Kanagawa ken shi, shiryo hen* (Yokohama: Dai Nihon insatsu, 1971), vol. 1, p. 230. It should be noted, however, that records concerning the incident in which Yoshikata was killed are taken from the *Heike monogatari* and the *Hyakurenshō*, a historical text of unknown authorship that is sometimes attributed to Sovereign Kameyama (r. 1259–1274). Thus our understanding of the cause of the falling out is a product of the narrative characterization of Yoshinaka woven in the *Heike*. Whether the cause of the fatal dispute is accurate or not, it clearly resonated with later audiences as a believable characterization of late Heian warrior activities in the Kantō. This suggests that it was meaningful as well in the context of contemporary, Kamakura- and early Muromachi-era concepts about warrior behavior, an issue that arises again in the discussion of Yoshinaka's Petition.

19. The assertion of Yoshihira's intent to have Yoshinaka killed is made in the *Jōsuiki*; the fact that he would be sent so far from home after his father's death implies this concern generally.

20. The concept of *sōryō* was part of the court structure of Heian Japan, and the Minamoto as an essentially aristocratic family was subject to this frame for inheritance practices. The *sōryō* was determined not by birth order but rather by family rank of both parents; a strong maternal family, especially, lent credence to a son's potential claim to this status. See Mass, *Lordship and Inheritance*, pp. 58–93. Yoritomo was the only of Yoshitomo's remaining sons whose mother came from an aristocratic family, and he was a clear favorite to inherit his father's mantle as clan head.

21. As described in the "Shimizu no kanja" episode that opens chapter 7.

22. Hero of the Later Three Years War, after which Yoshiie was forced to grant awards to his retainers from his own holdings after the court refused to compensate them, claiming that the war was a private affair and not under the jurisdiction of the government. Yoshiie's benevolence, so the legend goes, won the loyalty of his followers, whose descendents would then become followers of Yoshitomo and later Yoritomo.

23. For a discussion of variant explanations of Yoshinaka's taking of the name Jirō, see Tomikura, *Zenchūshaku*, vol 2, p. 202.

24. Tomikura, *Zenchūshaku*, vol. 2, p. 202.

25. Tomikura, *Zenchūshaku*, vol. 2, p. 203.

26. McCullough, *The Tale of the Heike*, p. 207.

27. In most *yomihonkei* texts, this moment is narrated a little differently, as we shall see below.

28. Kitahara and Ogawa, Enkyōbon, vol. 1, p. 597.

29. Mizuhara, *Jōsuiki*, vol. 3, p. 239.

30. Mizuhara, *Jōsuiki*, vol. 3, p. 240.

31. The origin of the term "ox-head" for these talismen is debated. One explanation is that "ox head" (*goō*) is a transcription error of "tutelary god" (*ubusuna*); another is that the original reference was to ox "tama" (*tama* meaning testicles, or gall or kidney stones—in the medieval period, the character *tama* was generally used where *ō* is found in modern parlance) and referred metaphorically to alleged curative powers of these medicinal objects. What is certain, however, is that the ox-head talisman is a conventional apparatus used for a number of purposes today. Ox-head talismen are closely affiliated with a number of significant religious sites, particularly the Kumano shrines. They are made of rectangular pieces of bark or rice paper and are inscribed on one side with the name of a specific deity or religious institution. The name is written in "crow characters," in which each stroke or group of strokes within each character takes on the shape of a stylized crow. This practice became associated with ox-head talismen in the Sengoku period. See *Nihonshi daijiten* (Tokyo: Heibonsha, 1992–1994), vol. 3, p. 187.

32. Horiike Shunpō, *Todaiji omizutori* (Tokyo: Shogakkan, 1996), p. 143.

33. Mizuhara, *Jōsuiki*, vol. 3, p. 241.

34. Kujō Kanezane's journal and Jien's seven-volume history of Japan, respectively. The former is a contemporary, day-to-day record while the latter is a reflective history stretching back to the age of the gods; both provide important additional narratives of the period.

35. I take the Kakuichibon as the base text for this consideration because of its availability in English translation and the familiarity of its narrative. The general chronology of the codification of these texts is as follows: the Enkyōbon, Hyakunijukkubon, and Nagatobon are all considered to be early; next come the Kakuichibon, the *Jōsuiki*, and finally the *kōwakamai*.

36. Modern pronunciation: *gansho*.

37. It is not the first document accredited to Yoshinaka in other variants, as evidenced in the *Jōsuiki* account that follows.

38. McCullough, *The Tale of the Heike*, p. 228.

39. Tomikura, *Zenchūshaku*, vol. 2, p. 309.

40. Kitahara and Ogawa, Enkyōbon, vol. 2, p. 32.

41. Kitahara and Ogawa, Enkyōbon, vol. 2, p. 32.

42. Mizuhara Hajime, Hyakunijukkubon, vol. 2 of his *Heike monogatari* (3

vols.) in *Shinchō Nihon koten shūsei* (Tokyo: Shinchōsha, 1979–1981), pp. 184–193. Hereafter cited as Mizuhara, Hyakunijukkubon.

43. Mizuhara, Hyakunijukkubon, p. 185.

44. Kokusho kankōkai, ed., Heike monogatari *Nagatobon* (Tokyo: Meishō kankōkai, 1974), p. 453. Hereafter cited as Kokusho kankōkai, Nagatobon.

45. McCullough, *The Tale of the Heike*, p. 228.

46. This is the kind of passage that scholars looking for indications of oral composition cite as demonstrative of an oral tradition, since orally composed works tend to be repetitive (see Ong, *Orality and Literacy*, especially pp. 38–39). Murakami Manabu discusses repetition of specific terminology in terms of the oral origins of *katari* in "*Heike monogatari* e no sasoi: kataru monogatari to yomu monogatari no aida," in *Aera Mook Special Number 31:* Heike monogatari *ga wakaru* (Tokyo: Asahi Shinbunsha, 1997), pp. 5–8. He argues that the Kakuichibon rendering, with its more subtle integration of repetition, reflects a honing of orally derived material by compilers who saw the creation of a text as a literary endeavor. I would suggest that, given the thematic centrality of knowledge possession and interpretation in this episode, compounded by the relative infrequency of this sort of exact repetition in the *Heike* generally (as well as in this episode), repetition stems more specifically from thematic rather than formal concerns here.

47. Kitahara and Ogawa, Enkyōbon, vol. 2, p. 33.

48. Mizuhara, Hyakunijukkubon, pp. 185–186.

49. Asahara and Kitahara, *Mai no hon*, p. 206.

50. This kind of advice is also common in the Chinese context; the ninth month follows the season for revering the dead (the eighth month), a particularly inauspicious time for causing death.

51. Kitahara and Ogawa, Enkyōbon, vol. 2, p. 33.

52. Sadayoshi, who had been successful in subduing Chinzei. Kageie feared that if the northern campaign were to pause at this point, Sadayoshi would in a better position than he, Kageie, to be rewarded for his actions.

53. Kitahara and Ogawa, Enkyōbon, vol. 2, p. 33.

54. Kitahara and Ogawa, Enkyōbon, vol. 2, p. 34; Kokusho kankōkai, Nagatobon, p. 455; Tomikura, *Zenchūshaku*, vol. 2, p. 310; Mizuhara, *Jōsuiki*, vol. 4, p. 67; Mizuhara, Hyakunijukkubon, vol. 2, p. 186; Asahara and Kitahara, *Mai no hon*, p. 206.

55. McCullough, *The Tale of the Heike*, p. 228; Tomikura, *Zenchūshaku*, vol. 2, p. 310. The response varies slightly in wording from variant to variant, but all identify the shrine as Hachiman's. Today, one can visit the Hanyū Gokoku Hachiman in Takaoka City, Toyama Prefecture, where there is a monument commemorating Yoshinaka's petition and an etching on a stone tablet of the *ganjo*.

56. Mizuhara, Hyakunijukkubon, vol. 2, p. 186; Mizuhara, *Jōsuiki*, vol. 4, p. 67; Asahara and Kitahara, *Mai no hon*, p. 207.

57. Kitahara and Ogawa, Enkyobon, vol. 2, p. 34; Kokusho kankōkai, Nagatobon, p. 455; Asahara and Kitahara, *Mai no hon*, p. 206; Mizuhara, Hyakunijukkubon, vol. 2, p. 186; Tomikura, *Zenchūshaku*, vol. 2, p. 310; Mizuhara, *Jōsuiki*, vol. 4, p. 67.

58. McCullough, *The Tale of the Heike*, p. 229; Tomikura, *Zenchūshaku*, vol. 2, p. 310; Mizuhara, Hyakunijukkubon, vol. 2, p. 186; Kitahara and Ogawa, Enkyō-bon, vol. 2, p. 35; Mizuhara, *Jōsuiki*, vol. 4, p. 68; Kokusho kankōkai, Nagatobon, p. 455; Asahara and Kitahara, *Mai no hon*, p. 207.

59. Mizuhara Hajime discusses Kakumei's role in *Enkyōbon* Heike mono-gatari *ronkō*, p. 336.

60. Tomikura, *Zenchūshaku*, vol. 2, pp. 310–312, discusses the various ver-sions of Kakumei's post-Yoshinaka existence. The most common of these recounts that he changed his name (again), went to Hakone Shrine, and remained there undiscovered for some years. Later, when Yoritomo realized that he has been Yoshinaka's scribe, Kakumei was forced to flee. See also Mizuhara, *Enkyōbon* Heike monogatari *ronkō*, pp. 336–341.

61. McCullough, *The Tale of the Heike*, p. 229.

62. Mizuhara, *Jōsuiki*, vol. 4, p. 70

63. Mizuhara, *Jōsuiki*, vol. 4, p. 70.

64. Asahara and Kitahara, *Mai no hon*, p. 209.

65. Kenneth Butler, in "The *Heike monogatari* and the Japanese Warrior Ethic," *Harvard Journal of Asiatic Studies* 29 (1969): 93–108, notes the prevalence of this sort of formula in his discussion of the *Heike* as oral literature. While it is hard to endorse an assessment of the *Heike* as a purely or even primarily oral lit-erature, this is one of a number of formulaic usages found throughout the vari-ants that, whether oral or not, consistently serves the function of introducing a warrior as he prepares to do battle (and frequently heroic last battle). Here, it is most noteworthy for its seeming incongruity, as discussed above.

66. Mizuhara further notes the similarity of Kakumei's appearance here to that of Benkei, Yoshitsune's trusted retainer (and sometimes scribe) and raises the possibility that the (possibly fictional) character of Benkei is modeled on the description of Kakumei here. (NHK koten kodoku: *Heike monogatari*, tape 32).

67. Because it is not part of the *Heike biwa* performance tradition, the Dream Interpretation narrative discussed in Chapter Two is not considered in terms of musicality.

68. Komoda Haruko, "Heikyoku kyokusetsu to ongaku kōzō," p. 178. The names of *kyokusetsu* are not always written with the same *kanji*, so translations of the names into English remove us one step further from their meaning in the *Heike* con-text; they should be used advisedly, but are translated here for general reference.

69. *Hiroimono* (martial pieces) are conventionally juxtaposed with *fushimono* (lyrical pieces), and each group is musically marked by the employment of various specific *kyokusetsu*. Both the *hiroi* and *kō no koe kyokusetsu* are associated with *hiroi-mono*, and they share the characteristic of being high-pitched and commonly used in military descriptions. This said, *hiroimono* and *fushimono* are general categories, and therefore not always definitively descriptive. The Ganjo episode, for instance, contains no military actions, but it is generally "military" in both its narrative con-tent and in the *kyokusetsu* comprising it.

70. Most battle dressing sequences are shortly followed by name-announcing and/or recitation of military lineage.

71. This passage is performed in *shiragoe* (plain voice) *kyokusetsu* followed by *hazumi* (breaking), *kudoki* (narrating), and *kowarisage* (descending) *kyokusetsu*, modes commonly associated with the sort of straightforward narration found in descriptions of lineage for warriors as well. Komoda, "Heikyoku kyokusetsu to ongaku kōzō," p. 168.

72. As exemplified most memorably by Tsunemasa (and his biwa), Atsumori (and his flute), and Tadanori (and his poetry).

73. The petition can be found in: Kitahara and Ogawa, Enkyōbon, vol. 2, pp. 35–36; Kokusho kankōkai, Nagatobon, pp. 455–456; Tomikura, Zenchūshaku, vol. 2, pp. 315–316; Mizuhara, *Jōsuiki*, vol. 4, pp. 68–69; Mizuhara, Hyakunijukku-bon, vol. 2, pp. 188–189; Asahara and Kitahara, *Mai no hon*, pp. 207–209.

74. Even in "*kanabon*," or texts intentionally rendered into *kana* (probably to facilitate ease of reading/performing), documents including this *ganjo* exhibit a much higher concentration of *kanji* words and phrases than in the surrounding text.

75. Highly conventional, *kanji*-heavy expressions also comprise the main content of recited liturgy and some forms of spoken narrative.

76. For a thorough discussion of the role of battlefield invocation during the Muromachi period, see Thomas D. Conlan, *State of War: The Violent Order of Fourteenth-Century Japan* (Ann Arbor, MI: Center for Japanese Studies, University of Michigan, 2003), pp. 165–182. While this passage describes a less formalized ritual than those like the "five altars" ritual Conlan mentions, the general mind-set regarding the role of the sacred on the battlefield adheres for these texts (so formative for the warrior culture Conlan describes) as well.

77. Conlan, *State of War*, p. 168.

78. *Nihonshi daijiten*, vol. 2, pp. 600–601.

79. McCullough, *The Tale of the Heike*, p. 230.

80. McCullough, *The Tale of the Heike*, p. 229.

81. The sovereign Ōjin was a legendary ruler said to have reigned from 270–310. He undergoes apotheosis and becomes Hachiman. The association between the deity and a sovereign (however legendary) is the basis upon which Hachiman comes to be seen as the ancestor of sovereigns.

82. Tomikura, Zenchūshaku, vol. 2, p. 315.

83. See, for example, Kuroda Toshio, Obō to Buppō (Kyoto: Hōzōkan, 1983), especially pp. 7–22.

84. McCullough, *The Tale of the Heike*, p. 229.

85. McCullough, *The Tale of the Heike*, p. 229.

86. McCullough, *The Tale of the Heike*, p. 230.

87. "I am like a child measuring the vast oceans with a seashell" is from the *History of the Former Han*; "[I am] like a praying mantis opposing a mighty chariots with its forelimbs" is found both in the *Chuangzi* and the *Anthologies*.

88. In the Kakuichibon, it is delivered to the Shinden, in the Enkyōbon, Nagatobon, and *Jōsuiki*, to the Shadan, in the Hyakunijukkubon to the Hōden.

89. Top arrows (*uwaya no kabura*) are the "humming bulb arrows" (*kaburaya*) fired at the outset of a battle to intimidate the enemy; they emit a high-pitched whistling sound when fired. A perforated bulb attached to the arrow shaft catches the air and vibrates when in flight, causing the whistling sound. They are referred to as "top arrows" because their shafts are longer than regular arrows so they protrude further from the top of a quiver. Attaching top arrows to a petition to the gods is also described in connection with Yoshiie and Yoritomo in *Hakonesan engi*. See Tomikura, *Zenchūshaku*, vol. 2, p. 318.

90. Kitahara and Ogawa, Enkyōbon, vol. 2, p. 35; Kokusho kankōkai, Nagatobon, p. 456; Mizuhara, *Jōsuiki*, vol. 4, p. 70.

91. Sacred to Hachiman.

92. McCullough, *The Tale of the Heike*, p. 230.

93. *Futagokoronaki kokorozashi* in the Enkyōbon, *kokorozashi no futastunaki* in the Hyakunijukkubon, *futatsunaki kokorozashi* in the Nagatobon, *kokorozashi futatsunaki* in the Kakuichibon, and *makoto no kokorozashi no fukasa* in the *Jōsuiki*.

94. McCullough, *The Tale of the Heike*, p. 230; Tomikura, *Zenchūshaku*, vol. 2, p. 319; Mizuhara, Hyakunijukkubon, vol. 2, p. 190.

95. *Kono hitobito no senzo*. McCullough, *The Tale of the Heike*, p. 230.

96. McCullough, *The Tale of the Heike*, p. 230.

97. Although Yoshiie was present at the battle, the *Mutsuwaki* attributes this invocation to Yoriyoshi. Mizuhara, Hyakunijukkubon, vol. 2, p. 190.

98. Saeki, Heike monogatari *sogen*, pp. 350–358.

99. McCullough, *The Tale of the Heike*, p. 230; Tomikura, *Zenchūshaku*, vol. 2, p. 319; Mizuhara, Hyakunijukkubon, vol. 2, p. 190.

100. Kitahara and Ogawa, Enkyōbon, vol. 2, p. 35; Mizuhara, *Jōsuiki*, vol. 4, p. 70; Kokusho kankōkai, Nagatobon, p. 456.

101. For a discussion of epic teleological narrative, see Quint, *Epic and Empire*, p. 9. Epic narrative is characterized by a straightforward plot pointing toward a specific conclusion. Epic is traditionally associated with narratives of the victors, whose victories are the basis for the political or cultural order of the writer(s) or performer(s) of the epic. Epic is juxtaposed with romance, which is exemplified by meandering, circular plot lines that threaten never to reach a conclusion.

102. This characterization operates within a larger rubric governing the war tales, in which the Taira and Minamoto stood side-by-side in defense of the throne. Because the Taira have created unbalance in that order, the logic goes, the Minamoto must reassert their role by reclaiming it for themselves alone.

103. Further, *yomimono* as a category are set aside as special; they are "Lesser Secret Pieces" (*shōhiji*), among the last category of piece learned by students in the sighted tradition. The episode discussed in Chapter Four, "Koshigoe," is also designated a *yomimono*.

104. Mass, *Lordship and Inheritance*, especially p. 53. I return to this subject in more detail in Chapter Four.

Chapter 4: Yoshitsune at Koshigoe

1. See Yamashita Hiroaki, "*Gikeiki* no *Heike monogatari* jūyō," *Kokugo to koku-bungaku* 713.3 (1996): 28–42, for a general discussion of the multiple relationships between the texts, including the *Gikeiki*'s parodic role.

2. Literature (often parodic) and art, particularly woodblock prints, from the Edo period also frequently take him as their subject.

3. The theory of the triad of heroes (Kiyomori, Yoshinaka, and Yoshitsune) as a structural element of the *Heike* was first proposed by the early *Heike* scholar Yamada Yoshio in Heike monogatari *kō* (Tokyo: Kokutei kyōkasho kyōdō hanbai sho, 1911). This remains an important paradigm for textual studies even today.

4. Yamashita Hiroaki discusses this omission in terms of parody: See Yama-shita, *Ikusa monogatari no katari to hihyō*, pp. 241–266. He argues that the *Gikeiki* in-verts the narration of the *Heike* at a number of points, including the obvious exclusion of the war itself.

5. A more comprehensive list of narratives about Yoshitsune's life is provided in McCullough's *Yoshitsune*, pp. 30–66. Yamashita, cited above, provides provocative readings of *Gikeiki* within the context of the war tales. For his most recent work, see Yamashita, *Ikusa monogatari to Genji shōgun*, pp. 47–51.

6. McCullough, *Yoshitsune*, p. 6.

7. Included among the list of Kiyomori's well-placed daughters in the "Kiyo-mori's Flowering Fortunes" episode of the *Heike* (McCullough, *The Tale of the Heike*, pp. 28–30), is one allegedly born to Tokiwa.

8. See Chapter One, note 17 for a discussion of the fates of Yoshitomo's sons. The story of Tokiwa's tribulations is also included in the *Gikeiki* as well as the *kōwaka-mai* and *otogizōshi* repertoires.

9. In keeping with the tradition of upper-class males of the day, Yoshitsune was given a name at birth (Ushiwaka), one later in his youth (Shanaō), and finally his adult name, Kūro Yoshitsune, at his capping ceremony (*genbuku*), which was performed relatively late, when he was sixteen years old. Kūro means "ninth son," which, indeed, Yoshitsune was.

10. McCullough, *Yoshitsune*, p. 72.

11. McCullough, *Yoshitsune*, p. 75.

12. McCullough, *Yoshitsune*, p. 75.

13. Asahara and Kitahara, *Mai no hon*, pp. 295–304.

14. The presence of *tengu* in this body of legends is itself layered with mean-ing. One formulation describes *tengu* as the spirits of dead priests, thus inscribing them with a sort of religious authority as well as a supernatural one. See Waka-bayashi Haruko, "Tengu: Images of the Concepts of Evil in Medieval Japan" (Ph.D. dissertation, Princeton University, 1995).

15. Asahara and Kitahara, *Mai no hon,* pp. 305–311.

16. From Asahara and Kitahara, *Mai no hon,* p. 311. Translation by author. In addition to this reference to discord between the brothers, the "Tsurugi sandan" (Praise for the Swords) of the *kōwakamai* canon and the *Heike*'s "Tsurugi no maki" (Chapter of the Swords) both include brief references to Kajiwara causing discord between Yoritomo and Yoshitsune. They are discussed in more detail in Chapter Five.

17. Kishi Shōzō, trans. and Nagahara Keiji, ed. *Zen'yaku Azuma kagami* (To-kyo: Shinjinbutsu ōraisha, 1976–1985), vol. 1, p. 81. Hereafter cited as Kishi and Nagahara, *Azuma kagami.* All translations by author unless otherwise noted. This source is cited here as the most specific reference to this event. Although the date of the meeting may not be entirely accurate, given the questionable veracity of the *Azuma kagami*'s record of the Genpei period, a meeting did take place on or near this date.

18. Tomikura, *Zenchūshaku,* vol. 3, p. 92.

19. Kishi and Nagahara, *Azuma kagami,* vol. 1, p. 166 (1184/6/20).

20. In English, see McCullough, *Yoshitsune,* p. 18; Sansom, *Japan to 1334,* p. 81.

21. Kishi and Nagahara, *Azuma kagami,* vol. 1, p. 166 (1184/6/21).

22. Kishi and Nagahara, *Azuma kagami,* vol. 1, p. 170 (1184/8/8).

23. Kishi and Nagahara, *Azuma kagami,* vol. 1, pp. 170–171 (1184/8/23).

24. The Kajiwara were originally descendents of the Kanmu Heike. In the ini-tial phases of Yoritomo's uprising, Kagetoki sided with Ōba Kagechika against Yori-tomo, but in the battle of Ishibashiyama, he came to the assistance of Yoritomo, earning him a place as one of Yoritomo's most trusted retainers. He was an impor-tant member of Yoritomo's Bureau of Samurai Affairs (*Samurai dokoro*), and contin-ued to be an influential member of the warrior government even after Yoritomo's death. He incurred the wrath of other powerful retainers, however, and was re-moved from office; he died fighting in Suruga (present-day Shizuoka Prefecture) in 1200. The *Azuma kagami* and legend ascribe his removal from office to slandering another retainer; whether this is true or not, it fits nicely into the portrayal of him we shall see below.

25. Kishi and Nagahara, *Azuma kagami,* vol. 1, p. 198 (1185/3/24).

26. See McCullough, *The Tale of the Heike,* pp. 389–390.

27. The accounts of Yoshitsune's death in the *Gikeiki* and the *kōwakamai* "Fukumi jō" (The Inserted Letter) relate that the child who died at his side was a boy, but the *Azuma kagami* reports that it was a four-year-old girl (Kishi and Naga-hara, *Azuma kagami,* vol. 2, p. 83). The reason for the discrepancy is unclear, but the elevated poignancy of the death of an heir rather than a daughter probably contributes to the literary license taken here.

28. The vilification of Kagetoki as a thematic concern is clearly enough marked to make it useful in differentiating variant texts under the *Heike* rubric. See, for example, Suzuki Jun, "*Heike monogatari* Kakuichibon to Yasakabon no aida:

Yoritomo no sonzaikan to kataribon no tenkai," *Kokubungaku kenkyū* 116 (1995): 12–23. See also Sakurai Yoko, "*Heike monogatari* no henshū hōhō: shohon no ryūdō to bunseki wo kangaeru tame ni," *Kokugo to kokubungaku* 713.2 (1996): 28–42.

29. Kajihara and Yamashita, Kakuichibon, vol. 1, p. 261.

30. McCullough, *The Tale of the Heike*, pp. 359–360.

31. Chapter 6, part 3. Kitahara and Ogawa, Enkyōbon, vol. 2, pp. 370–373.

32. Chapter 41, episode 20, "The Sorrow of the Heike and Kagiwara Kagetoki and the Reverse Oars," in Mizuhara, *Jōsuiki*, vol. 6, pp. 234–237.

33. Tomikura, *Zenchūshaku*, vol. 3, part 1, pp. 419–422.

34. Kishi and Nagahara, *Azuma kagami*, vol. 1, p. 205.

35. Kishi and Nagahara, *Azuma kagami*, vol. 1, pp. 205–206.

36. Kishi and Nagahara, *Azuma kagami*, vol. 1, p. 206.

37. The Ōsaka barrier is located in present-day Ōtsu city. It stood as the easternmost extreme of the capital environs; beyond it lay "the East." The conceptualization of it as the border between civilization and the outback (to which provincial officials often had to travel), combined with the characters used to write it ("the slope of meeting") earned it a prominent position in the lexicons of classical poets, who played upon the separation passing it implied and the non-separation its name invoked; it is often used as a poetic trope to signify the impermanence of worldly relations and attachments. In addition, it was associated with famous classical figures including the blind *biwa* player Semimaru, who was said to have resided there. Susan Matisoff, in *The Legend of Semimaru, blind musician of Japan* (New York: Columbia University Press, 1978), provides a complete study of the historical and legendary presence of this figure.

38. Kitahara and Ogawa, Enkyōbon, vol. 2, p. 438.

39. Kitahara and Ogawa, Enkyōbon, vol. 2, p. 438.

40. Kitahara and Ogawa, Enkyōbon, vol. 2, p. 438.

41. See McCullough, *The Tale of the Heike*, pp. 338–341. An encounter between Munemori and Jijū (Yuya in the Yashirobon; "Jijū, the daughter of Yuya," in the Kakuichibon) is embedded within the narrative of Shigehira's journey in the Kakuichibon and Enkyōbon texts. In the Kakuichibon, Shigehira is told of the romance between the two while Munemori was governor of Tōtomi Province. In contrast, in the *Jōsuiki* Munemori simply meets Jijū here, they exchange poems and lament his fate, and he continues on his journey. The *nō* play "Yuya," attributed to Zeami, is only loosely based on the *Heike* texts.

42. The stations are listed in order, a technique known as *monotsukushi*, literally "an exhaustive listing of things." This technique is not limited to listing place names, but is also used to list people or weaponry or items in any category. It bears a strong resemblance to the cataloguing of items (ships, warriors, etc.) in the Western epic tradition. This is one of many techniques accredited to oral performance and composition—the catalogue being a mnemonic device. The *michiyuki* framing it, however, is of course a well-established convention in poetic and literary aesthetics of the Heian period, which complicates the oral/written dimensions of the

technique here. It is perhaps most productive to look at this listing as a function of performativity, either textual or dramatic, as it clearly serves the specific function of moving the story forward both temporally and spatially, in a direction that implies alienation from the familiar and the likelihood of an unhappy end to the journey. The particular list of stations along the Tōkaidō seems to originate with the *Kaidōki*, a Kamakura-period work.

43. Mizuhara, *Jōsuiki*, vol. 6, p. 90.

44. Mizuhara, *Jōsuiki*, vol. 6, p. 129.

45. The *ku* laid out in the *Heike mabushi* (1776) are gradated to reflect the narrative and ritual significance of the pieces as well as their difficulty. *Ku* are arranged in the order in which they are learned, one *ku* from each *Heike* chapter per *Mabushi* chapter. Certain kinds of *ku*—*yomimono*, secret pieces, etc.—are separated out and delineated as special. The *Mabushi* includes musical markings and was widely used in the Tokugawa period; it is still the base text for the sighted lineage today.

46. Kajihara and Yamashita, Kakuichibon, vol. 2, pp. 321–326.

47. Kajihara and Yamashita, Kakuichibon, vol. 2, p. 323.

48. Kajihara and Yamashita, Kakuichibon, vol. 2, p. 323.

49. Kajihara and Yamashita, Kakuichibon, vol. 2, pp. 324–326.

50. McCullough, Yoshitsune, pp. 132–134; Kajihara Masaaki, ed., *Gikeiki*, vol. 31 of *Nihon koten bungaku zenshū* (Tokyo: Shogakukan, 1971), pp. 187–192. Hereafter cited as Kajiwara, *Gikeiki*. This narrative is composed of two named episodes: "How Yoshitsune Marched Against the Heike" and "The Letter from Koshigoe."

51. Kajihara, *Gikeiki*, p. 195.

52. Kajihara, *Gikeiki*, p. 196.

53. Kajihara, *Gikeiki*, pp. 196–197.

54. Kajihara, *Gikeiki*, pp. 197–198.

55. Kajihara, *Gikeiki*, p. 202.

56. Asahara and Kitahara, *Mai no hon*, pp. 340–346. Also found in Agō and Fukuda, *Kōwaka bukyoku kenkyū*, vol. 5, pp. 176–216. All translations by author.

57. Asahara and Kitahara, *Mai no hon*, p. 340.

58. Asahara and Kitahara, *Mai no hon*, p. 340.

59. Asahara and Kitahara, *Mai no hon*, p. 341.

60. Asahara and Kitahara, *Mai no hon*, p. 344.

61. Asahara and Kitahara, *Mai no hon*, p. 344.

62. Asahara and Kitahara, *Mai no hon*, pp. 344–345.

63. Asahara and Kitahara, *Mai no hon*, p. 345.

64. Asahara and Kitahara, *Mai no hon*, p. 345.

65. Asahara and Kitahara, *Mai no hon*, p. 346.

66. Asahara and Kitahara, *Mai no hon*, p. 346.

67. Asahara and Kitahara, *Mai no hon*, p. 346.

68. Asahara and Kitahara, *Mai no hon*, p. 346.

69. Kishi and Nagahara, *Azuma kagami*, vol. 1, p. 211 (1185/5/4).

70. Kishi and Nagahara, *Azuma kagami*, vol. 1, p. 211.

71. Kishi and Nagahara, *Azuma kagami*, vol. 1, p. 211.

72. Kishi and Nagahara, *Azuma kagami*, vol. 1, p. 212.

73. Kishi and Nagahara, *Azuma kagami*, vol. 1, p. 213.

74. Kishi and Nagahara, *Azuma kagami*, vol. 1, p. 213.

75. Kishi and Nagahara, *Azuma kagami*, vol. 1, p. 219.

76. One of the early arguments used by proponents of oral-formulaic theory for oral composition of Homer's works was the repetition of epithets for specific characters: Odysseus is a "man of twists and turns," Achilles is "Peleus' son" and "godlike," dawn is "rosy-fingered." The explanation theorists proposed for this phenomenon was that an epithet and its various (case-based) permutations allowed a poet to complete a foot appropriately as he composed in performance. The issue of the degree of this theory's viability aside, the differences between the Japanese performance traditions and the ancient Greeks' are significant: the structural vicissitudes of the epic form in Greek are counterpointed by the much more forgiving general 5/7/5/7 syllable alternation in the Japanese poetic (or here, semi-poetic) line; the cases of Greek are absent in classical Japanese; and the great degree of variation in vocal expression (some sung, some spoken) in Japanese all make the rules for composition in Japanese different.

77. See the Glossary for *kanji* used to write these terms.

78. Michizane's life is detailed in Borgen, *Sugawara no Michizane and the Early Heian Court*. In chapter 7, he discusses various theories concerning the causes for Michizane's banishment; he notes that from the time of the *Ōkagami* on, unjust slander by Fujiwara Tokihira became a standard explanation for Michizane's unfortunate fate. See pp. 284–285.

79. Kitahara and Ogawa, Enkyōbon, vol. 2, p. 439.

80. Quint, *Epic and Empire*, p. 50, discusses narrative as driven by repetition compulsion; this issue is explored more fully in Chapter Five.

81. For treatments of Yoritomo's portrayal in the war tales as a power holder, see Saeki, Heike monogatari *sogen*, pp. 385–414 (a discussion of Yoritomo as law-giver) and Yamashita, *Ikusa monogatari to Genji shōgun*, pp. 198–205 (a discussion of Yoritomo's apotheosis [*shinkakuka*]).

82. See Otsu Yūichi, "Yoshinaka kō," *Nihon bungaku* 39.7: 35–44 for a discussion of the sanction of the *kami* for Yoritomo's rule.

83. For a discussion of kin-group rivalries during the late Heian period, see Jeffrey P. Mass, *Yoritomo and the Founding of the First Bakufu* (Stanford, CA: Stanford University Press, 1999) p. 45.

84. Consolidation of families under one primary heir was the trend. This is discussed in more detail in Chapter Five. See Mass, *Lordship and Inheritance*, pp. 37–39, 58–114. For a discussion of how this system disenfranchised women, see Hitomi Tonomura, "Women and Inheritance in Japan's Early Warrior Society," *Comparative Studies in History and Society* (1990): 592–623.

85. Throughout the early and middle parts of the Kamakura period, however, secondary sons and all daughters, though granted smaller portions than

the designated heir (*sōryō*) and required to pay dues to Kamakura through him, nevertheless were granted portions of their parents' holdings, often in perpetuity. See Mass, *Lordship and Inheritance*, chapters 2–3, pp. 37–93.

86. Shinoda, *The Founding of the Kamakura Shogunate*, p. 10.

87. In addition to the "original document," visitors also can purchase souvenir replicas. The materiality of the petition within the texts is thus translated into concrete artifact further adding a flavor of historicity, of actuality, to the event commemorated and reified by the artifact.

88. This is particularly true in *kabuki* during the Edo period, but interestingly in modern adaptations of his story as well. In Kurosawa Akira's *Men Who Tread on the Tiger's Tail* (1945), for instance, the director carefully shapes his story as a critique of post-war Japan, but the conventional characterization of Yoshitsune remains essentially intact. And although conventional villains like Kiyomori are reinterpreted through a psychoanalytical lens in Yoshikawa Eiji's *Shin Heike monogatari* (New tale of the Heike, 1962–1963), the interiority of the prototypical warrior hero is not the topic of popular modern scrutiny.

89. Prasenjit Duara, "Superscribing Symbols: The Myth of Guandi, Chinese God of War," *Journal of Asian Studies* 47.4 (1988): 780.

Chapter 5: The Soga Brothers

1. Both the *Soga monogatari* and the *Azuma kagami* record that the vendetta occurred on the final day of the hunt (the twenty-eighth day of the fifth month), which concluded with an evening of revelry. The Soga brothers stole into camp after the festivities had died down and attacked Suketsune in his tent, where he lay sleeping in the company of a close retainer and two courtesans. For the *Soga monogatari* account, see Mihashi, *Soga monogatari*. The events are also recorded in Kishi and Nagahara, *Azuma kagami*, vol. 2, pp. 279–280. The Itō family originally descended from a branch of the Fujiwara family. The name Kudō originated with the bestowal of the position of *shugo* (constable) of Tsuruga and Izu to the seventh-generation heir, and it was passed by Suketaka to Suketsugu who passed it to Suketsune.

2. Vendettas are an important feature of dramatic genres of the Edo period, in particular. Along with the revenge of the forty-seven *rōnin*, the Soga brothers' story is among the favorite topics for the *kabuki* and *bunraku* stages.

3. Although Gorō asked permission to commit suicide, Yoritomo forbade it, responding that Gorō's crime of disrupting the Kamakura Lord's hunting party and carrying out a private vendetta required punishment by execution. See Laurence R. Kominz, *Avatars of Vengeance: Japanese Drama and the Soga Literary Tradition* (Ann Arbor, MI: Center for Japanese Studies, The University of Michigan, 1995), p. 1. This work provides a lengthy study of dramatic interpretations of the Soga story during the Edo period.

4. Yoritomo began appointing *jitō* (land stewards) in 1185, and *shugo* (constables) by 1193. Mass, *Lordship and Inheritance*, pp. 38–39.

5. The Kamakura rule only came to fruition after his death; and it expanded further after the Jōkyū War of 1221. Mass, *Lordship and Inheritance*, pp. 37–57.

6. Two variants are referred to throughout this chapter. The Echizen text is included in Asahara and Kitahara, *Mai no hon*, pp. 511–517. The Daigashira text is found in Murakami Mitoshi, annot., "Tsurugi sandan," in Agō Torashin and Fukuda Akira, et al., eds., *Kōwaka bukyoku kenkyū*, vol. 9 (Tokyo: Miyai shoten, 1979), pp. 296–320. Hereafter cited as Agō and Fukuda, *Kōwaka bukyoku kenkyū*, vol. 9. Translations are by the author.

7. Found in Mizuhara, *Jōsuiki*, vol. 1, pp. 59–88.

8. The Russian romantic Mikhail Lermonotov underlined the useless conventionality to which Tsar Nicholas I's obsession with the military parades had reduced the sword by wearing a toy sword when the Tsar was reviewing the troops in 1839. His sarcastic play with the symbolizing function of the sword earned him a twenty-one-day sentence. See Laurence Kelly, *Lermontov: Tragedy in the Caucasus* (New York: George Braziller, Inc., 1977), p. 114.

9. The few females-at-arms are exceptions. Joan of Arc, one of a handful of historically verifiable women warriors, and her literary sisters (Tomoe, Camilla, Bradamante, et al.) are acknowledged as anomalies. They are notable both for their unusual male bravery and their adoption of male garb. Their appearance, in other words, can only be articulated in terms of their assimilation into the masculine domain of the battlefield.

10. For descriptions of Japanese tales in which needles are used to thwart otherworldly foes, see Ikeda Hiroko, *A Type and Motif Index of Folk literature* (Helsinki: Suomalainen Tiedeakatemia Academia Scientiarum Fennica, Folklore Fellows Communications, No. 209, 1970), pp. 103, and 119–120.

11. Masamune, the most famous of premodern swordsmiths, was active in Sagami Province during the end of the Kamakura period. He is credited with founding the Soshu school of swordsmithing and is thought to have been trained by Shintogu Kunimitsu.

12. See Edward Norbeck, "Little-Known Minority Groups of Japan" in George De Vos, ed. *Japan's Invisible Race: Caste in Culture and Personality* (Berkeley, CA: University of California Press, 1966), pp. 188–189. The liminal/outsider status of metalworkers in Japanese folklore is discussed as well in Matsumoto Nobuhiro, "Japanese Metalworkers: A Possible Source for their Legends," in Richard M. Dorson, ed., *Studies in Japanese Folklore* (Bloomington, IN: Indiana University Press, 1963), pp. 147–161. This article focuses on the origins of metalworkers' folk knowledge, tracing folk tales about them to other countries of origin. Pertinent to this study is the association between metalworkers and special fates.

13. The relationships between orality and writing have been important topics of critical inquiry for performative traditions for over a century, the Parry-Lord model of orality representing a starting place for investigations into contemporary oral traditions as well as temporally remote contexts (including the medieval worlds of Europe and elsewhere). The complexity of medieval contexts has proven

extremely fertile ground for investigating performance genres in milieus exhibiting varying degrees of literacy, like the one discussed here. For pertinent discussions of European medievality, see D. H. Green, "Orality and Reading: The State of Research in Medieval Studies," *Speculum* 65.2 (1990): 267–280 and Brian Stock, *Listening for the Text.*

14. See Matusmoto, "Japanese Metalworkers," especially pp. 148–151.

15. Schools and lineage became important for many arts, from poetry and tea ceremony to *nō*, calligraphy, the martial arts, and other crafts.

16. Guild documents, most prominent among them the *Tōdōyōshū*, date from the Tokugawa period, when practitioners of various trades trying to gain recognition and sanction from the government for their art or craft justified both its longevity and its connections to the upper echelons of society through written histories and explications of the practices of the art, etc. The idea of a guild, concretized at this point, has its origins in the Muromachi period; practitioners of *Heike biwa* saw themselves as possessing an "art" (*michi*), although perhaps one not as exclusionary as its Tokugawa period descendant. A printed version of another guild document, the *Tōdōdaikiroku* transcribed by Suzuki Takatsune, is included in Kamisango, ed., *Heike biwa: katari to ongaku*, pp. 227–309. A genealogy for the guild is provided on pp. 235–238. See also Gerald Groemer, "The Guild of the Blind in Tokugawa Japan," pp. 346–380, for a discussion of the development of the guild from the *tōdō* of the Muromachi period.

17. Including most prominently Shōtoku taishi, who is claimed as the ancestor of turners and smiths, among others.

18. See Stith Thompson, *Motif Index for Folk Literature* (Bloomington, IN: Indiana University Press, 1955–1958), pp. 137–138 for a listing of tales in various world cultures that include magical swords. For Japan, see Ikeda, *A Type and Motif Index.*

19. Folktales concerning magic swords are collated in Ikeda, *A Type and Motif Index*, pp. 68–70 and 193–194. Included among these is Kusanagi, the sword Susanō-o liberates from the tail of an eight-headed serpent. Kusanagi, lost at sea in the battle of Dan-no-ura, might also be seen to represent a magic sword—both its mythic history and its cyclical return to the dragon king with the fall of the Heike suggest its supernatural powers, a topic returned to below.

20. Cogan, *The Tale of the Soga Brothers*, p. 8. Toin Kinsada, ed, *Sonpi bunmyaku*, vol. 59 of *Shintei zōhō kokushi taikei* (Tokyo: Yoshikawa Kōbunkan, 1964), p. 37. The source for this information is unclear, and may in fact originate in the *Soga monogatari*, thus leaving us with potentially circular proof.

21. The *Soga* comments that Suketsugu died in 1160 because of curses that Sukechika had coerced the intendant at Hakone Shrine to perform. Before he died, Suketsugu, ignorant of his kinsman's rancor, designated guardianship of his son, Suketsune, to Sukechika. Cogan, *The Tale of the Soga Brothers*, pp. 7–12.

22. The boys were then adopted by Soga, from whom comes the name.

23. The Soga brothers on the other hand languished in obscurity; they had no hereditary holdings and were completely reliant on their stepfather for support.

Although their mother had tried to hide their father's tragic past from them (according to the *Soga* and other legendary materials, which are the only references we have to the boys' youth), they learned of their identities and planned revenge from early on. Gorō, the younger brother (at the time known by his childhood name, Hakoō) was sent to Hakone to become a priest, but, with the assistance of his brother and other sympathetic warriors, he was able to escape, undergo *genbuku*, the formal initiation rite into the adult world for young men, and join his brother in their attack in 1193.

24. Sukechika opposed Yoritomo in battle at the Fuji River, was captured, and expected to be executed. Instead he was pardoned and released into the custody of his son-in-law, Miura Yoshizumi, an important retainer of Yoritomo. He was pardoned on 1182/2/14, an act which is portrayed in the *Azuma kagami* as demonstrating Yoritomo's generosity toward former enemies; it should be remembered, however, that the pardon occurred during the pregnancy of Yoritomo's wife, Masako, and that the pardon may in fact have been a preemptive measure against the potential threat of a dissatisfied enemy (not unlike the pardon of the Kikaigashima exiles in the *Heike* during Kenreimon'in's pregnancy with Antoku). After the pardon, Sukechika immediately committed suicide, allegedly because he was "conscious-stricken" over his former treatment of Yoritomo (see Kishi and Nagahara, *Azuma kagami*, vol. 1, p. 121 [1182/2/14]). On 1194/3/25, Yoritomo ordered sutra recitations dedicated to the repose of his spirit. Coming as it did so shortly after the death of the Soga brothers, we can postulate that not only they but their grandfather also posed a threat as malicious spirits (Kishi and Nagahara, *Azuma kagami*, vol. 2 [1194/3/25]).

25. The story of Senzuru's birth and murder, recounted in book 2 of the *Soga monogatari*, provides an important frame tale for the primary narrative of the Soga brothers' revenge. See Cogan, *The Tale of the Soga Brothers*, p. 48.

26. In the eighth of twelve chapters, where it is treated as either the first or first through third episodes of that chapter. Cogan's translation includes the entirety of the Swords narrative in the first episode of this chapter under the title "The Farewell Visit to Hakone." In other versions (including that used in the Soga monogatari *chūkai*), this episode is broken down into "The Farewell Visit to Hakone," "Meeting the Intendant," and "The Origins of the Swords."

27. Mihashi, *Soga monogatari*, p. 434.

28. The translation of Mijin as "Crusher" is taken from Cogan for consistency. Other places where his translations are used, he is cited. All uncredited translations of names are my own.

29. Yoshinaka's son, Shimizu Onzōshi (Master Shimizu, sobriquet for Yoshinaka's son, Yoshishige) did not serve as a general during the Genpei War; I have not encountered this version elsewhere. A separate cycle of stories exists concerning Yoshishige's attempt to escape from Yoritomo after his father's defection.

30. Mihashi, *Soga monogatari*, pp. 434–435.

31. The Hyōgo-chain style was a style created by artisans in Hyōgo. It consists

of a chain made of either gold or silver attached to the sword at the hilt that was used to secure the sword at the wearer's waist.

32. Minamoto Yorimitsu, also known as Raikō (the Chinese-style reading of "Yorimitsu"), was a popular hero known for his prowess as a warrior and an archer. He and his younger brother, Yorinobu, were known as the "claws and teeth" of the regent Fujiwara Michinaga. Yorimitsu died in 1021. He is the ancestor of Yorimasa.

33. One *shaku* equals approximately one foot; one *sun* equals 1.2 inches.

34. Cogan, *The Tale of the Soga Brothers*, p. 199; Mihashi, *Soga monogatari*, p. 435.

35. Minamoto Yorinobu (968–1048). Yorimitsu's younger brother. Father of Yoriyoshi, and thus the progenitor of the line that produced Yoritomo, Yoshitsune, and Yoshinaka. Note that this passage moves to a brother, not a son, a topic that will be addressed more specifically in other variants.

36. Cogan's translation.

37. One *jō* equals approximately ten feet.

38. Mihashi, *Soga monogatari*, p. 435.

39. Because Yoshiie is referred to as Lord Hachiman consistently throughout this text, I have chosen to use that moniker. In addition to remaining faithful to the original, this also serves to remind the reader of the strong identity between the Minamoto and the deity Hachiman.

40. For a discussion of the Hashihime legend, see Terry Kawashima, *Writing Margins: The Textual Construction of Gender in Heian and Kamakura Japan* (Cambridge, MA, and London: Harvard University Press, 2001), chapter 5. See especially pp. 255–288, for an analysis of Hashihime's demonic incarnation.

41. The reference to five *sun* rather than six here appears to be a transcriptional or recitational error.

42. Mihashi, *Soga mongatari*, p. 436.

43. The Daigashira version contains the histories of both swords, where the Echizen only traces the history of Gorō's. The differences between lineages are generally minute, especially compared to the differences among *Heike* variants, so I rely primarily on the Daigashira text here, making reference to the Echizen where necessary.

44. Of the fifty extant pieces in the repertoire, forty are about the Genpei War, the life of Yoshitsune, or the lives of the Soga brothers. Of the remaining ten, one recounts the Izanami and Izanagi myth, three more describe acts of undue self-sacrifice for the good of the realm or one's lord, three involve mostly fantastic journeys and heroic struggle, one is a love story, and two, "Miki" and "Honnōji," describe the good deeds of Toyotomi Hideyoshi. In the first, he shows mercy on an enemy after their surrender, and in the second, he crushes the Akechi and secures his control of the realm.

45. See Araki, *The Ballad-drama of Medieval Japan*, pp. 133–139. This method of categorization is somewhat problematic; I mention it here primarily because of the clear narrative plot through the Soga revenge that *Mai no hon*'s organization of

the *Soga-mono* creates. By arranging them in the same order that they appear in *Soga*, the idea of *Soga-mono* as a discrete set of texts becomes meaningful.

46. Hyōgozukuri refers to the same style as Hyōgogusuri; Hyōgogusuri appears in the Echizen text. Note that both terms contain the same number of syllables, making them interchangeable in recitation.

47. Agō and Fukuda, *Kōwaka bukyoku kenkyū*, vol. 9, p. 300.

48. The Echizen text has this as "on both banks of the waterfall" (*taki no sōgan ni*). Asahara and Kitahara, *Mai no hon*, p. 512.

49. Sovereign Heijō (774–824, r. 806–809).

50. Fl. ca. mid-Heian period; famous smith. The *nō* play "Kokaji" recounts that, based on a prophetic dream, the sovereign Ichijō commanded that he make a sword.

51. A reference to where it is stored. In addition to being written with the character for "above" (in the Echizen text), it is also written with the character for "god" (at places in the Daigashira text).

52. *Kyūman hassenno uchi no shugo no kamitachi*. The Echizen text omits "*shugo no*." Agō and Fukuda, *Kōwaka bukyoku kenkyū*, vol. 9, p. 303; *Mai no hon*, p. 513.

53. Agō and Fukuda, *Kōwaka bukyoku kenkyū*, vol. 9, p. 304.

54. Second ancestor of the Seiwa Genji (913–997). Mitsunaka served as governor in several provinces and also established an alliance with the regent Fujiwara house at court.

55. Agō and Fukuda, *Kōwaka bukyoku kenkyū*, vol. 9, p. 310.

56. Agō and Fukuda, *Kōwaka bukyoku kenkyū*, vol. 9, pp. 312–313.

57. As discussed in Victor Turner, *The Ritual Process: Structure and Anti-Structure* (Ithaca, NY: Cornell University Press, 1974), pp. 95–96.

58. Mizuhara, *Jōsuiki*, vol. 1, pp. 259–288.

59. McCullough's translation. Elsewhere translated as "The Water Consecration Scroll."

60. Shida Itaru, "*Heike* tsurugi no maki," in *Nihon koten bungaku daijiten* (Tokyo: Iwanami shoten, 1984), vol. 5, p. 389.

61. The account of the loss of Kusanagi is very similar to that provided in the *Gukanshō*, which recounts that the sovereign Antoku was in fact a reincarnation of the daughter of the Dragon King (*ryūō*), who had lost the sword to Susanō-o in the legendary past. By taking the blade to the bottom of the sea at Dan-no-ura, Antoku was in fact returning it to its proper home. See Shida, "*Heike* tsurugi no maki," p. 389.

62. Agō and Fukuda, *Kōwaka bukyoku kenkyū*, vol. 9, p. 317.

63. This name appears to be a variant on Hizakiri. Maru is a character sometimes used in naming; it has traditionally been used as the final character in male names (Semimaru), for example, and today it is commonly found as the final character in the names of ships.

64. The association of early warriors with swords is of particular interest, since most contemporary accounts identify warriors as bearers of bows and ar-

rows rather than swords. The emphasis on the sword as the symbol of warrior identity reflects the changing characterization of warriors during the medieval period, a movement that would culminate with such ruminations upon the centrality of the sword as Miyamoto Musashi's *Book of Five Rings* or Yoshimoto Tsunetomo's *Hagakure* during the Edo period.

65. The speed with which this feat is accomplished suggests the miraculousness of the deed; note the lengths of times the swordsmiths from "Praise of the Swords" spent in their labors—three years, or three years and three months.

66. The *nō* play *Kanawa* is related to the legend of her origin recounted here.

67. A narrative most famously known from the *nō* play *Tsuchigumo*. Note the expansion of the narrative found in the *kōwakamai* as well.

68. Mizuhara, *Jōsuiki*, vol. 1, p. 72.

69. Where his maternal grandfather was the head priest (*taigushi*).

70. Mizuhara, *Jōsuiki*, vol. 1, p. 75.

71. The narrative comments that Yoshitsune's victories were all due to the greatness of his sword (Usumidori). Mizuhara, *Jōsuiki*, vol. 1, p. 76.

72. Mizuhara, *Jōsuiki*, vol. 1, p. 87.

73. Mizuhara, *Jōsuiki*, vol. 1, p. 88.

74. See Quint, *Epic and Empire*, p. 50. Quint builds his models of romance and epic narratives on Peter Brooks' theories of narrative outlined in *Reading for the Plot: Design and Intention in Narrative* (New York: A. A. Knopf, 1984). Brooks stresses the repetition compulsion as an important underlying drive for narrative generally.

75. See, for example, in Cogan, *The Tale of the Soga Brothers*, book 5, episode 2, "The Quarrel Between Gorō and Kagesue" (pp. 117–119); book 5, episode 8, "Gorō Falls in Love with a Courtesan" (pp. 129–132); book 8, episode 3, "The Hunt on Fuji Plain" (pp. 202–212). Interestingly, however, Kajiwara Kagetoki is one of the retainers whose pleas convince Yoritomo not to kill the brothers when they are brought before him as children, in "Warriors Petition Yoritomo" (pp. 80–82).

76. Cogan, *The Tale of the Soga Brothers*, p. 246.

77. Throughout the early and middle parts of the Kamakura period, however, secondary sons and all daughters, though granted smaller portions than the designated heir (*sōryō*) and required to pay dues to Kamakura through him, nevertheless were granted portions of their parents' holdings, often in perpetuity. See Mass, *Lordship and Inheritance*, pp. 37–93. For a discussion of the *sōryō* system as a post-1220 development, see Mass, *Antiquity and Anachronism*, pp. 53–54.

78. See Mass, *Yoritomo and the Founding of the First Bakufu*, pp. 254–255.

79. For a discussion of document forms and judicial practices of the Kamakura government, see Mass, *Antiquity and Anachronism*, pp. 139–141.

80. Yoritomo's council sets the scene for his decision not to execute the boys in book 3 of the *Soga* (Cogan, *The Tale of the Soga Brothers*, pp. 80–82), when they are still very small. Following the vendetta, Yoritomo hears Gorō's case before deciding to execute him—against his personal inclination, but for the good of society. This is true as well of his interrogation of the brothers' youngest male sibling, Ombō,

whom he summons after Gorō's death (book 10; Cogan, *The Tale of the Soga Brothers*, p. 260). Throughout, we are given the impression of a fair-minded lord who regrets having to make decisions, but is obligated by his duty to punish the Soga brothers' excessive behavior by imposing the death penalty. While altercations in the judicial arena so central to framing the *Soga* account fall away from retellings in other genres, they remain an important impetus for the revenge; Yoritomo in this adjudicatory role remains an important presence in both *kōwakamai* and later early modern performance texts about this period.

81. The idealization of the warrior world, the very idea of warrior and later specifically samurai identity, and finally the identification of something known as *bushidō* (the way of the warrior) were all developments within narrative and dramatic traditions; they reflected an ideal rather than a norm. This ideal, of course, emerged in large part as a response to the complexities of a society as it changed over the centuries of the Muromachi, Sengoku, Tokugawa, and even modern periods; it always involved a degree of nostalgia for an romanticized, fictional time. It is not surprising, therefore, to find such rich and elaborate retrospective fallacies concerning the Genpei era.

82. I am grateful to Yasuko Arai for this insight. Secret pieces in the tradition are special both in their content and form. Their musical structure differs from the rest of the repertoire in the organization of *kyokusetsu* and the use of the most difficult of them in secret pieces. The secret pieces are longer and more melodically variegated than other *ku*, and they contain fewer passages in the *shirague* or *kudoki kyokusetsu* associated with straight narration.

Conclusion: Warrior Rule in Medieval Japan

1. Although the Mongol invasions are the subject of a picture scroll and other records, the actions of this conflict did not successfully move into other genres; this is generally true for the *Taiheiki* as well. For a translation and critical essay on the Mongol invasion scrolls, see Thomas D. Conlan, *In Little Need of Divine Intervention: Takezaki Suenaga's Scrolls of the Mongol Invasions of Japan* (Ithaca, NY: East Asia Program, Cornell University, 2001). For a translation of the *Taiheiki*, see Helen Craig McCullough, trans., *The Taiheiki: A Chronicle of Medieval Japan* (New York: Columbia University Press, 1959).

2. See, for example, Yamashita, *Ikusa monogatari to Genji shōgun*, pp. 32–52 and Hyōdō, *Heike monogatari: katari no tekusuto*, pp. 72–89.

3. For a discussion of Yoritomo in the *kōwakamai* tradition, see Fukuda Akira, "Kōwaka bukyoku no seikaku: gunki monogatari to no kakawari kara (jō)," in Agō and Fukuda, eds., *Kōwaka bukyoku kenkyū*, vol. 1, pp. 21–37.

4. Both the Ashikaga and later the Tokugawa invented or elaborated their own genealogies to connect themselves to the Seiwa Genji, emphasizing the importance of being Minamoto long after the end of Yoritomo's line. See Hyōdō, *Heike monogatari no rekishi to geinō*, pp. 8–30.

5. Extracanonical *nō* plays focusing on, for example, Yoshinaka's Petition do exist. Their felicitous content and other characteristics, however, contribute to their exclusion from the canon. Works like these suggest another interesting interstice that might help us better articulate the idea of the *nō* canon.

6. Asahara Yoshiko, in the "Kaisetsu" from Asahara and Kitahara, *Mai no hon*, pp. 589–619, discusses the solidification of narrative style in *kōwakamai* (p. 592) and its close musical relationships to *Heike biwa* (p. 596).

7. The first actual references to "*kōwakamai*" per se appear in journals around 1550. The general assumption among scholars is that the art was adapted from *kusemai. Kusemai* performances by the Echizen Kōwaka troupe are recorded a century earlier. Although firm evidence tracing the development of *kōwakamai* as it is recorded in the *Mai no hon* is non-existent, scholars generally trace the origins of the *kōwaka* back to the *kusemai* of Zeami's time and then through various developments of the *kusemai*. See Araki, *The Ballad-drama of Medieval Japan*, pp. 71–77.

8. Yamashita in *Ikusa monogatari to Genji shōgun* (pp. 2–46) discusses Yoritomo's apotheosis in narratives of the period, especially the *Heike.*

9. Hyōdō, Heike monogatari: *katari no tekusuto*, pp. 89–92, for example, discusses the portrayal of Ashikaga Yoshimitsu as "king" (*kokuō*) and the degree of specialness and even divinity that adheres to this portrayal. The apotheosis of Tokugawa Ieyasu is figured in the Tōshogū at Nikko. In all cases, these deifications of shōguns are affiliated with the idea of the country of Japan (Nippongoku).

Appendix A: The Hōgen and Heiji Uprisings

1. Usually, a *tenjōbito* was a person of fourth or fifth rank. The high aristocrats, the very small number of power holders at second and third rank, were sometimes indicated by this term as well, but they were more conventionally referred to as *kugyō.*

2. The general circumstances of both the Hōgen and Heiji disturbances are outlined in Varley, *Warriors of Japan as Portrayed in the War Tales.*

Glossary

This list includes Japanese characters for important terms appearing in this book. Where they have been identified most prominently by their English equivalents (Hakone Shrine, The Three Sacred Regalia), the English term is followed by romanized Japanese in parentheses. Further explanatory descriptions are enclosed in brackets. Proper names are capitalized; titles of works and general terms are italicized. Japanese names of texts included in this study can be found in Appendix C.

General Terms and Characters

Ashikaga[family]　足利
biwa [lute]　琵琶
biwa hōshi　琵琶法師
daihiji　大秘事
dan　段
Genpei War　源平合戦
Gukanshō　愚管抄
gunki monogatari　軍記物語
Gyokuyō　玉葉
Hakone Shrine (*Hakone jinja*)　箱根
　神社
hentai kanbun　変体漢文
hiroi　拾
hiroimono　拾物
hitatare　直垂
hōgan biiki　判官びいき
Hōgen monogatari　保元物語
Hōjō [family]　北条
jōruri　浄瑠璃
Kajiwara Kagetoki　梶原影時

Kakumei　覚名
kana　仮名
kanabon　仮名本
kanamajiri　仮名交じり
kanbun　漢文
kataribonkei　語本系
Kiso Yoshinaka　木曾義仲
kō no koe　強声
konkōbun (*wakan konkobun*)　和漢混
　交文
kōwakamai　幸若舞
ku　句
kudoki　口説
kusemai　曲舞
kyokusetsu　曲節
maki　巻
mana　真名　or 真字
Manabon　真名本
Minamoto Noriyori　源範頼
Minamoto Yorimasa　源頼政

201

Minamoto Yorimitsu　源頼光
Minamoto Yorinobu　源頼信
Minamoto Yoritomo　源頼朝
Minamoto Yoriyoshi　源頼義
Minamoto Yoshihira　源義平
Minamoto Yoshiie　源義家
Minamoto Yoshitomo　源義朝
Minamoto Yoshitsune　源義経
Mochihito　以仁
Musashibō Benkei　武蔵房弁慶
Nagatobon *Heike monogatari*　長門本
　　平家物語
nō [drama]　能楽
Ōkagami　大鏡
onnade　女手
otogizōshi　御伽草子
otokote　男手
rekishi monogatari　歴史物語

Retired Sovereign Go-Shirakawa　後
　　白河院
Rikkokushi　六国史
rufubon　流布本
shōdan　小段
Sovereign Antoku　安徳天皇
Sovereign Ōjin　応神天皇
Taiheiki　太平記
Taira Kiyomori　平清盛
Three Sacred Regalia (*sanshu no
　　shingi*)　三種神器
tōdōza　当道座
Tsurezuregusa　従然草
wabun　和文
wakan konkōbun　和漢混交文
yomihonkei　読本系
yomimono　読物

Terms Specific to the Narratives in Chapters Two to Five

annai(sha)　案内（者）
buannai　不案内
chakushi　嫡子
Chichugiri　蜘蛛切
Chōka　てうか
chōka　朝下
chōteki　朝敵
Dokuhebi　毒蛇
ebisu　夷
ganjo　願書
ganmon　願文
gōsu　号す
Higekiri　姫切
Hizamaru　膝丸
ichimon　一門
ikon　遺恨
iware　謂れ
jō　丈
kaimyō su　改名す
kan to naru　冠となる
Keitangoku　契丹国
Kikaigashima　鬼界島

kishōmon　起請文
Kōrai　高麗
Kumokiri　蜘蛛切
megurashibumi　廻文
Mijin　微塵
Mushibami　虫食
na o aratamu　名を改む
na o tsukeru　名をつける
naginata　長刀
Nippongoku　日本国
Onimaru　鬼丸
ox-head talisman (*goō hōin*)　牛王法
　　印
reimu　霊夢
saikoku　西国
sato no hito　里の人
sato no osa　里の長
sayamaki　鞘巻
sei-i taishōgun　征夷大将軍
settō　節刀
shaku　尺
Shishi no ko　獅子の子

Sotonohama　外浜
sun　寸
tachi　太刀
tenka　天下
tōgoku　東国
Tomogiri　友切
urami　恨み，憾み，怨み
Usumidori　薄緑

Yagura Peak　矢倉が岳
yurai　由来
zangen　讒言
zansha　讒者
zanshin　讒心
zanshin[a]　讒臣
zanso　讒訴
zansu　讒す

Bibliography

Primary Texts and Translations

Agō Torashin, Fukuda Akira, and Manabe Masahiro, eds. *Kōwaka bukyoku kenkyū*. 10 vols. Tokyo: Miyai shoten, 1979–.

Asahara Yoshiko and Kitahara Yasuo, eds. *Mai no hon*. Vol. 59 of *Shin Nihon koten bungaku taikei*. Tokyo: Iwanami shoten, 1994.

Atsumi Kaoru, Maeda Mineko, and Ubukata Takashige, eds. *Omura-ke zō Tōdōza, Heike biwa shiryō*. Kyoto; Daigakudō shoten, 1984.

Cogan, Thomas J., trans. *The Tale of the Soga Brothers*. Tokyo: Tokyo University Press, 1987.

Fukuda Toyohiko, ed. *Shintei zōho kokushi taikei-bon* Azuma kagami, Gyokuyō. Tokyo: Yoshikawa kōbunkan, 1999.

Fukuda Toyohiko and Hattori Kōzō. *Genpei tōjōroku: Bandō de umareta* Heike monogatari. 2 vols. Tokyo: Kōdansha gakujutsu bunko, 1999–2000.

Ichiko Teiji, ed. *Heike monogatari*. Vols. 45–46 of *Shinpen Nihon koten bungaku* zenshū. Tokyo: Shogakkan, 1994.

Ishimoda Shō, ed. *Heike monogatari. Iwanami shinsho*. Tokyo: Iwanami shoten, 1957.

Kajihara Masaaki, ed. *Gikeiki*. Vol. 31 of *Nihon koten bungaku zenshū*. Tokyo: Shogakkan, 1971.

Kajihara Masaaki and Yamashita Hiroaki, eds. *Heike monogatari*. Vols. 44–45 of *Shin Nihon koten bungaku taikei*. Tokyo: Iwanami shoten, 1991–1993.

Kishi Shōzō, trans., and Nagahara Keiji, eds. *Zen'yaku Azuma kagami*. 8 vols. Tokyo: Shinjinbutsu ōraisha, 1976–1985.

Kitagawa, Hiroshi and Bruce T. Tsuchida, trans. *The Tale of the Heike*. 2 vols. Paperback reprint. Tokyo: Tokyo University Press, 1977.

Kitahara Yasuo and Ogawa Eiichi, eds. *Enkyōbon* Heike monogatari: *honmonhen*. 2 vols. Tokyo: Benseisha, 1990.

Kokusho kankōkai, eds. Heike monogatari *Nagatobon*. Tokyo: Meicho kankōkai, 1974.

Kondō Heijō, ed. *Tōdōyōshū*. Vol. 27 of *Kaitei shiseiki shūran*. Kyoto: Rinsen shoten, 1984.

Kuroita Katsumi, ed. *Hyakurensho*. Vol. 9 of *Shintei zōho kokushi taikei*. Tokyo: Yoshikawa kōbunkan, 1977-.

McCullough, Helen Craig, trans. *The Taiheiki: A Chronicle of Medieval Japan*. New York: Columbia University Press, 1959.

————, trans. *The Tale of the Heike*. Stanford, CA: Stanford University Press, 1988.

————, trans. *Yoshitsune: A Fifteenth-Century Japanese Chronicle*. Stanford, CA: Stanford University Press, 1971.

McCullough, Helen C., and William H. McCullough. *Tale of Flowering Fortunes: Annals of Japanese Aristocratic Life in the Heian Period*. 2 vols. Stanford, CA: Stanford University Press, 1980.

Mihashi Tokugen, ed. Soga monogatari *chūkai*. Tokyo: Zoku gunshoruishō kanseikai, 1986.

Mizhuhara Hajime, ed. *Heike monogatari*. 3 vols. *Shinchō Nihon koten shūsei*. Tokyo: Shinchōsha, 1979-1981.

————, ed. *Shintei Genpei jōsuiki*. 6 vols. Tokyo: Shinjinbutsu ōraisha, 1988-1989.

Nagazumi Yasuaki, ed. *Heike monogatari*. Vol. 9 of *Nihon no koten*. Tokyo: Shūeisha, 1979.

Okami Masao and Akamatsu Toshihide, eds. *Gukanshō*. Vol. 86 of *Nihon koten bungaku taikei*. Tokyo: Iwanami shoten, 1967.

Sadler, Arthur. "The Heike Monogatari." *Transactions of the Asiatic Society of Japan* 46.2 (1918): 1-278; 49.1 (1921): 1-354.

————. The Ten Foot Square Hut *and* Tales of the Heike: *Being two thirteenth-century Japanese classics, the "Hojoki" and selections from "The Heike Monogatari."* Sydney: Angus & Robertson Limited, 1928.

Saeki, Ariyoshi, ed. *Zōhō Rikkokushi*. Tokyo: Asahi shinbunsha, 1940-1941.

Satake Akihiro and Kubota Jun, eds. *Hōjōki, Tsurezuregusa*. Vol. 39 of *Shin Nihon koten bungaku taikei*. Tokyo: Iwanami shoten, 1989.

Tachibana Kenji and Kato Shizuko, eds. *Ōkagami*. Vol. 34 of *Shinpen Nihon koten bungaku zenshū*. Tokyo: Shogakkan, 1996.

Takagi Ichinosuke, Ozawa Masao, Atsumi Kaoru, and Kindaichi Haruhiko, eds., *Heike monogatari jō*. Vol. 32 of *Nihon koten bungaku taikei*. Tokyo: Iwanami shoten, 1959-1960.

Tochigi Yoshitada, Kusaka Tsutomu, Masuda Takashi, and Kubota Jun, eds. *Hōgen monogatari, Heiji monogatari, Jōkyūki*. Vol. 43 of *Shin Nihon koten bungaku taikei*. Tokyo: Iwanami shoten, 1992.

Tokieda Motoki, Iwasa Masashi, and Kido Saizō, eds. *Jin'no shotoki*. Vol. 87 of *Nihon koten bungaku taikei*. Tokyo: Iwanami shoten, 1965.

Tomikura Tokujirō, ed. Heike monogatari *zenchūshaku*. 4 vols. Nihon koten hyōshaku: zenchūshaku sōsho. Tokyo: Kadokawa shoten, 1966-1968.

Wilson, William R. *Hōgen monogatari: Tale of the Disorder in Hōgen*. A Monumenta Nipponica Monograph. Tokyo: Sophia University Press, 1971.

Critical Studies

Amino Fumihiko. *Umi to retto no chūsei*. Tokyo: Nihon edita sukuru shuppanbu, 1992.

Amino Yoshihiko. "Deconstructing 'Japan.'" *East Asian History* 3 (June, 1992).

———. *Rekishigaku to mizokugaku*. Tokyo: Yoshikawa kōbunkan, 1992.

———. *Umi to retto no chūsei*. Tokyo: Nihon edita sukuru shuppanbu, 1992.

Anderson, Benedict. *Imagined Communities: reflections on the origin and spread of nationalism*. Revised and extended edition. London and New York: Verso, 1991.

Araki, James T. *The Ballad-drama of Medieval Japan*. Berkeley and Los Angeles, CA: University of California Press, 1964.

Asakawa Kan'ichi. *Documents of Iriki*. Society for the Promotion of Science, 1955.

Bialock, David T. "Peripheries of Power: Voice, History, and the Construction of Imperial and Sacred Space in 'The Tale of the Heike' and other Medieval and Historical Texts." Ph.D. dissertation, Columbia University, 1997.

Borgen, Robert. *Sugawara no Michizane and the Early Heian Court*. Cambridge, MA: Council on East Asian Studies, Harvard University, 1986.

Brennan, John. "Dreams, Divination, and Statecraft: The Politics of Dreams in Early Chinese History and Literature." In *The Dream and the Text: Essays on Literature and Language*, edited by Carol Schreier Rupprecht, 73–102. Albany, NY: State University of New York Press, 1993.

Brooks, Peter. *Reading for the Plot: Design and Intention in Narrative*. New York: A. A. Knopf, 1984.

Butler, Kenneth Dean. "The *Heike monogatari* and the Japanese Warrior Ethic." *Harvard Journal of Asiatic Studies* 29 (1969): 93–108.

Conlan, Thomas D. *In Little Need of Divine Intervention: Takezaki Suenaga's Scrolls of the Mongol Invasions of Japan*. Ithaca, NY: East Asia Program, Cornell University, 2001.

———. *State of War: the Violent Order of Fourteenth-Century Japan*. Michigan Monographs in Japanese Studies Series 46. Ann Arbor, MI: Center for Japanese Studies, University of Michigan, 2003.

Duara, Prasenjit. "Superscribing Symbols: The Myth of Guandi, Chinese God of War." *Journal of Asian Studies*, 47.4 (1988): 778–797.

Field, Norma. *The Splendor of Longing in the* Tale of Genji. Princeton, NJ: Princeton University Press, 1987.

Finnegan, Ruth. *Literacy and Orality: Studies in the Technology of Communication*. New York, NY: Basil Blackwell, 1988.

———. *Oral Poetry*. Cambridge: Cambridge University Press, 1977.

Foley, John M. *Immanent Art: From Structure to Meaning in Traditional Oral Epic*. Bloomington and Indianapolis, IN: Indiana University Press, 1991.

Friday, Karl. *Hired Swords: The Rise of Private Warrior Power in Early Japan*. Stanford, CA: Stanford University Press, 1992.

Fukuda Akira. *Gunki monogatari to minkan denshō*. Tokyo: Iwasaki bujutsu sha, 1987.

Gomi Fumihiko. *Azuma kagami no hōhō.* Tokyo: Yoshikawa kōbunkan, 1990.

Green, D. H. "Orality and Reading: The State of Research in Medieval Studies." *Speculum* 65.2 (1990): 267–280.

Groemer, Gerald. "The Guild of the Blind in Tokugawa Japan." *Monumenta Nipponica* 56.3 (Autumn 2001): 349–380.

Halbwachs, Maurice. *On Collective Memory.* Trans. Lewis A. Coser. Chicago, IL: University of Chicago Press, 1992.

Hayakawa Kōichi. *Heike monogatari wo yomu: seiritsu no nazo wo saguru.* Tokyo: Izumi shoin, 2000.

Horiike Sunpō. *Todaiji omizutori.* Tokyo: Shogakkan, 1996.

Howell, Thomas R. "Setsuwa, Knowledge, and the Culture of Reading and Writing in Medieval Japan." Ph.D. dissertation, University of Pennsylvania, 2002.

Hyōdō Hiromi. Heike monogatari: *katari no tekusuto.* Tokyo: Chikuma shinsho, 1998.

———. Heike monogatari *no rekishi to geinō.* Tokyo: Yoshikawa kōbunkan, 2000.

———. "Kakuichibon *Heike monogatari* no denrai o megutte." In *Heike biwa: katari to ongaku,* edited by Kamisangō Yūkō. Kasube-shi: Hitsuji shobō, 1993.

———. Taiheiki *"yomi" no kanōsei; rekishi to iu mongatari.* Tokyo: Kodansha, 1995.

Ichiko Teiji, ed. Heike monogatari *kenkyū jiten.* Tokyo: Meiji shoin, 1978.

———, ed. *Nihon koten bungaku daijiten.* 6 vols. Tokyo: Iwanami shoten, 1984.

Ikeda Hiroko. *A Type and Motif Index of Folk-literature.* Helsinki: Suomalainen Tiedeakatemia Academia Scientiarum Fennica, Folklore Fellows Communications, No. 209, 1970.

Inui Yoshihisa, "*Heiji monogatari* no seiritsu – hito to toki no ba." In Heiji monogatari *no seiritsu,* edited by Tochigi Yoshitada et al., 180–201. Tokyo: Kyūko shoin, 1998.

Iser, Wolfgang. *The Implied Reader: Patterns of Communication in Prose Fiction from Bunyan to Beckett.* Baltimore: Johns Hopkins University Press, 1974.

Kajihara Masaaki, ed. Heike monogatari *hikkei.* Vol. 15 of *Bessatsu kokubungaku.* Tokyo: Gakutōsha, 1982.

Kamisangō Yūkō, ed. *Heike biwa: katari to ongaku.* Kasube-shi: Hitsuji shobō, 1993.

Kanagawa ken kiga chōsa kenshi henshū shitsu, ed. *Kanagawa ken shi, shiryo hen,* vol. 1. Yokohama: Dai Nihon insatsu, 1971.

Kawashima, Terry. *Writing Margins: The Textual Construction of Gender in Heian and Kamakura Japan.* Cambridge, MA, and London: Harvard University Press, 2001.

Keirstead, Thomas. "The Gendering and Regendering of Medieval Japan." In *U.S.-Japan Women's Journal,* English Supplement no. 9, 1995.

Kelly, Laurence. *Lermontov: Tragedy in the Caucasus.* New York: George Braziller, Inc., 1977.

Kindaichi Haruhiko, Shimizu Isao, and Kondō Masami. *Heike monogatari sōsakuin.* Tokyo: Gakushū kenkyūsha, 1973.

Kobayashi Kenji, "Eirihanpon 'mai no hon' no sashie no keisei." In *Kōwaka bukyoku kenkyū,* edited by Fukuda Akira and Manabe Masahiro, vol. 10. Tokyo: Miyai shoten, 1998.

Kominz, Laurence R. *Avatars of Vengeance: Japanese Drama and the Soga Literary Tradition.* Ann Arbor, MI: Center for Japanese Studies, The University of Michigan, 1995.

Komoda Haruko. "Heikyoku no kyokusetsu to ongaku kōzō." In *Heike biwa, katari to ongaku,* edited by Kamisangō Yūkō, 161–193. Kasube-shi: Hitsuji shobō, 1993.

Komori Yoshiaki. *Kanagawa no rekishi to densetsu.* Tokyo: Akatsuki in shokan, 1977.

Konishi Jin'ichi. "*Heike monogatari* no gentai to kato-keitai: honmon hihyō no kihonteki taido." In Heike monogatari: *katari to gentai,* vol. 7 of *Nihon bungaku kenkyū shiryō shinshū,* edited by Hyōdō Hiromi, 64–79. Tokyo: Yūseidō, 1987. [Originally published in 1969.]

Kuroda Toshio. *Obō to Buppō.* Kyoto: Hōzōkan, 1983.

LaFleur, William. *The Karma of Words.* Berkeley, CA: University of California Press, 1983.

LaMarre, Tomas. *Uncovering Heian Japan.* Durham, NC: Duke University Press, 2000.

Lord, Albert Bates. *The Singer of Tales.* Cambridge, MA: Harvard University Press, 1960.

Lurie, David. "Nara and Heian Reading/Writing Practices and the Foundations of Japanese Culture." Paper delivered at the Association for Asian Studies Annual Meeting, March 28, 2003.

Mass, Jeffrey P. *Antiquity and Anachronism in Japanese History.* Stanford, CA: Stanford University Press, 1992.

———. *The Development of Kamakura Rule, 1180–1250.* Stanford, CA: Stanford University Press, 1979.

———. *Lordship and Inheritance in Early Medieval Japan.* Stanford, CA: Stanford University Press, 1989.

———. "The Missing Minamoto in the Twelfth-Century Kanto." *Journal of Japanese Studies* 19.1 (Winter 1993): 121–145.

———, ed. *The Origins of Japan's Medieval Age.* Stanford, CA: Stanford University Press, 1997.

———. *Warrior Government.* New Haven, CT, and London: Yale University Press, 1974.

———. *Yoritomo and the Founding of the First Bakufu.* Stanford, CA: Stanford University Press, 1999.

Matisoff, Susan. *The Legend of Semimaru, Blind Musician of Japan.* New York: Columbia University Press, 1978.

Matsumoto Nobuhiro. "Japanese Metalworkers: A Possible Source for their Legends." In *Studies in Japanese Folklore,* edited by Richard M. Dorson. Bloomington: Indiana University Press, 1963, 147–161.

Mizuhara Hajime. *Enkyōbon Heike monogatari ronkō.* Tokyo: Katō chūdōkan, 1979.

————. NHK koten kodoku: *Heike monogatari*. Audio recordings of radio program.

Murakami Manabu. "*Heike monogatari* e no sasoi: kataru monogatari to yomu monogatari no aida." In *Aera Mook Special Number 31*: Heike monogatari *ga wakaru*, 5–8. Tokyo: Asahi Shinbunsha, 1997.

————, ed. *Nihon bungaku kenkyū taisei Gikeiki/Soga monogatari*. Tokyo: Kokusho kankō kai, 1993.

Nagahara Keiji. *Minamoto no Yoritomo*. Tokyo: Iwanami shoten, 1995.

Nihonshi daijiten. 7 vols. Tokyo: Heibonsha, 1992–1994.

Norbeck, Edward. "Little-Known Minority Groups of Japan." In *Japan's Invisible Race: Caste in Culture and Personality*, edited by George De Vos, 188–189. Berkeley, CA: University of California Press, 1966.

Ojima Yoshiyuki. "*Shintōshū* to *Soga monogatari* to no kankei." In *Nihon bungaku kenkyū taisei Gikeiki/Soga monogatari*, edited by Murakami Manabu. Tokyo: Kokusho kankō kai, 1993.

Okano Tomohiko. *Genji to Nihon kokuō*. Tokyo: Kōdansha gendai shinsho, 2003.

Okumura Mitsuo. *Heike mabushi*. 3 vols. Tokyo: Rinsen shoten, 1971.

Ong, Walter J. *Orality and Literacy: The Technologizing of the Word*. London: Methuen, 1982.

Orikuchi Shinobu zenshū. Edited by Orikuchi hakushi kinenkai. 30 vols. Tokyo: Chūō kōron sha, 1965–1966.

Orikuchi Shinobu. "Nihon bungaku no naiyō." In *Orikuchi Shinobu zenshū*, vol. 7. Tokyo: Chūō Kōronsha, 1965–1966.

Ōtsu Yūichi. "Yoshinaka kō." In *Nihon bungaku* 39.7 (1990): 35–44.

Quint, David. *Epic and Empire: Politics and Generic Form from Virgil to Milton*. Princeton, NJ: Princeton University Press, 1993.

Ricouer, Paul. *Time and Narrative*. Translated by Kathleen McLaughlin and David Pellauer. 3 vols. Chicago, IL: The University of Chicago Press, 1984.

Ruch, Barbara. "Medieval Jongleurs and the Making of a National Literature." In *Japan in the Muromachi Age*, edited by John W. Hall and Takeshi Toyoda, 279–309. Berkeley and Los Angeles: University of California Press, 1977.

————. "The Other Side of Culture in Medieval Japan." In *The Cambridge History of Japan, vol. 3: The Middle Ages*, edited by Yamamura Kōzō, 500–543. Cambridge: Cambridge University Press, 1990.

Saeki Shin'ichi. "'Chōteki' izen." In *Kokugo to kokubungaku* 74.11 (November, 1997): 94–102.

————. Heike monogatari *sogen*. Tokyo: Wakakusa shobō, 1996.

Sansom, George. *A History of Japan to 1334*. Stanford, CA: Stanford University Press, 1958.

Shida Itaru. "*Heike* tsurugi no maki." In *Nihon koten bungaku jiten*, vol. 5. Tokyo: Iwanami shoten, 1984, 389.

Shinkawa Tokio. *Kanji bunka no naritachi to tenkai*. Tokyo: Yamakawa tosho shuppan, 2002.

Shinoda, Minoru. *The Founding of the Kamakura Shogunate 1180–1185, with Selected*

Translations from the Azuma Kagami. New York: Columbia University Press, 1960.

Shirane, Haruo. *The Bridge of Dreams: A Poetics of 'The Tale of Genji.'* Stanford, CA: Stanford University Press, 1987.

Squires, Todd. "Reading the Kōwaka-mai as Medieval Myth: Story-Patterns, Traditional Reference, and Performance in Late Medieval Japan." Ph.D. dissertation, Ohio State University, 2001.

Steenstrup, Carl. *Hojo Shigetoki, 1198–1261, and His Role in the History of Political and Ethical Ideas in Japan.* London: Curzon Press, 1979.

Stock, Brian. *Listening for the Text: on the Uses of the Past.* Philadelphia: University of Pennsylvania Press, 1990.

Sugimoto Keizaburō, ed. Heike monogatari *to rekishi.* Vol. 3 of *Anata ga yomu* Heike monogatari. Tokyo: Yūseidō, 1994.

Suzuki Jun. "*Heike monogatari* Kakuichibon to Yasakabon no aida: Yoritomo no sonzaikan to kataribon no tenkai," *Kokubungaku kenkyū* 116 (June 1995):12–23.

Suzuki Takatsune. "Heikyoku." In Heike monogatari *hikkei,* edited by Kajihara Masaaki, 204. Tokyo: Gakutōsha, 1985.

Takagi Ichinosuke. Heike monogatari *ron.* Kōdansha gakujutsu bunko. Tokyo: Kōdansha, 1977.

Takehisa Takeshi. "Azuma kagami." In Heike monogatari *hikkei,* vol. 15 of *Bessatsu kokubungaku,* edited by Kajihara Masaaki, 14–18. Tokyo: Gakutōsha, 1982.

Thompson, Stith. *Motif Index for Folk Literature.* Bloomington: Indiana University Press, 1955–1958.

Tochigi Yoshitada et al., eds. Heiji monogatari *no seiritsu.* Tokyo: Kyūko shoin, 1998.

Toin Kinsada, ed. *Sonpi bunmyaku.* 5 vols. *Shintei zōho kokushi taikei.* Tokyo: Yoshikawa kōbunkan, 1964.

Tonomura, Hitomi. "Women and Inheritance in Japan's Early Warrior Society." *Comparative Studies in History and Society* (1990): 92–623.

Tsukasaki Susumu. "*Soga monogatari* denshō ron." In *Nihon bungaku kenkyū taisei Gikeiki/Soga monogatari,* edited by Murakami Manabu, p. 128. Tokyo: Kokusho kankō kai, 1993.

Turner, Victor. *Dramas, Fields, and Metaphors.* Ithaca, NY, and London: Cornell University Press, 1974.

———. *The Ritual Process: Structure and Anti-Structure.* Ithaca, NY: Cornell University Press, 1974.

Varley, H. Paul. *Warriors of Japan as Portrayed in the War Tales.* Honolulu: University of Hawai'i Press, 1994.

Wakabayashi Haruko. "Tengu: Images of the Concepts of Evil in Medieval Japan." Ph.D. dissertation, Princeton University, 1995.

Wakita Haruko. *Josei geinō no genryū.* Tokyo: Kadokawa shoten, 2001.

Watson, Michael G. "A Narrative Study of the Kakuichi-bon *Heike monogatari.*" Doctoral thesis, Queens College, University of Oxford, 2003.

Yamada Yoshio. Heike monogatari *kō*. Tokyo: Kokutei kyōkasho kyōdō hanbai-
    sho, 1911.
Yamaji Aizan. *Minamoto no Yoritomo*. Tokyo: Heibonsha, 1987.
Yamashita Hiroaki. "Gen 'Heike' no omokage." In Heike monogatari *hikkei*, vol. 15
    of *Bessatsu kokubungaku*, edited by Kajihara Masaaki, 14–18. Tokyo: Gaku-
    tōsha, 1982.
————. "*Gikeiki* no *Heike monogatari* jūyō." *Kokugo to kokubungaku* 713.3 (1996): 28–
    42.
————. Heike monogatari *kenkyū jōsetsu*. Tokyo: Meiji Sshoin, 1972.
————. *Ikusa monogatari no katari to hihyō*. Tokyo: Sekai shisōsha, 1997.
————. *Ikusa monogatari to Genji shōgun*. Tokyo: Miyai shoten, 2003.
Yanagita Kunio. "Ariō to Shunkan sōzu." In *Teihon Yanagita Kunio shū*, vol. 7. To-
    kyo: Chikuma shobo, 1967. First published in *Bungaku* (January 1940): 1–17.

Index

Adachi Tō Kurō Morinaga, 35–43, 58–59
annai(sha) (knowledge[able person]),
    72–75, 83, 141–142
Antoku, Sovereign, 3–4, 63–64, 91–92
Ariwara Narihira, 36
Ashikaga shōgunal house, 15–16, 160n.
    10, 200n. 9; connection to Seiwa
    Genji, 16, 47, 166n. 59, 175n. 76,
    176n. 83, 199n. 4
Azuma kagami, 2, 23–24, 67, 87; embed-
    ded documents in, 95, 104; Genpei
    War account in, 87–91, 94–96, 104;
    historical accuracy of, 94, 104, 110–
    111; Koshigoe account in, 104–105,
    110–111; relationship to medieval
    narrative, 94–95; style of, 94, 104,
    110; Yoshinaka's youth described in,
    67

Benzaiten, 71
biwa, 12–13, 71, 119, 162n. 20, 189n. 37
biwa hōshi, 4–5, 8–9, 12–13, 18–19, 162n.
    20, 164n. 41
blind guild (*tōdōza*), 9, 13, 15, 118–119,
    164n. 40, 194n. 16
bow and arrow, and military identity, 44,
    50–51, 77, 125, 197n. 65
buannai (lack of knowledge), 72, 83
bunraku, 87, 115

chakushi. See primary heir
"The Chapter of the Mirror" (*Kagami no
    maki*), 127

"Chapter of the Swords" (*Tsurugi no
    maki*), 116, 127–128
Chichugiri, 195
chinkon. See placation
Chōka (Book Cutter), 121
Chūshingura, 30. *See also* forty-seven *rōnin*
circular letter (*megurashibumi*), 65–68

daihiji. See major secret pieces
Dan-no-ura, 4, 86, 90–96, 130
divinations before battle, 74, 78–79
documents: embedded in narratives, 10,
    17–18, 78, 84–85, 99, 110–111, 142,
    148; as historical trope, 27, 61, 70,
    94, 174n. 51; as judicial evidence,
    70–71, 84–85, 110–114, 135, 139,
    144–148, 179n. 2, 198n. 79; and
    justification of arts, 118; Nagahara
    Kanetō and, 68–70; in read lineage
    texts, 11; Yoshinaka and, 78–80;
    Yoshitsune and, 10, 112–114
Dokuhebi (Poisonous Snake), 121
Dragon King (*ryūō*), 109, 121, 197n. 61
"The Dream Interpretation" (*Yume
    awase*), Dream Interpretation ac-
    count in, 42–43, 55–56
dream, prophetic: in Dream Interpreta-
    tion narrative, 37–44, 47–49, 51–57,
    139; as trope, 7, 27, 63, 89, 95–96,
    175n. 63, 178n. 108, 179n. 109

Enkyōbon *Heike monogatari*, 14; Dream
    Interpretation account in, 35, 40,

213

About the Author

ELIZABETH OYLER is assistant professor of Japanese at Washington University in St. Louis, specializing in medieval narrative and drama. She is also a student of *Heike biwa,* a performance art involving recitation of the Tale of the Heike to the accompaniment of the *biwa* lute. This is her first book.